In Praise of Charlie D

". . . a risk-taker who didn't know fear."

—Johnny Musso

". . . the 'Sultan of Scalp.' He refined the art of trading into a science. . ."

—Tom Bonen

"Charlie was a great risk-taker with great ability and his risk taking far exceeded the parameters most traders would even consider. I'm telling you—I couldn't even hold Charlie's jock. More important than financial success, I think it is appropriate to judge what a trader gives back to the exchange and his fellow traders. In those respects, Charlie was unique."

—Robert Goldberg
Former CBOT Chairman and grain trader

"Charlie was a model patient. He was never down. He dealt with all the problems associated with his illness with both optimism and courage. He always approached his illness from the perspective of what treatment would allow him to maintain the quality of life, not prevent him from dying. He's a cancer patient that many doctors, including myself, will never forget."

—Dr. Funmi I. Olopade
Pritzker School of Medicine, University of Chicago

Charlie D. Charlie D. Charlie D. Charlie D. Charlie D. Charlie D. Charlie D. Charlie D. Charlie D. Charlie D. Charlie D. Charlie D. Charlie D. Charlie D. Charlie D. Charlie D. Charlie D. Charlie D. Charlie D.

the story of the legendary bond trader

WILLIAM D. FALLOON

John Wiley & Sons, Inc.
New York • Chichester • Weinheim • Brisbane • Singapore • Toronto

For a man I never met, and his brother John,
my entrance and exit to his story

Copyright © 1997 by William D. Falloon
Published by John Wiley & Sons, Inc.

Library of Congress Cataloging in Publication Data:
Falloon, William D.
    Charlie D: the story of the legendary bond trader / William D.
Falloon.
        p.   cm.
    ISBN 0-471-15672-8 (cloth : alk. paper)
    1. DiFrancesca, Charles.   2. Floor traders (Finance)—United
States—Biography.   3. Chicago Board of Trade.   I. Title.
HG4928.5.D53F35   1997
332.64′273′092—dc21
    [B]   97-26539

Printed and bound by CPI Group (UK) Ltd, Croydon, CR0 4YY

C9780471156727_090724

contents

foreword

Fortunately for the futures industry, a tweed-suited banker came strolling into Goldberg Brothers at the Chicago Board of Trade and inquired about becoming a trader one day in 1980. One never knows who will be a great trader or merely a mechanic, but generally speaking, bankers do not make great pit traders. More often than not they are set in their ways—overly analytical, risk averse—and make trades with a "committee" mentality.

Charlie D was not of that persuasion. Although he educated himself about what it took to develop a "pit" mentality, he obviously had a natural sense for the trading arena and a competitive drive probably developed from his football days. Yet he still had to learn that there is a fine line between the game and the business. Once he understood the essential concepts he became a whirling dervish of activity. He did it bigger and better, but always with great dignity, humility, honesty, and integrity.

Charlie D was what every trader strives to be: talented, competitive, humble, exuberant, and charitable. Don't forget your roots, and make sure you take time to help the next young trader learn, just as someone helped you. Charlie D knew these lessons well. May this book teach all of us a few things about the beauty of life and how to live it—in and out of futures markets.

—Bobby Goldberg
Former Chicago Board of Trade Chairman

obituary

by johanna steinmetz

Charles P. DiFrancesca, 39, leading bond futures trader

Charles P. DiFrancesca, 39, considered the biggest individual trader in terms of contract volume in the Chicago bond futures pit, died Wednesday at the University of Chicago Hospital of complications from lymphoma.

Mr. DiFrancesca, of Wilmette, who always declined to give interviews, was a legend among his peers in the pit.

One of these, former Bears football player Johnny Musso, put it simply: "He was a risktaker who didn't know fear."

Another trader and friend, Thomas Fitzgerald, said, "When people at Merrill Lynch or PaineWebber wanted to know what was going on in the market, they'd say, 'What's Refco [a major trading company] doing? What's Charlie D. doing?' As an individual trader, he was on the same level as major companies in the world. And he did it with a sense of humor and always with integrity."

Mr. DiFrancesca, whose illness was diagnosed five years ago, continued to trade until April 26, sometimes wearing protective gear to shield parts of his body made tender by surgery and radiation treatment.

Mr. DiFrancesca underwrote the career of more than one neophyte trader and made countless anonymous donations to charitable causes.

His passions included poker and golf, which he sometimes played with Chicago Bulls star Michael Jordan.

"I'll never forget the first time he met Jordan," said Fitzgerald, who introduced the two. "He says to Michael, 'Do you know Dave Corzine? Think you could get his autograph for me?' Michael turns to me and says, 'Who is this guy?'"

Mr. DiFrancesca, who grew up in Waukesha, Wis., attended the University of Wisconsin and Carroll College in Waukesha, where he played football for his father, the coach.

He graduated from Colorado State University, where he also played football. He attended graduate school at Northwestern University's Kellogg School of Management.

After college, he held a variety of jobs before a lucrative condominium conversion in 1980 enabled him to buy a seat on the Board of Trade.

Survivors include his wife, Ann; a daughter, Maggie; a son, Jake; his parents, Vincent and Margaret; a brother; and a sister.

A memorial service for Mr. DiFrancesca will be held at 4 p.m. Tuesday in Northwestern University's Alice Millar Chapel, 1870 Sheridan Rd., Evanston.

cigar smoke | 1

The first time I heard about him he appeared as a phantasm of smoke—big-shouldered, fearless, and cocky—rising from the smoldering ashes of a fine Cuban cigar. I was in a city named after a bird that also had risen out of fire, and a band of us had just broken away that evening from a cocktail party next to a backlit pool, rippling cool blue and mercurial. Two days earlier, a bellhop had handed me two oranges to eat from the trees of paradise and then grabbed my golf clubs and luggage, telling me this luxury resort in Phoenix had once been the private hideaway for blue-blooded General Motors executives until the Internal Revenue Service shut down its utility as a corporate tax shelter. Now the Wigwam Resort was simply plush host to the Eighth Annual Risk Management Conference sponsored by two of Chicago's largest futures and options exchanges, the Chicago Board of Trade and the Chicago Board Options Exchange. As usual, press credentials had made it largely a free ride. For the cost of a plane ticket and room, we had four days of parties, golf, sunshine, and (dare I mention work?) educational seminars with brokers, institutional investors, market regulators, and top exchange brass.

That late Friday evening on January 22, 1993, some of us at the cocktail reception already were feeling the effects of too much free drink. I had just stationed myself in a lounge chair away from the party with what I thought was a final, last-call Heineken in hand. It was from this cushiony perch, with four of us surrounding a former Merrill Lynch broker whose name escapes me, that a bond trader whom I had never met was summoned in genie-like fashion by a simple question.

"So who's the best trader you've ever seen?"

With a cigar clenched between his teeth, the broker struck a match. He leaned back in a smooth leather lounge chair identical to mine, inhaled, the cigar tip aglow, and then exhaled a mammoth cloud that wafted from his lungs and seemed to take human form. He tilted forward and spoke a foot or so from my ear, the clamor of the party still coming from the patio.

"I'll tell you who the best trader ever was, but you certainly aren't going to have heard about him. He never cared about interviews. Even when the *Wall Street Journal* came knocking at his door, he turned them down. So you can't even read about him in any library. But he is still the greatest trader who ever lived. No question."

He handed me a handmade Cuban cigar, as if it were physical evidence of his credibility.

"Better than Tom Baldwin?" I asked.

Baldwin was perhaps the best known of the big hitters currently playing on the floors of Chicago's exchanges. He trades enormous size in the bond pit and is known around Chicago for rolling his wealth into a real estate partnership that restored the Rookery, a red-stoned historical landmark on LaSalle Street. Surviving a plane crash in the 1980s on the way to his Michigan mansion only added to tales of his mystique as a gutsy and seemingly invincible trader. But the broker didn't hesitate.

"The best. Larger than life. He was the first big trader in the bond pit. He made that pit what it is today, the largest in the world. But you aren't going to read about him anywhere, or get an interview."

"Oh yeah. What's his name?"

"We called him Charlie D. His real name was Charles DiFrancesca."

"And he doesn't do interviews?"

"He passed away a couple of years ago. But he wouldn't if he was still around. That was just his style."

So much for trying to work at night, I thought. My next question about a possible interview obviously had been foiled. But the night was still young, and I was in need of some amusement.

"I see. What made him so much larger than life? Do you know any stories about him?"

As the broker's narrative began, my mind started to wander. My questions had been on impulse. I was skeptical that I would learn anything new about any Chicago trader, much less one who was being cast as an undiscovered and publicity-loathing legend. Perhaps he was speaking of a small clique of hotshot bond traders, whose newly discovered wealth burned brighter than an SOS flare for a year or so during the go-go 1980s. These flashes in the pan often disappeared before anyone had a chance to learn their names and hear their tales of fleeting glory, their skills as traders defined more by good luck than talent and skill. Success quickly went to their heads, but not without exacting a toll—more often than not they were slaves to their wealth, not students of market subtleties. Was Charlie D one of them, or something else entirely? Nursing a nearly full beer, I had plenty of time to listen.

Masked by a mist of cigar smoke, I planned a quick path to bed if the broker's story-telling did not live up to its billing, my chair strategically close to the patio door. At the mention of the trader's nickname, Charlie D, I found myself repeating it a few times under my breath. It had a ring, at least in my ear. I imagined, through the smoky haze, a flamboyant wild man donned in a Hawaiian trading jacket. Filling it was a dark Italian figure with a bolder and even wider striped trading tie hanging loosely around his neck. From the sound of the opening bell, he left his collar unbuttoned, sometimes crossing his arms to wait for the market to come his way. He timed his attacks in the trading pit with all the stealth of a black panther.

He most likely worked out with weights at the East Bank Club and lived in some Gold Coast condo, where Lake Shore Drive in Chicago makes a bend directly north to one of the wealthiest stretches in the city. I might even have seen him being whisked off in a cab from the corner of LaSalle and Jackson to some Rush Street hot spot. That's if I had known to stop and look for him while he was still alive. No doubt he carried a silver money clip, as many successful and unsuccessful traders do, neatly packing a wad of $100 and $50 bills in the front pocket of some loose-fit Dockers. On this particular day, after the market close, he held the cab door for his clerk, a golden blonde with silky hair cascading straight down to her waist. For all I knew she was as stunning as American muralist John Warner Norton's *Ceres*, a partially cloaked Greek goddess on canvas who symbolized the allure of trading and the bounty of American farmlands, shafts of wheat in her right hand and gold coins dropping like priceless seeds from her left. I had walked past her many times in the Chicago Board of Trade's atrium. Maybe marriage was in the cards for these two. Or, someone better might come along for such a playboy. Next stop: a Lake Forest mansion on the North Shore. Golf on the weekends at the prestigious Bob O'Link.

But this image quickly faded. The more I was told that evening and in later recountings with friends, family, and traders, the more my preconceived visions faded—the bond trader known as Charlie D still eluded me. The stereotypical image of a commodities trader kicked up in the 1990s by Barings-buster Nick Leeson, who lost $1 billion trading financial futures in Singapore and Osaka, or by someone like Red Bone, the Little Rock broker with Refco who helped Hillary Clinton to a $100,000 nest egg trading live cattle futures, was not to be. He simply did not fit any mold. And unlike young Nick, he had never made newspaper headlines or the evening news because of his ignominy as a speculator or something worse. The best I could conjure through the smoke was an image of a capitalist John Belushi trading bond futures, but even that picture dissolved after a few more sips of beer and conversation.

I sunk deeper into my chair, staring at my cigar and flicking the ashes. It was clear this trader was not just another nameless face wearing a brightly colored trader's jacket in a pulsating psychedelic sea of jackets, the chaotic open-outcry abstraction that many of us have seen from the Chicago Board of Trade's visitors' gallery.

When the broker's voice cracked during his storytelling, a day from the past burning much brighter than the tip of his cigar, I sensed this trader was different. "He died about a year ago in his thirties. Cancer. But I tell you, no one took his spot in the pit, and he traded up until he died. Coming back to the pit after his first round of chemo, he took off his baseball cap and we all threw our trading cards up and cheered. The pit parted like the sea in the Bible. Nobody ever took his spot on the top step, even when he was dying in the hospital. Wouldn't dare. That was *his* spot—and still is in my mind. At his funeral in Evanston, even the bellhops and stickmen in Las Vegas sent flowers. You couldn't breathe in the church there were so many flowers and people. We all respected him, whether we were traders or not. He made everyone feel like he was their best friend."

The edges of my image of Charlie D at the Wigwam started to blur like the colors of a desert skyline at sunset. I can no longer remember all of the specifics of that night. But as the broker's story continued, I do remember losing interest in finding a bellhop to drive me in a golf cart to my room. By the end of the evening, the genie-trader wafting from the broker's cigar had me drinking a few more Heinekens and buying a round of cigars for the broker's late-night audience. The story of Charlie D's death, in fact, had been told in such detail that it sobered me into remembering my mother's final year with ovarian cancer. But unlike her death, the complexity and mysteriousness of Charlie D's life and death I found oddly spiriting.

The genie-trader in the cigar smoke had me laughing and smiling. I found myself traveling with him on one of his trips to Las Vegas to roll the dice at the craps table and play unlimited stakes poker with Amarillo Slim and Los Angeles Lakers owner Dr. Jerry Buss. We won, of course. I was then transported to a Chicago hospital with him to donate blood to save his brother and mother from their own personal bouts with cancer. I traveled to Waukesha, Wisconsin, where Charlie D had been a star high school quarterback, student council president, honor student, and All-American boy, leading his team to a state regional championship. Waukesha would be the site where his eventual fate with cancer was written—Charlie D throwing passes with his father, a college football coach, under high-tension wires that ran past their home built on Wisconsin farmland. The electromagnetic field from those wires led in time to the cage of cancer that trapped Charlie D later in life, or so I was told that evening. I had no idea if this were true.

The broker was on a roll, and the intimacy of his story has never really left me. Charlie D would take me back to the University of

Chicago, where I once had been a student visiting the hospital during a stressful week of finals. It was that same hospital from which Charlie D later finagled his way out of a hospital bed, over and over. On many occasions after chemotherapy, he often quick-released his catheter connections to a metal tree of experimental drugs—the moment the contents emptied—to catch a cab for the bond market's opening bell. Who needed a doctor or nurse to give him permission to leave? He then traded for his own account and sometimes for the "cancer research account" of leading U of C researchers, splitting the winnings he made on such hospital-escape days. And winnings came often, I was told—in increments of $30,000 or more.

Then there were stories in the Chicago Board of Trade trading pit, where Charlie D's trading positions in his prime would rival the size of proprietary traders at major Wall Street firms. He would often make more in a day than most of us made in a year, if it was a good day. After the close, he would retire to his nondescript cubbyhole of an office on the 12th floor for a quick bite, typically a burger and fries, Milk Duds, and a nap. After all, the night trading session started at 6:00 P.M., and his internal alarm clock was set for the appropriate hour. I was told that more than a few traders who had blown out or run on hard times owed Charlie D a wealth of gratitude for his generosity in the face of their adversity, not his. Everyone, I was told, owed him their thanks (and in many cases, money) for what always seemed to be his sympathetic ear to other people's problems and his open checkbook. Once he gave, I was told, he never looked back.

Some of the other legends I heard that evening sounded even more far-fetched. First was a story about some anonymous gifts Charlie D had made, including the purchase of a camper for a retiring high school football coach and a high-powered microscope for cancer researchers at the University of Chicago. I was told that he had funded the college education of many people, including his housemaid's son. And, of course, there was a legendary party he had thrown for his wife in New York, which the broker described as a party to end all parties. Mixed in with all these tales of generosity and merriment were stories of his Midas touch as a risk-taker, a touch that reportedly had been passed on to at least one unidentified lottery winner who had parlayed a Ben Franklin from

Charlie into great fortune. If I believed every story, it seemed to me, it no longer seemed to be a question of who had been touched by him, but rather who hadn't.

And finally there was that one last joyride on his Harley to someplace in Michigan, which the broker used to close the curtain on the evening. It was this fearless trip in the dead of winter that projected in my mind the face of James Dean, as he might have appeared if genetically and comically mutated into an Italian sex symbol with a somewhat less-than-perfect nose. The cold air from that motorcycle jaunt, I was told, had further weakened his immune system and had finally killed our hero. The legend ended there on a fittingly jazzy and unpredictable upbeat, high-tension wires always omnipresent in the broker's fertile mind. Charlie D was screaming down a highway in a hell-bent ride with destiny, leaving high-tension wires in his wake, laughing at all of our sadness and pity for him. He was prepared to die, but why stop living in the meantime? Sitting in my leather chair, I swear I heard the motorcycle's engine roar past. He was riding full throttle to somewhere for who knows what—an experimental cure for his cancer, perhaps, or a golf game with Michael Jordan?

This man couldn't be real, I thought. But I was told that one of the story's fortunate survivors, Charlie D's brother John, still traded in the bond pit at the Chicago Board of Trade, as if that were proof enough of the legend's authenticity. I thought back to my mother's plight with cancer: Something was missing in the story I had just heard, but I had enough drinking and cigars for the night, and had heard enough about big-shot traders. Anticipating a hangover, I excused myself, searched every suit pocket for my electronic key, and found my way to my room thanks to a bellhop in search of guests like me who could use a ride. Off we went in a golf cart to my own private desert cottage, a refreshing breeze blowing against my face. The next morning, all I remembered about that night was my surprise that somehow I had found my room and that I might still have a chance to meet Charlie D in the image of his brother. What a fun encounter that might be, I recall daydreaming, even if Charlie D was only a half truth concocted by a rumormongering broker.

And so, a few months later, I began my search for a man who emerged hazily from a broker's cigar smoke—a man named Charles Paul

DiFrancesca, born September 13, 1951, in Macomb, Illinois. Back in Chicago, I tried paging his brother John on the trading floor of the Chicago Board of Trade to see if any of what I'd heard was true. Three times, no luck. Was he still alive? Or had his cancer spread out of control and killed him, too? I would try once more. I tracked down his home phone number with the help of a Chicago Board of Trade staff member who was also overtaken by the power of the cigar smoke that night. I finally met John and a friend of the DiFrancesca family, technical trading wizard Tom DeMark, for dinner at Berghoff's, a German restaurant on Adams Street that brews its own beer. From that point on, I realized that the legend of Charlie D would always have a powerful way of growing, not shrinking, the more human and truthful the story of his life became.

Indeed, sobriety and time have had a way of adding clarity to what seemed real in the haze of smoke. Only some of the Wigwam folklore translated into fact. So many questions about Charlie D's life and death still need to be mended or answered, but I believe his story is a better one because of it. For the record, Charlie D was clean-cut, not a cigar smoker or drinker like the Wigwam apparition. He sometimes bought a cigar and a drink during a round of golf, but the indulgence was more often than not for friends. He never smoked and his cup almost always remained full. Neither did he donate blood to save anyone as the broker had suggested, though I would argue that was open to further debate based on what was actually meant by "giving blood." And, of course, he is forever remembered for his willingness to battle the odds.

At this point, I correct one important factual error that troubles me most because I'm the one who created it late that evening: His trading jacket wasn't Hawaiian, but light blue, like a clear Midwest sky and lightly starched, at least in the first video image I ever saw of him. His ties: the antithesis of loud, the same ones he wore as a middle-market Harris banker before wandering over to the Chicago Board of Trade to watch grown men scream and throw elbows and take risks that would send nine out of ten back from where they came. It wasn't a place for those who lacked courage or the desire to compete. The moment Charlie D saw the trading pits, they felt like home, and it didn't take him long to make the bond pit his castle.

Of course, his trading badge number for nine years—666—is a bizarre coincidence around which rumors have circulated to explain his death. I guess that happens sometimes when someone so special dies young. Truth is often stranger than fiction, I've come to discover, especially where Charlie D was concerned—but not that strange. On occasion, as with the 666, mythology about his death has mutated in ways that seem to me to be beyond superstitious, although I don't think anyone has the answers to explain all the forces of mind and body running beneath the surface of his life. Even I am superstitious to a degree when it comes to Charlie D, though certainly not about the 666. To be sure, the real Charlie always had his own inconsistencies and imperfections, as all of us do. But by grace of something that even I can't put a finger on, he has never completely been forgotten, despite the market's inclination toward a very short attention span. Just the other day, a couple of traders in the bond pit told me that a petition had been drafted to have the exchange's new $180 million trading floor (which could serve as a garage to at least one Boeing 747) named after him. That a bond trader would be remembered for something worth more than any money he made or lost, it seems to me, is perhaps the strangest truth of all.

larger than life | 2

O n Friday, June 16, 1986, an amazing party began, with Charlie D yanking the chains, banging the drums, blowing the horns, and ringing the bells from behind his curtain of success like the Wizard of Oz. The yellow brick road to the party began in Chicago and led to the Plaza Hotel in New York. Along the way, it meandered by chartered bus to Atlantic City for the men and Bloomingdale's for the women, reaching its crescendo with dinner at Tavern on the Green on Saturday evening. The so-called wind-down period afterward included more merriment and embraces back in the Plaza's presidential suite. As the curtains for the memories of that party rose and fell, it was Charlie who made its machinery hum. No one thought about the cost to throw this carnival, and they didn't have to. That was part of the joy and fun for Charlie. He wanted people to scratch their heads and smile for years after the party was over—enjoy it forever really—and no one more than his wife Ann. He handled virtually every aspect short of packing his guests' bags. The party was top secret: a covert surprise as big and glorious as the top floor of the Plaza Hotel itself.

Behind the scenes, Charlie D's business manager, Susie Smider (Braman, after marriage), worked quiet as an elf, making the arrangements as the date for the party fast approached. Charlie never gave her a budget. He didn't have to as she knew conceptually what he had in mind. After all, it was Ann's 40th birthday, and Susie knew Ann as a friend, perhaps in some ways even better than Charlie knew Ann. Susie knew what made Ann happiest, staring down the big 4-0, and she also knew what made Charlie D happiest: focus on his whirlwind business life inside and out of the pit but still bring joy to those he loved.

Charlie D looked forward to all the age jokes he could muster when the big day arrived. But in the back of his mind there was an important reason (perhaps counterbalancing his need to needle those he loved) not to put a budget on his wife's 40th birthday party. He remembered their wedding in 1980: It, too, had been one of the best days of his life, but it hadn't been anything to write home about. The lowest of low-budget affairs, it took place in Ann's apartment. Her children from a previous marriage and now Charlie's by love, Jake and Maggie, then ages 4 and 2, served as attendants to the bride and groom. The smiles on their faces told a story of great happiness. They now had a dad to replace the one who had walked out on the family. This one added something else to their lives and to Ann's that was missing—he was fun and upbeat. Ann's niece Laura joined them as a third in the wedding party troika, standing up as a flower girl. Bible in hand, the judge gave them their vows with heart, but not much in the way of fanfare. A small table in Ann's living room, decorated with crêpe paper, held a modest but tasty wedding cake. Smiling at Ann, who snapped a picture of Charlie and the kids next to the cake, Charlie promised her that some day he would re-create the happiness of that day but in a bigger way. The next day, he was back at it again. He dove deeper into the bond pit, in search of more gold, remembering his promise, just taking enough time to have a honeymoon celebration with some close friends, John Bollen and his wife, along the New Jersey coastline.

This birthday/belated wedding celebration, compared to the first, was as different as night and day. Susie called 65 of Ann's closest friends and family to New York, inviting guests from as far away as London. Only a handful couldn't make it; it was just too tempting. The entire top floor of the Plaza Hotel was rented, with 35 suites giving everyone a comfortable place to stay. A surprise reception would be held Friday night. Every detail had been attended to, right down to the insurance policies Charlie D bought from Mutual of Omaha, on a paranoid whim, to protect the families of the guests should their plane crash. It was Charlie D's curious way of thinking like a responsible parent, done in his snap-of-the-finger style.

While most of the guests flew together on a raucous flight out of O'Hare Airport, whooping it up long before they touched down in New York, Ann and Charlie D left on a later flight. Ann had no idea why she was going to New York to celebrate her birthday. On the plane, the depression of turning 40 set in. She bordered on being cranky, but Charlie pampered her. On the drive to O'Hare, Ann made it clear to him that she really did not want to go. If she had her choice, she would be happier spending her 40th with a few close friends and family in Wilmette. But even that was now out of the question. Charlie D brushed off the complaints, coaxing his irritated wife onto the plane with promises of fun in the Big Apple.

"Ann, I don't think we'll have any problem finding things to do in New York. Let's just see how it turns out when we get there."

Ann's willpower to resist the trip was broken. Still depressed about her birthday, she began planning how to cover her losses on the weekend, making the most of what seemed to be one of her husband's impulsive and poorly planned trips. He should have let her do the planning.

"Charlie, we don't even have theater tickets. What are we going to do when we're there? If you're going to drag me to New York, maybe we could have dinner at Tavern on the Green. I've always wanted to go there."

"Fine, we'll give it a try, honey. We'll do whatever you want. I have a good feeling we might run into a couple of friends in New York. Your birthdays are always good luck."

"Oh sure, Charlie, a few friends among the millions of people wandering the streets of New York. I don't think so."

"OK, I'll take that bet, if you want to make it. It's a very big town. You never know. Stranger things have happened in the bond market."

"Sure. If we meet more than four people who we know in a city the size of New York, I'll fulfill your wildest sexual fantasy at the hotel."

Things were falling into place—maybe getting better.

"Is that a bet, Ann? Let me whisper my favorite into your ear, my dear. I like my upside, even if the odds aren't in my favor. There are a lot of people in New York. We'll run into at least someone who we know, I'm sure."

"Sure? Charlie, you've got a birthday bet. But if you lose, you're buying theater tickets, sitting through the whole show on Saturday with a smile, and then taking me to Tavern on the Green."

"OK, honey. A kiss seals it. Let's go have some fun in New York. The way I see it, neither of us can lose now."

Ann flipped the pages of a magazine; Charlie asked the stewardess for a round of Cokes. Thinking of Tavern on the Green, a famous restaurant and old haunt of the Kennedys, at least piqued Ann's interest. She always had wanted to dine there. The flight breezed by, with the DiFrancescas mellowed by the sight of New York glimmering in the night. Happy Birthday, New York.

Ann and Charlie gathered their luggage at LaGuardia Airport and jumped into a limousine. The party entourage had landed that Friday afternoon and settled in their rooms a couple of hours earlier. A home video camera was already rolling to chronicle parts of the party that Ann would miss as she was caught in the whirlwind. While most of the guests came from the Chicago area, a couple of chartered planes brought in special guests from out-of-the-way places, including Ann's eightysomething grandmother from Athens, Ohio. Lights out, they gathered quietly in the palatial presidential suite at the Plaza Hotel. Ann's sister Francie greeted the guests as they arrived, passing out yellow T-shirts that read, "It's Great to be 40. Let's Celebrate!" on the front and "Happy 40th Birthday, Ann!" on the back. Guests wore them over their party attire, like T-shirts worn by jocks just after winning a championship game. Charlie D called the hotel from the limousine to confirm their expected time of arrival, information which would be relayed to the guests in the presidential suite. At approximately 6:55 P.M. the lights in the suite were turned off and the room went silent. Charlie D and Ann were being escorted from the lobby to their room. A stay in the presidential suite had already improved Ann's outlook about New York. Charlie gave her the key to the door. The bellhop pulled the luggage cart behind them.

"I can still remember the day that Charlie invited me to the party," says Wilmette neighbor and friend J. B. Dougherty. "He came over in person and said he wanted me and my wife to attend Ann's 40th birthday party, that it was going to be a surprise. I said fine. So then he tells us that it's going to be in New York. He must have seen the look on my face because he said, 'No, no, don't worry about the kids or the expense, I'm taking care of everything.' I was working at Baxter at the time, so I was accustomed to these big-time corporate deals, but this was one step beyond that. This was truly a Great Gatsby kind of affair. He rented out the entire top floor. The hors d'oeuvres buffet at the party was over 40 feet long, and cocktails were being served in every corner of the room. Every guest was given their own suite. The dinner party was at Tavern on the Green, and Charlie had already made reservations for all the guys to hit the tables at Atlantic City the following day, while all the girls shopped at Bloomingdale's on Fifth Avenue. Susie told me the whole thing probably cost him $300,000. Only Charlie would go to this kind of trouble. He even had a mariachi band come serenade Ann."

When Ann opened the door to the presidential suite and the lights came on, she saw 65 people appear before her like waxen figures frozen in the explosion of one of those old-fashioned camera lights. For a brief second she stood confused, wondering if she had somehow been beamed up in a never-never land in between childhood in Ohio and her current life in Chicago. Follow the yellow brick road.

"Suuuurrrrrppppprrrrriise!" the flashes of yellow shouted.

Charlie stood behind Ann at the door and placed his hand on his wife's shoulder and kissed her. Mission accomplished. Beneath the shouting and commotion, he whispered into her ear something no one else heard.

"Ann, I haven't counted, but I think there's more than four people you know in this room. We can settle the bet later. Happy Birthday, honey." His Cat-in-the-Hat smile spoke volumes, and so did hers.

That room, in some sense, was a time machine, the type we all wish we could live in for a day or two, with our favorite people from every period of our lives. All Ann saw were neighbors from around Chicago: the Shlaes, the Mussos, the Youngs, the Gallaghers, the Doughertys. There was her mother, father, and sister, friends from college. There was her old boyfriend from California. Oh my God!—and some college chums who used to skinny-dip with her. Her grandmother from Athens, Ohio! Her hands rose involuntarily to her mouth, in shock. She felt like a woman who had just been given a dream wrapped in a box the size of a 40-story hotel. She looked at Charlie speechless. He was obviously enjoying the pricelessness of a secret well kept and a promise fulfilled.

The memories of that party remain eternal in the hearts of the guests who attended. Ann had never felt so loved. The mariachis, dressed in sombreros and black costumes studded with silver, gently showered *la chica mas bonita* with their voices and guitars at Tavern on the Green the following evening. That evening at the dinner party, Charlie D lifted his champagne glass, pinkie finger dangling, toasting his wife's birthday and their marriage of six years. After the mariachis had turned Ann a finer color of crimson with another *canción romántica,* he explained to his guests that this was the wedding party he had wanted to give her years ago when they met, but couldn't. When Ann heard his words, time seemed to stop as eyes wandered the room looking at family and friends. It was never better sitting with Charlie for dinner.

Indeed, her smile and occasional giggle said it all. And why not indulge in smiling and laughing and perhaps even pinch yourself to see if you were still alive? Of course, she remembered the low-budget wedding, too, which took place not long after Charlie came to her apartment with most of his clothes in plastic bags. For a long time, he was lower than low emotionally, but Ann DiFran and the Bond Trading Man had each other and were looking ahead.

In a world of forking paths, Charlie D had many parties and celebrations and personal goals within his periscope. In his mind, there was absolutely no question he could continue being one of the best bond traders at the Chicago Board of Trade. He never doubted his abilities once he stepped foot in the bond pit. The pit was his goal line, the place to run the proverbial quarterback sneak if he needed to move himself a yard for glory. But it was never the be-all and end-all in his life, and his personal goals both financially and spiritually far exceeded anything he had accomplished to date. This interlude of prosperity was simply a chance to enjoy with others the fruits of his hard work. From 1980 to 1986, he had proven his uncanny ability to amass enormous positions in the bond pit and to trade such size successfully. Rarely, in his own words, was he the one "to puke his position all over his shoes." In the minds of most traders at this time, no one grabbed the hot potato of price risk in the bond pit more times during the day than Charlie D, and no one passed it off with as much grace and nimbleness under pressure. It was a fine art that few other traders had the steely nerves or intangible "court awareness" to pursue as successfully.

One man who witnessed Charlie D's meteoric rise on the trading floor firsthand was David MacLennan, head of customer service and risk management at Goldberg Brothers from 1982 to 1987. In his mid-20s at the time, it was MacLennan's job, in his words, to act as a conscience or the hook for large traders in the pit, if their emotions, ego, or fear ever got the best of them. "I was the closest thing that large floor traders have to a boss," said MacLennan. "I reported to John Ruth [one of the executives at the clearing firm], and it was my job to go to the floor for John if he wanted to discuss a large trading position with any trader, or to persuade them to reduce it if he thought that was necessary."

How large was Charlie D's trading activities at the time? According to MacLennan, a Goldberg Brothers trade checker could typically handle dozens of independent traders—known as *locals*—on the trading floor. Because none of them traded large positions, it was no problem for the trade checker to keep tabs on dozens of traders at once, and still have time to relax at some point during the trading day. Not so in the case of Charlie D and fellow pit trader Rob Moore, who cleared through a separate division of Goldberg Brothers known as B&D, coined from the first names of the Goldberg Brothers, Bob and Dave. Clearing account 666 had been created specifically for these giants in the pit because it was such an easy number to remember. On the trading floor, large outtrades in which traders get their signals crossed when buying and selling are considered the devil's work, but not something resonating with Biblical mystery. Outtrades on the size that these big dogs traded could cost a pretty penny. All big traders on the floor depended on having clearing numbers that were no-brainers to remember—747, 151, 007—so that their competitors would not have to think when consummating a trade and jotting it down on a trading card. Charlie D and Rob Moore liked 666 exactly for this reason. After all, who was going to forget it? And if you were a trader who had a lucky baseball cap from childhood or one who never stepped on a sidewalk crack outside the Chicago Board of Trade, all the better for the big dogs from the land of 666. They had you, because it certainly did not faze either lightning-fast Charlie D or Rob Moore, who banged around in the bond pit like bats out of hell. While the number sometimes drew jokes from other traders, Charlie D just laughed along with them. It wasn't something he thought twice about. It was just a number that made markets move faster because of the speed at which it could be written with pencil and trading card in hand. It was an edge—however small.

Given the way that Charlie D traded, every edge was key. "We had just one trade checker for those two guys alone," admits MacLennan. "When I was there, Charlie D's stack of trading cards at the end of the day was twice the size of any other trader's, and he was usually soaked with sweat by the time he came off the floor. I'm telling you—this guy worked for his living. He used to come in to our offices with his tie hanging down to his belly button after a day on the trading floor. The way he traded was physically and mentally exhausting. But if I ever came down to the floor to talk to him, he always treated me with respect."

It was during the early 1980s that Charlie D began to show the generosity that later became fabled. Hard work and a whimsical way of sharing defined Charlie D's reputation in the pit from that point forward. "Charlie treated most people better than they would treat themselves," says fellow bond trader Tom Gallagher. First in line would be the six or seven employees at Goldberg Brothers who interacted with him on a regular basis. At Christmas, Charlie made it a habit of rewarding them with packaged vacation tours to places such as Hawaii. Nothing to pay for but your meals. Charlie D's trade-checking clerk, a bespectacled bearded man in his forties named Richard Newman, received a Rolex watch after one of Charlie D's best years. Raki Mehra, maitre d' at Morton's Steakhouse, a near North Side restaurant known for the Hollywood and sports celebrities it attracts, puts Charlie D in the Hall of Fame of tippers. A who-is-keeping-tabs philosophy seemed to be in his nature, but he always had a purpose. He enjoyed bringing others pleasure—from his wife and friends to other traders and colleagues and beyond. "I found it unbelievable that he could be that generous with people he didn't know all that well," noted one Goldberg employee. As a private tribute to a man who ate once or twice a month at Morton's, Raki has left Charlie D's photo up with Arnold's, Frank's, and MJ's. "It will be above *his* table until they fire me," said Raki at the steakhouse, pointing at a photo he took of Charlie and his wife. "You'll never find another one like him. I saw him a few weeks before he died. He kissed me on the cheek and said, 'See you next week.' That was the last time we saw each other."

Like Elvis, Charlie D wanted to do things for his parents as well, sometimes to their embarrassment. Vince and Marge received the keys to a luxury condo in Wilmette, initially an awkward situation. One neighbor thought Vince was a janitor and asked him if he could take care of some trash. Wilmette, an affluent community, wasn't like Vince's old neighborhood, but what parent wouldn't be proud? Charlie D had no problem finding needs and lacks, in himself or others, on which to spend his money. He would buy a beautiful tan brick home on Wilmette's Greenwood Avenue in 1983, a "starter" home, as he liked to call it. Not too long afterward, he bought a summer cabin in Michigan, not far from Point O' Woods Country Club in Benton Harbor. He also dabbled with investments outside of the bond pit, including a company named Sencon.

Charlie D also aided the bond pit indirectly with donations of a different sort. Once he had his legs under him as a trader, he began to bankroll other traders with accounts of $30,000 or more in an attempt to get them started in the business. More traders meant more liquidity for him, or so he reasoned. It was good for the market, his market now, if you thought about it. It didn't take long before he roped his brother into the business along with several of his colleagues at Harris Bank. Not everyone took him up on the offer, but more than a few did. His enthusiasm persuaded a few Harris friends, including Tom Young, John Pelling, and Mark Droegemueller, to get into the business, even if they didn't accept his bankroll. He also backed Jim Perkaus, who suffered a sports-related spinal injury that confined him to a wheechair, to trade from off the floor. Charlie's sincerity persuaded others that they could take risks and profit just like him. Perhaps the strangest introduction of all was Charlie D reintroducing Gordon Larsen, a Ph.D. in psychiatry and close friend of his mother Margaret, to the futures markets by scheduling a meeting for him with Dave Goldberg. A mad hatter himself in so many ways with a heart of gold, Larsen had lost a bundle in silver futures when the Hunt Brothers tried to corner the silver market, but he was honest and decent and a friend. Charlie D thought Larsen's understanding of human nature might make him an excellent trader. One talk with Goldberg, however, was as far as Larsen went with reentry into the world of speculation and risk. "Charlie sincerely believed that just about anybody could become an excellent trader," says Larsen. "His enthusiasm probably got the best of him with me, but I did enjoy the meeting with Dave."

These were fast times for Charlie D. More than a few traders who blew out of the market came to depend on him to get them back into the game, and more often than not he was happy to do it. For the right person and sometimes for the wrong one, he signed a check in his office, after the close, giving most people the benefit of the doubt. As far as he was concerned, there was no shame in taking a risk and losing, so long as you learned from the experience and came back stronger. At the time, he hardly missed the money. He was almost printing it, if you believe the buzz that surrounded the pit. One former Goldberg employee points out that Charlie D was "making well into the seven figures" each year over this time period and, as if to make his point without spilling the beans entirely, adds: "and I'm not talking just a one with six zeroes."

What was so remarkable during this stretch was the consistency with which he made money, and his ability to control the risk associated with futures trading. Charlie D the contrarian always seemed to have one eye on potential exits to a big trade when fast markets made the pit chaotic, and he was able to turn a profit on a position more often than not before the market stranded other less savvy traders in its wake. He scratched his trades before they got out of hand with monkish discipline. He rarely left the pit during trading hours, and almost always closed out his positions before the final bell. He did double-duty in the pit at night, when the Chicago Board of Trade launched an evening trading session.

"He was a good, fast trader," explains MacLennan. "The other big guys down here had more of a tendency to speculate—to hold positions longer than a day. Charlie loved to buy and sell, and usually went home even. I'm not saying he didn't speculate at times, because he did. But while others may have traded two 200- or 500-lot positions in a day, Charlie was doing 50 lots and 100 lots up to 100 times in a day. He was clearly the biggest trader in terms of volume. If he was long 500 bonds and needed to move, he could get the trade off."

Clearing firms never comment on trader activities, nor do exchanges, so Charlie D's bottom line relative to his competitors will never be known exactly, except by those who saw his profit and loss statements. But anecdotal evidence of his consistency does show outside the pit. From March 1983 to January 1987, he parlayed his trading revenues into outside investments. He would regularly take out in excess of $100,000 each month to fund investments outside the pit. In June 1986, for example, he contributed $262,000 in working capital to outside investments alone. For nearly four years, there was not a single month in which profits from the Treasury bond pit were not reinvested in other investments he saw as his business future. It was a track record of making money consistently as a trader only a handful of others in the pits could claim to match.

Those who saw him trade throughout the mid-1980s say it was a thing of beauty. "If I were to use one word to describe him," says Tom Young, a friend from Charlie's days at Harris Bank and a fellow bond trader, "it would be 'fearless.' It was like he was a vacuum cleaner up there on that top step, sucking in all this information that no one else could really see. He knew which traders were underwater, which traders were short or long, and by how much, and which traders would puke their positions under certain scenarios. He was intense up there, always concentrating on his next move, the movement of outside paper coming into the pit. And he always had a position on, every minute of the day. If he had a fault, I suppose it was his belief that others had the brains that he did to trade that way. Not everyone had the talent or the nerve to do it."

From 1980 to 1982, competing traders say that Charlie D made most of his money as a pure spreader. At the time, there were two-tick margins in most calendar spreads in bonds, which was an opportunity for someone willing to accommodate outside paper. Two ticks was a large profit margin for someone trading huge size like Charlie. He jumped all over that type of trading, particularly at a time when laws allowed year-end straddles and rolls at tax time. Those outside the pit looking for such trades frequently found Charlie D in the middle of the market, providing liquidity. The two-tick spreads, which later narrowed to one tick as the bond futures market became more efficient, made him his first small fortune because of the size he traded to accommodate other traders in and out of the pit. But just because it was sometimes a tax play at the end of the year did not mean it was riskless. Charlie D did it year round. He understood that futures positions called spreads have lower risk than simple long or short positions, and that he could control his risk by constructing spreads (combined long and short positions) so that much of what is lost on one position is gained back on the opposite position. He was one of the quickest, perhaps, at getting both legs of such trades off under the pressure of live market conditions. But if you weren't fast and didn't understand that spread relationships sometimes go awry, you could also lose your shirt, caught in between one leg of a trade and the other. Charlie D moved in the pit; he didn't stand still. On that basis he built up a sizable capital base in less than three years.

As the size of his bankroll grew, so too did Charlie D's confidence in the pit. Young and other bond pit brokers and locals saw it on a daily basis, amazed as they watched him begin to trade large positions that others didn't dare touch. Big brokers with thick decks always came looking for him from all directions in the pit, because of this reputation and his ability to digest or toss the hot potato. "His deal was size," explains Young. "It worked well for him, but it wouldn't work well for everybody, let me tell you. To trade that way, you had to be absolutely confident in your abilities."

Young's favorite memory of Charlie D in the pit was during an early night trading session in the late 1980s. During the session, Young saw Charlie D short the market in size, buying it back 20 ticks lower. He worked the pit to get in and out of this position like a well-oiled robo-trader, seemingly emotionless on the top step. "It was like he was just pushing the rest of the traders in the market off a cliff that night," says Young. "It was the most beautiful thing to watch as far as trading goes, particularly if you're a trader in the pit and can appreciate his awareness about the surrounding action that was taking place at the time. Charlie was the liquidity in the market in many of those early night trading sessions."

News of Charlie D's gift soon made its way out of the pit, and it was during the night trading hours that Charlie D was introduced to Japanese bond traders in Tokyo. Making a trip to Tokyo with other big hitters in the bond pit, Tom Baldwin and James Heinz (known jokingly as the "Prince of Darkness" because he traded only at night to help promote the night session), Charlie D made a lasting impression on Japanese traders. On the trip, he orally committed to trade 500-lot and up positions if the Japanese came into the market in the evening to conduct their business. The Japanese traders knew from their squawk boxes that he was one of the key traders on the floor. It was a commitment that left some traders in Tokyo scratching their heads, while it pulled others into the market. Charlie D was always a man of his word on the trading floor. It would not take long before the Chicago Board of Trade was trading millions of contracts at night and cut a lightbulb-shaped cake on the trading floor to celebrate. By 1991, the Japanese accounted for 50 percent of overall trading volume in bonds during the night trading session. On that particular public relations trip to Tokyo, Charlie D became even more of an enigma because of his uncanny ability in the eyes of the Japanese to make money in the bond pit. Some tried to ascribe special powers to explain his skill, which was hard to translate from a different time zone. "Excuse me, Mr. D," said one green trader at a Chicago Board of Trade–sponsored cocktail party in Tokyo, obviously searching for a sound reason for Charlie D's trading success. "Are you a relative of Fed Chairman Greenspan?"

Charlie D laughed at impressions used to explain his success inside the pit and turned it into a polite joke. "No sir, I'm not. But he sometimes does call me at home at 6:00 A.M." The Japanese never knew if he was serious or not. One trader, who witnessed his impact on the market, noted: "Almost single-handedly, he made the Japanese believe that there was going to be a level of liquidity that would allow them to trade at night."

Charlie D was more than just a moving target for the Japanese, with whom he regularly matched wits and positions in the early night trading sessions. His reputation at home also had spread through the tight-knit trading communities of Chicago and New York. Rumors abounded that powerful colleagues of off-the-floor speculator Paul Tudor Jones had tested the waters to see if Charlie D might come work for him. Charlie D, at the time, was interested in trading just his own money—at least at this point. He saw no need to work for anyone but himself.

One trader who well remembers Charlie D's early days in the bond pit is Dana Oberlin, an upstairs trader at Morgan Stanley in Chicago. Oberlin claims to be a direct beneficiary of Charlie D's largess when they were both at Harris Bank. It was there that Charlie D took a personal interest, while Oberlin was making his way through the bank's training program, to find him a position in the bank's trust department. Oberlin gravitated to Charlie D from the beginning because he saw something even then that was unique. It was a small invisible thing to do for Oberlin, but it has pushed him down his own yellow brick road.

"At the bank, he was the type of guy who always had something witty or intelligent to say," says Oberlin. "He gave me the heads up to help me get a job in the Harris Bank trust department one time, simply because I told him about a research paper I had written on the performance of low-price stocks versus high-price stocks. He knew I wanted to be a portfolio manager and he wanted to help me do it. Like many others who knew him at Harris, I was struck by his knack for making the right moves in life for himself and others. It's strange how in the middle of the trading day I will sometimes think about him, even to this day. I can't explain it. He just pops up in my head."

A phone call from Charlie D in 1980, when Oberlin was working at Morgan Stanley, was the first Oberlin heard about Charlie D leaving Harris Bank. About three years later, he introduced Charlie D to his wife Marie, a real estate agent, to help Charlie D shop for a new house in Wilmette. Obviously he had risen far above the $800-per-week salary that new Harris bankers were making in the late 1970s.

"He had an aura about him," explains Oberlin. "I knew Bill Kissinger who owned the house next to him since I was a kid, because I went to school with Bill's kids. I remember Bill saying, 'Who is this guy?,' not soon after he moved in. You heard in the neighborhood that he worked at the Board of Trade, but you also heard that he was a pretty young guy to be paying the kind of money he had to pay to buy that house on Greenwood. His reputation started to precede him a little bit in the neighborhood. But once the neighbors got to know Charlie, any negative perceptions, jealousy, or suspicions were gone. He wasn't the type of guy having caterers do parties at his house every other weekend. He wasn't pretentious at all. But there was definitely a little buzz about him running through the neighborhood."

Charlie D's savvy as a trader by then was finely honed. Unbeknownst to Oberlin's wife the real estate agent, his Mona Lisa lips hid his housing preference. While Charlie D's wife Ann loved the two-story, tan brick house on Greenwood next to Kissinger, Charlie D saw his dream home elsewhere. He declared his love for a large wooden house, owned then by the Earlywine family, across the street on Greenwood. Also for sale, the Earlywine house had a wraparound front porch that Charlie D would not let real estate agent Marie Oberlin forget. While shopping for houses, he seemed reluctant even to go inside the tan brick home on Greenwood, and had to be coaxed not to judge the house's character prematurely.

After all these years, Oberlin still didn't know of Charlie D's true desires during the real estate negotiations. He was buying the house for his wife Ann, not himself. The tan brick house was the one his wife wanted, but he sure wasn't going to tell his friend Dana or his real estate agent wife that. It was a bit of harmless gamesmanship that befuddled both the Oberlins, a wide receiver reverse with Charlie running with a football made of air while his wife walked into the front door of her dream home for a touchdown.

"Oh, he was heartbroken," says Dana, recounting the incident, as if it had happened yesterday. "He used the phone in my folks' house and kept talking about offering more than the asking price for the other house, even though it was sold. He just wouldn't give up. I don't know what he specifically liked about it; I think he said he liked its vintage and style. If he couldn't buy that house, he told us that he would buy the one across the street so that he could at least look at it."

Sorry Dana and Marie, Charlie D was just having some fun. It was his nature.

"Charlie D loved that tan brick house," says his wife Ann, knowing her husband's impenetrable poker face was never easy to decipher whether he was buying and selling bonds or houses. "He always called it our first 'starter' home. It was the type of home you could just walk into and start living. It was great."

That house, like the party, was just a sign of Charlie D's bigger plans in life outside of the bond pit. During the mid-1980s Charlie D, according to some friends, took a casual observer's interest in the deal-making powers of leveraged buyout (LBO) acquisition specialist William F. Farley. Formerly a native of Pawtucket, Rhode Island, who had transplanted to Chicago, Farley was making serious waves in Chicago business circles by the relatively young age of 42. Beginning his career as an encyclopedia salesman in 1969, Farley parlayed his savings of $25,000 into possibly 10,000 times that by 1985. After buying Northwest Industries in 1985, he controlled a company with $2 billion in revenues and was listed in the Forbes 400 list of richest men, with an estimated net worth of $250 million. He was also a minority shareholder in the Chicago White Sox, a director at the Goodman Theater, and a governor of Bowdoin College.

Farley in 1985 was lighting up the business pages as Chicago's LBO guru. Charlie D saw a parallel between his life and that of Farley's, fashioning himself not just the biggest bond trader but potentially something more. For one, Farley sprang from humble beginnings as a postman's son, while Charlie D started as the son of a college football coach. No glitter in either profession, really. Both Farley and Charlie D had been divorced once, and later remarried, starting with whatever they could scrum together themselves. In their respective markets, both had proven their skills in buying value cheaply. Finally, both men seemed always to be searching for bigger competition and bigger risks.

LBO specialist William F. Farley was a feared and respected industrialist. A venerable Republican, Illinois Senator Charles Percy, touted him as an "exceptional" candidate for the U.S. Senate in 1986, against Democrat incumbent Senator Alan Dixon. It was quite a compliment to Farley, who had built Farley Industries into a highly leveraged conglomerate of manufacturing companies and, as a result, had also become a controversial figure in Chicago business as an upstart newcomer who played by his own rules. On August 10, 1989, the *Chicago Tribune* would ask a question about him in a headline: THE FRUITS OF INDUSTRY: CAN UNDERWEAR KING WILLIAM FARLEY STRETCH HIS SAVVY TO THE WHITE HOUSE?

Noted the Tribune's James Warren in his "Magazines" column about Farley after the LBO king's August 7 interview with Connie Bruck in the *New Yorker*: "His striving verges on the comical, but don't discount him. He's got nerve, as shown by long-shot corporate victories and, on a different level, showing up for an interview with Bruck wearing a Fruit of the Loom sweatshirt and red briefs."

The same might have been said about Charlie D's competitiveness. While he never imitated Farley's interview theatrics, Charlie D's mindset as a businessman was not so different. Publicity didn't seem to interest him; he preferred to go about his business, planning for bigger days when he truly would be worth talking about and keeping his trading reputation private. Something deeper ran through his nature, and it didn't involve image consultants. Initially on a smaller scale, Charlie D probably saw no reason why he couldn't transition from being the bond pit's best trader into another type of creative dealmaker, perhaps even becoming an industrialist himself. He had crossed paths with many businessmen of stature, including Bulls and White Sox team owner Jerry Reinsdorf, while working at Reinsdorf's real estate development company, Balcor, prior to trading. He certainly did not see himself in the bond pit forever, and there were parts to Farley's and Reinsdorf's characters that he found charismatic and inspiring. He paid close attention to their business acumen and style, and aspired to reach their level of success as mavericks.

No one at Ann's party doubted Charlie D's ability to do the same as Farley and to perhaps do it even bigger and better, especially Charlie. While his trading had put him on the top step of the bond pit at the Chicago Board of Trade, he was already contemplating his next move to turn his first $10 million into his first $100 million or more. After all, his compensation in the trading pits was right up there with Farley's annual salary, and he was building his wealth without debt. It would not be long before Charlie D began to look for investments and tax shelters that could lead him down other paths and on to new and greater challenges. As part of this goal, Charlie D started to invest in start-up companies he thought showed promise. In 1982, he acquired controlling interest in the outstanding capital stock of a company named Sencon, based in Northbrook, Illinois. Throughout the '80s, he also loaned $120,000 to a company called Cytodiagnostic Laboratory in Chicago and dabbled in other start-ups, some of which were tax shelters.

Sencon, ultimately, became the company on which Charlie D focused his most intent interest. This company was marketing a product known as "The Sencon System," an exterior wall insulation system comprised of Styrofoam or polystyrene insulation board mechanically fastened by metal fasteners to the exterior of commercial buildings. Over the insulation board a fiberglass mesh was fastened, over which was then applied a bonding agent and two coats of the combined cementitious Sencon products. Both the Sencon wet and dry mix contained latex polyvinyl acetate polymers. The company had not yet turned a profit, but Charlie smelled opportunity. His days traveling to shopping malls and commercial centers for Balcor's Reinsdorf told him there was a market for this stuff. From 1982 to the first few months of 1984, all goods for Sencon were manufactured by Dayton Superior Corporation, at its plant in Oregon, Illinois, using a commercially available polymer called Hornweld. The market for such a product was wide open in the Midwest and other regions of the United States, and it would not be long before Charlie D began to invest working capital into the company and to aid its legal defense against competitors who sought to prevent its entrance into the market. In the process, he continued to push the concept of marketing such a product nationwide and globally, trading and channeling some of his wealth to this purpose. In 1985, Sencon changed its formula to a wholly factory-blended dry mix wherein dry powdered polymers were factory-blended to eliminate the need to ship liquid admix to the job site, and to simplify job-site mixing. The revolutionary dry mix required the use of low-alkali cement and the proper ratio of sand and other components. Over a five-year period, Charlie D invested approximately $5 million of his bond pit profits into this company.

The road Sencon traveled had been anything but smooth during its early history, but the company was making a name for itself. Through a head hunter in Chicago, Charlie first met a man named C. Randal Rushing, who had previously been national sales manager for Dryvit Systems, a Warwick, Rhode Island–based firm. Rushing had left the company in March 1983 and began marketing an exterior wall finish and insulation system. This product would compete against Dryvit System's own trademarked exterior wall insulation and finish system, called "Outsulation." Since shopping malls, casinos, hotels, airports, and churches were going up just about everywhere that Charlie D looked, Sencon's product had endless uses. Exterior wall and insulation systems were an essential part of the construction process for large buildings from coast to coast, and beyond. The U.S. military was even using this stuff for barracks at home and in Hawaii and Korea.

Charlie D saw good news on many fronts. The Sencon System, through 1983 and 1984, had already won many bids away from Dryvit, including the Stapleton International Airport project in Denver, the Omni Hotel project in St. Louis, the U.S. Army's Schofield Barracks project in Oahu, Hawaii, a Target store project in Fridley, Minnesota, and the Bor-Son Tower West project in Minneapolis. Dryvit was not the least bit happy. In court, Dryvit had sought injunctive relief and monetary damages from C. Randal Rushing, then president of Sencon. It also sought to enforce certain noncompetition and confidentiality covenants and to enjoin Rushing from conducting the business of Sencon. But Charlie D, who signed an unconditional agreement on September 21, 1984, to further support the company, aided Rushing's and Sencon's legal defense against such accusations. The injunction sought by Dryvit against Sencon had been voluntarily dismissed by Dryvit Systems on April 19, 1985, in federal court and in January 1987 in state court. Things were looking up for the new company in what would grow to be a multibillion-dollar industry.

The risks of an entrepreneurial start-up company and battling cancer later did not mix well for Charlie. Down the road, Sencon accused its product manufacturer, W. R. Bonsal, of not manufacturing its product in conformity with specifications and for breach of contract, while W.R. Bonsal countersued for money owed for the manufacture of product just before this dispute. Charlie ultimately agreed to pay a judgment in favor of W. R. Bonsal for $316,437.88 on May 10, 1989, and Sencon was dealt a serious blow. Fighting cancer, Charlie was never able to turn the company around after these early problems with its product and the subsequent lawsuit.

In 1986, however, the future, in Charlie D's optimistic eye, could not have seemed brighter for Sencon as it cleared Rushing's legal wrangle off its plate and began manufacturing its products through a third-party arrangement with W. R. Bonsal. From March 1984 to December 1985, W. R. Bonsal was principal manufacturer of Sencon's product. Sencon entered into this agreement in January 1984 and ordered $600,000 of manufactured product to be delivered to various job sites all across the country. Life was made complex because of Sencon's nature as a start-up company, but it was also promising. Charlie D used the word "global" to describe Sencon, whenever he met with his lawyers or company executives. His optimism was contagious. Still the underdog in this battle, Charlie D never doubted the company's ability to compete if it could find its place at the starting line. Like Farley, he knew he could find a way to become even bigger and more successful. Some day he planned to hang up his trading jacket, but not just yet. Trading was his ticket to a brighter future.

Not everyone at the New York birthday celebration, however, knew what Mr. D did for a living. Charlie D played up his mystique as a successful businessman from Chicago like a fiddler on the roof, enjoying it, but also making light of it whenever he had the chance. He had an ego for sure when it came to being a trader, but he was not too full of himself. He still could have fun whenever there was a crowd.

"I remember when he took everybody to New York for Ann's 40th," says Gallagher. "It was such a party that the caterers at the Plaza thought he was with the mob, since he came from Chicago and had that fine Italian name. Typical of New Yorkers to think that, I suppose. There were bellhops who took care of him in the presidential suite, and they were all kids who were on call for 24 hours. As we're coming down the elevator with one of the bellhops, the kid says, 'Hey, Mr. D, I would like to come to work for you in Chicago.' So Charlie says, 'You would? You know what I do for a living, don't you?' 'Yes, I think I do, Mr. D,' the kid said. So Charlie gets real serious, looking him directly in the eye, 'Maybe you can come to work for me? Have you ever killed anybody?' The blank look on that kid's face. He says, 'No, but I think I could.' Charlie and I went up the elevator just pissing in our pants after that. It was classic Charlie D. You never knew what he was going to come up with next."

Every good party must come to an end. As the guests returned home on Sunday, Charlie D seemed slightly concerned about a pain beneath his right arm. He was much too busy to worry about it for too long, but he did take the time to ask a friend at the party, Dr. Jim Matthews, head cardiologist at Northwestern University Hospital, about it. Occasionally it seemed to act up, and it was hell on a trader who had to lift his arms above his head a fair part of the trading day. Dr. Matthews suggested that it was probably muscle strain that could be cured with a little rest, but if it bothered Charlie, he might consider going for an X ray back in Chicago. Who had time for an X ray? Certainly not Charlie. The plates on his table were spinning fast and furious.

"It was as if Charlie was taking his hot air balloon higher and higher every year," says one bond trader who knew him well. "At some point, you're up there pretty high in the air—and some people might wonder when to stop filling the balloon with hot air. But Charlie was so confident. He was going to take his balloon up as high as it would go and see where it would take him. It wasn't in his nature as a person to worry about all the possible places that life takes us before we land. He loved his work and was always gearing up for tomorrow."

unstung by | 3
the sting

Almost five years to the day after Charlie D's death on Thursday, May 23, 1991, a letter from the Chicago office of the Federal Bureau of Investigation (FBI) came to me and confirmed what other locals and brokers in the bond futures pit had told me repeatedly in casual conversation. Many of Charlie D's competitors had argued that he was not only the biggest risk taker and largest market maker in the pit in terms of the contract volume traded on any given day but also the pit trader with the most integrity. The FBI's letter had not come out of the blue; I had requested it because of a fear that I might find out something about Charlie D's trading that would tarnish his Mr. Clean reputation. With a reporter's skepticism garnered from years of covering financial markets, I figured no one could be as snow white as the broker and Charlie's friends and family made him out to be.

The letter had come after I had already requested a face-to-face interview with an FBI agent. That random request alone must have sounded somewhat bizarre to the first FBI agent who fielded my call, since it was not always easy finding a proper and concise way to request an interview about a dead man without sounding like a screwball. The death factor alone was probably a red flag with any investigator. But there was nothing to lose by trying, so I explained the story as best I knew it. At the FBI agent's suggestion, I attempted to go directly to the source, figuring that another FBI agent named Michael Bassett would be able either to put to rest or to confirm my fear. For two years he had frequented the shadows of the same trading pit in which Charlie D had made millions. Bassett began trading in 1987 and continued until an FBI sting operation made the front page of the *Chicago Tribune* on January 19, 1989. By that time he had disappeared from the Board of Trade without a trace. I hoped he would talk with me off the record, just to assure me that I was pursuing the story I thought I was. I simply wanted verification that what I had heard about Charlie D was true—or, conversely, to discover what the collective memory of all my other sources may have missed or omitted. If I needed to punch holes in the memories of well-meaning friends, I would call it as I saw it, like an umpire.

FBI mole Michael Bassett, known as bond trader Mike McLoughlin during the FBI sting operation at Chicago's two largest futures exchanges, had been stationed in the bond futures pit at the Chicago Board of Trade. His job hadn't been an easy one. He was wired for sound many times when he encountered traders in and outside the pit. At the time, the bond futures pit was the world's largest, trading 70.3 million contracts by the end of 1988, or 28.6 percent of all volume in the 49 largest U.S. futures contracts trading over 100,000 contracts for that year. He had been dropped into the futures industry's largest contract market, where it was uncontrolled pandemonium in the pit on the most active days and nonsensical chaos even in quiet moments. With the din of voices in the pit often roaring like a jet engine, it was not uncommon for this machinery of traders to push and shove during the heat of battle, or to spit and sometimes stab with their pencils if tempers sparked. While the protective railing covered with soft black rubber foam encircling this human hurricane prevented traders from falling off the outer edge of the pit as they jostled for position or relief from constant bumping in the pit, it couldn't contain the volatile emotions or quiet the bombastic voices. The air was heavy in the pit's epicenter and the surrounding area, and the overcrowded exchange floor wafted the same odors as a men's locker room.

There, Bassett stood in proximity to some of the largest bond traders, who matched wits with some of the world's largest investment and commercial banks, insurance companies, institutional bond managers and, on occasion, central bankers such as the Federal Reserve. In total, his undercover investigation would lead to three convictions by the time he disappeared in January 1989. Broker Howard J. Groberstein, then 33, was charged with treble monetary damages under the Racketeer Influenced and Corrupt Organization Act (RICO) and 127 other counts; local trader Melanie Kosar, 25, was charged with one count of mail fraud and one count of prearranged trading; and John Myskowksi, 36, pleaded guilty to single counts of mail fraud and prearranged trading. The FBI suspected more, but these three traders were all they could convict—at least in the bond pit.

Tracking Bassett down, I discovered, was simple—just one phone call. Conveniently, he was still in the agency's Chicago office and hadn't skipped town to live and work somewhere else, as I was told some FBI agents did after a major investigation of this magnitude. Or perhaps my call was a little behind the times. In September 1987, Bassett had started trading under an assumed name after first working as a clerk for Archer-Daniels-Midland (ADM) at the Chicago Board of Trade for several months. This ADM floor position put him in direct contact with other traders, matching and confirming the details of their trades.

During our conversation, I ended up doing most of the talking, speaking about a man whom Bassett would never hint he had encountered. This seemed hard to believe since everyone in the pit knew who the big traders were, especially the one whose story I was chasing. The only things worth recollecting about that ten-minute conversation were Bassett's advice on how I might request information about Mr. DiFrancesca, as he chose to call him, under the Freedom of Information Act, and an odd feeling that came over me during our discussion. As he spoke, I sensed that Bassett was visualizing the trader in question. I listened intently to the only thing worth hearing: his inflection. It wasn't what he said so much as how he said it that caught my attention, particularly when I mentioned that "Mr. DiFrancesca" had died a few years ago. His words seemed delicately chosen, his sentences paced. He became almost overly polite. While speculation on my part, his tone of voice gave shape exactly to what it was he may have wanted to but could not tell me, even if I could never prove that he was actually telling me anything about anyone. So many others in the futures industry had given me the behind-the-scenes thumbs up about something that seemed to be on the tip of Bassett's tongue before he swallowed it. Had he seen firsthand the same honest, hardworking trader about whom I had heard so much?

Bassett's bureaucratic courtesy had been worth something, if only another shroud to add to Charlie D's dimension and shape. My formal attempt to investigate whether Charlie D was as squeaky clean as one attorney representing a few traders prosecuted by the FBI had suggested he was, elicited a reply more assuring than Bassett could professionally or legally volunteer. It was essentially a form letter, but then again, writing it had at least forced some FBI agent to rattle a filing cabinet in some nondescript government building in Chicago to check on a name.

"This is in response to your request for records under the Freedom of Information Act (FOIA)," stated this letter from FBI special agent Herbert L. Collins, Jr. "Your request about Mr. Charles P. DiFrancesca was received by this office on May 1, 1996. A search was conducted of our indices to the central records system as maintained by the Chicago Division. Based upon the information you furnished no records were located regarding your FOIA request."

That letter, thankfully, gave me the right to an appeal to the U.S. Department of Justice. I fired off a second query, this time sounding more confrontational. Tell me something I don't know, to paraphrase, was the letter's basic theme. Richard L. Huff, codirector of the Justice Department's Office of Information and Privacy, replied in writing with an official looking rubber-stamped date in the right-hand corner, June 24, 1996, obviously the work of Huff's hand and ink pad. Just below it was Re: Appeal No. 96-1516 RLH: DAH: LAD. I assumed the initials meant that at least three agents had looked at the appeal, and that the official appeal number would be used by a district court if I ever decided to option what now seemed to be my perpetual right to appeal. This time, however, the tone of the letter assured me that I would only be creating unnecessary paperwork for a court clerk in the Northern District of Illinois. The shape beneath the shroud of my fear—the criminal or, at any rate, questionable trader—had all but disappeared with all this written hocus-pocus.

"You were advised by the Chicago Field Office on May 10, 1996, that no records responsive to your request could be located in the indices of that office," wrote Huff. "It has been determined by my staff that its response was correct. Inasmuch as appeals can be taken only from denials of access to records which exist and can be located in Department of Justice files, I am closing your appeal in this office."

If the FBI ever kept a file on Charlie D during its sting operations at the Chicago Board of Trade or the Chicago Mercantile Exchange (CME), I was certain I would never see it. I could only rely on the honesty of the FBI agents, coming to me in the shape of form letters, who processed my request and told me that Charlie D did not have a file. The contents of these two letters—as boilerplate and impersonal as they seemed—were at least a hook to hang my hat on. Viewed in tandem with the anecdotal testimony of competitors in the U.S. Treasury bond futures pit and other sources familiar with the FBI investigation, they collectively confirmed that Charlie D's integrity wasn't questioned by those who were paid to walk into the pit wired, to question and to probe, and to prosecute any trader they caught breaking the law. Perhaps Bassett had told me something by saying nothing, for I knew from a handful of other traders that Charlie D had crossed trails with at least one FBI agent, long before anyone including Charlie D himself knew of their actual identities, on more than one occasion. I had also been told by at least one reliable source that he had seen an FBI agent ask Charlie D for some advice on how to trade on a couple of occasions. Charlie D had never been one to pass up the opportunity to offer some friendly advice to a new trader struggling as he had in his earlier days. McLoughlin clearly was a neophyte. Perhaps they had spoken.

Given Charlie D's stature in the pit, odds are the FBI, at minimum, looked into his trading. The FBI doesn't spend time on major investigations hoping to catch a few small fry. But, as far as I could tell, they found nothing untoward. If they conducted as thorough an investigation as they claimed later at a major press conference, they surely examined Charlie. Perhaps they determined that he was clean, and later attempted to glean what they could from him as traders do in casual conversation—without revealing their true identity. While FBI agents had knocked on the doors of many traders in the wee hours of the night and delivered subpoenas just a few months before Charlie D gave his final videotaped lecture on trading in March 1989, they had not rung the doorbell of the DiFrancesca's attractive tan-brick home in Wilmette.

Later I discovered that two of Charlie D's three videotapes on trading could not be found. One theory proposed for the displacement of these two early tapes by those who knew about them is that Charlie's original clearing firm, Goldberg Brothers, was bought up by LIT America, which was later sold to the proprietary Wall Street trading firm, Spear Leeds & Kellogg. During all these corporate shuffles, the possibility that these first two tapes were lost or tossed in some box the new corporation's executives no longer knew to save seems highly plausible. To my knowledge, only a third and final tape which Charlie did in March 1989 for LIT America still exists. Charlie's brother John had been the only one who saved a copy of one of the three tapes—the one done for LIT—that I could find. Another explanation for the two missing tapes, I suppose, is the possibility that some anonymous trader borrowed them and simply forgot to return them. I queried at least a half dozen Goldberg and LIT executives who might know of their whereabouts and came up empty. One of these executives at LIT did give me a tape that was supposed to be Charlie D lecturing, but turned out to be someone else entirely. This search (along with things I heard from others in the process) led to my own more sensational theory: that Charlie D's videotaped educational seminars and "sermons" about trading had included enough wisdom that the FBI agents may have put them to good use to train themselves as moles on the nuances and proper ethics of pit trading. There is no question that the FBI visited the large clearing firms and no doubt looked at the big traders like Charlie.

Still, it is all open to question what the FBI agents actually discovered during their probe of Chicago's futures exchanges. The investigations, which FBI agents called Operation Hedgeclipper and Operation Sourmash, ultimately led to 46 indictments and 14 guilty pleas by traders at the Chicago Board of Trade and Chicago Mercantile Exchange on August 3, 1989. Wendy Gramm, chairman of the Commodity Futures Trading Commission (CFTC) at that time, traveled to Chicago with

Attorney General Richard Thornburgh and FBI Director William Sessions to emphasize the importance of the FBI's two-and-a-half year investigation. Flanked by these men and U.S. Attorney Anton Valukas, who spearheaded the investigation, Gramm told a standing-room-only crowd of journalists, photographers, and TV cameramen that the FBI's undercover activities represented "the most extensive and aggressive law enforcement effort in the financial area, ever."

Once the dust had settled on the investigation, eight of 14 traders who agreed to plead guilty signed their names to civic consent decrees offered as part of legal plea bargaining between investigators and defense attorneys. These decrees prevented them from ever holding membership privileges at a U.S. futures exchange again. Of the 46 traders charged, a total of 24 came from the CME's Japanese yen and Swiss franc pits. The remainder came from the Chicago Board of Trade's soybean futures trading pit, where Ostrom had stationed himself under the alias Richard Carlson, and McLoughlin's turf in the bond futures trading pit. Carlson bagged 19 traders for illegal trading activities; McLoughlin nabbed three.

For those familiar with the mercurial trading pits in Chicago, and the economic Darwinism that takes place within its cramped quarters, it is not enough for a trader to be praised simply because the FBI does not have his name on some list that may or may not have made its way into the public eye. In reality, such praise can be earned only by the natural frisking that takes place among competing traders who take on one another and the market forces on a daily basis. Alone among themselves, they rely on *lex mercatoria*, or law merchant, a system of mercantile ethics developed during the Middle Ages that resonates still in all of the Board of Trade's rules. In a nutshell, a trader's word is his bond and should not be broken, if it is to stay golden. If it is broken or twisted to that trader's advantage, exchange rules allow fellow members who are also traders to function in much the same way as a court—to expedite decision making and disciplinary actions so that business life doesn't become the domain of lawyers or the corrupt. It's a delicate balance to be sure, but an effective one. If the crime is serious enough to be deemed unmercantile, the trader who broke his word can be denied the right to trade, be fined, or even expelled. It is the purpose of this time-tested system of law by and for traders of all types that keeps the wheels of futures markets greased and running smoothly.

That is obviously what caused FBI agents and Board of Trade officials to butt heads, the latter pointing out that the treble damages and seriousness of RICO was never intended to be applied to all types of business misconduct or petty crimes, as it sometimes appeared to be in the FBI's investigation of traders in the pit. The FBI investigation, and the question of whether it had worked in uncovering significant crime, prompted a debate in the *Columbia Journalism Review* that made the press, not the traders, the more interesting topic of discussion. In a July/August 1989 issue, that story's headline gibed the press and read: FRONT PAGE: THEY CAN DISH IT OUT, BUT THEY CAN'T TAKE IT. Neither the FBI nor the press, like futures markets, would come out of the investigation unscathed.

Many traders and reporters, shortly after the investigation surfaced, complained that the FBI had not even scratched the opaque surface of what goes on in Chicago's futures markets, which still depend largely on the self-regulatory law merchant for their success, despite the formation of a federal agency, the Commodity Futures Trading Commission, designated to oversee them by congressional action in 1974. Melanie Kosar, one of the traders convicted, was one of many who downplayed the quality of the work done by the FBI and the press, even though she was convicted for infractions in the Chicago Board of Trade's bond pit. Said Kosar of Bassett in a *Chicago Lawyer* cover story, "In the Pits," appearing on May 19, 1989, which retold her career-ruining experience with an FBI agent and a *Wall Street Journal* reporter at the Board of Trade: "I felt sorry for him because he regularly lost money. He had minimal trading abilities. He was awkward and not coordinated with his hand signals. I kind of looked out for him."

Those without an ax to grind and a journalist's eye for detail made similar accusations, albeit for different reasons than Kosar. Their remarks reached closer to the market's higher—and perhaps less-perfect—mercantile law. "Newcomers inevitably must either make large trades and demonstrate their ability to ride major risks, or be relegated to the farther fringes of the action," noted David Greising and Laurie Morse, in *Brokers, Bagmen and Moles,* an expose on the FBI investigation and corruption in Chicago's futures markets. "As an inexperienced newcomer, Bassett never made it to the top tier of the bond pit. His investigation netted only three traders."

As for Charlie D's life immediately after the investigation, there was nothing different or curious about his actions, other than perhaps being more vocal about his displeasure that life in the pits had sunk to such low levels in the public's eye. The FBI sting was a topic, quite frankly, that embarrassed him—whether the investigation had proven or disproven anything about the overall integrity of traders in the futures markets. In a lecture before his peers on March 23, 1989, he openly admitted to his audience that he hadn't identified himself as a commodities trader while vacationing in Florida when someone had asked, a sign that he felt stigmatized. Sometime after the FBI investigation broke in 1989, his son Jake watched his father's face turn crimson after his Porsche had stalled on the side of the Eden's Expressway. A trailing taunt flew from one of many cars whizzing past, "Serves you right, you fucking commodities trader." Charlie D and Jake locked eyes and said nothing. The next day, Charlie D sold the car. Jake could laugh about it seven years later, but his father hadn't seen the humor in the situation. Trading was a career he loved, a profession that in some sense had saved him. In the early days of his marriage, he was known to stop his car next to a soybean field and lecture his children about the economic purposes of the Chicago Board of Trade. With futures trading always seemingly an incomprehensible abstraction even to the most well-educated adults, Charlie D placed soybeans in the hands of his young children, saying "This is one of the commodities we trade." The confused looks given to him by Jake and stepdaughter Maggie, at such a young age, made it a very short lecture.

Even though his platonic relationship with the Goddess of Ceres atop the Board of Trade had always been strong, he was not as zealous about his craft in 1989, except on one point. "You know, I don't like the idea of standing in the pit not knowing if the guy next to me is a thief," he said to an audience of traders. "I don't like that."

Perhaps the knowledge of one's imminent death that overcomes the cancer patient is what prompted him to challenge his fellow trading peers attending his lecture in March 1989 to buy and sell in a manner above reproach—and then to rise to their defense later in the same speech, as someone who identified intimately with the difficulties and misperceptions about the relative value of their jobs. Embarrassed about the FBI sting, he also seemed embarrassed that he would ever try to speak so reverently about his chosen profession. F---ing commodities trader? Yep. That's all he was. That media criticism of his peers pissed him off, even if a handful of his ilk were bad apples, was not difficult to understand. He had been stereotyped and stigmatized along with those with whom he labored each day under horrific stress. Shady characters existed in every profession. As a result, his anger on the subject practically boiled. Didn't anyone realize that if one-tick spreads became two in U.S. Treasury bond futures, the U.S. government and thus taxpayers faced the potential burden of $1 billion in additional interest costs per year on the debt it financed through the issuance of government bonds? This was hardly a consumer-pays-in-the-end fact that was making any headlines. He defended his fellow traders for just this reason. So much for John Q. Public's notion that commodities traders preyed on the outside public and printed money by stealing from those who weren't part of the club. Had the FBI agents or newspaper reporters ever tried to make a living trading futures? It wasn't easy, despite the potential rewards. Traders like him were the grease that made markets hum.

"I don't understand for the life of me why anybody would want to be a commodities trader, given the publicity we've gotten and some of the conditions we work under, with one exception—you want to make money," he intoned, stiff-lipped and pacing. "So we *are* here to make money. That's an important thing to remember. When you walk into that pit, there's not going to be any psychic reinforcement. Nobody's going to come up to you and say you're a helluva trader, and you don't give a shit if they do. Because if it isn't in your [trading] statement, you can't eat it, OK. It's like checking in your personnel file; nobody cares about that anymore. You're independent operators. You're sleaze balls and slime bags and your neighbors think you cheat. OK, and they think they are taken advantage of every time they put an order in. They think you stole from their aunt. I like to think we do our job, provide a service, but we are economic animals. When you walk into that pit, you're there. There isn't any more glamour associated with being a commodities trader. That all went out the window with all that FBI stuff. You're a commodities trader because you want to make money. So when you walk into that pit, you've got to have some rules. . . ."

As Charlie D no doubt knew, there was more sizzle than steak when it came to public perception about futures markets. And it would not change overnight—perhaps never—and certainly not in what he worried might be his short lifetime. A trading pit, after all, is no simple place in which to conduct an undercover investigation—much less to be an honest guy trying to make a decent living. Despite the perception resulting from the FBI investigation, he knew the reality is that far more traders blow out of the market long before even a few of them have any success. With a noise level that can deafen and destroy a trader's voice, and stress that can manifest itself into bleeding ulcers and heart conditions, traders often rely on hand signals and eyesight alone to make trades, which are then scribbled on a card. Despite the efforts of trading clerks to verify the accuracy of trades made on the steps of the pit, a trader's honesty is paramount. It cannot be regulated by exchange committees, laws, or regulations, and for that reason is valued above all else by other traders. It is on the basis of law merchant, and the traders who put their faith and actions within the spirit of this higher creed, that the market can function efficiently to the point that billions of dollars of business are transacted in a single day, on average, at the Chicago Board of Trade. When a trader makes a mistake—taking the wrong side or inadvertently making an outtrade—it is often the "slime bag" or a clearing firm who eats the loss, not the slime bag's neighbor's aunt. And as an economic animal, Charlie D was comfortable saying this to anyone who questioned the honorability of his jungle. He had slimed himself on more than one occasion, or had been slimed by others, at his own expense. It was for this reason that traders euphemistically referred to trading cards as "bullets." During a bad spell, they could be as dangerous as a handgun every time you picked one from your pocket and fired.

Charlie D did not live in fear of the FBI, as perhaps the extremely small, crooked percentage of his fellow traders might. That Charlie D set the standard for integrity in the largest trading pit at the world's largest and oldest futures exchange is affirmed by many of his competitors. So important was Charlie D's contribution that Tom Bonen, then a popular market commentator at Discount Corporation of New York Futures, sat in front of his computer screen on May 24, 1991, and typed a message that would not make any of his clients money that day. It was not even a message he was sure any of them would care to read, less than two years after the FBI investigation. But his own observations and experiences as an executive at the Chicago Board of Trade had surprisingly overwhelmed him when the reality set in that Charlie D had heard his final closing market bell.

Between sips of coffee, Tom Bonen's emotions turned to metaphors on his computer screen as he watched his children play in the back yard, thinking of Charlie D's kids on that fateful day: "Just like the day that Babe Ruth died . . . it rained yesterday morning in Chicago. In fact, it poured Thursday morning, because even the heavens wept at the passing of Charlie D.

"There are incredible parallels between Charlie D and Babe Ruth. Yes! Both were legends. Both were 'incomparable superstars' as their respective enterprises were beginning to move into an important new era. In future decades, market analysts will be able to appreciate (and comment about) the incredible contribution 'Charlie D' made to the development of the bond pit during the 1980s. He was awesome.

"Without any hesitation, I would consider 'Charlie D' the 'Sultan of Scalp.' He refined the art of trading into a science during the past five years. The liquidity that the bond market now enjoys is, in large part, due to his imagination and execution as a legendary scalper and trader.

"I think the clubhouse speech following the death of Babe Ruth by Waite 'Schoolboy' Hoyt, who was a Hall of Famer and teammate of Babe Ruth, says more than many of us would want to admit about Charlie D. Hoyt's comments followed a quip by a brash, young rookie who said, 'The big fellow's dead? I guess we'll have to chip in flowers.'

" 'Listen, punk. Ruth has meant more to ballplayers than any man who ever lived. You ought to get down on your knees and thank God that a man like Babe existed. Where do you think you'd be if it hadn't been for the big fellow? Or where would I be? Or where would baseball be if it hadn't been for the Babe?' "

When people read that commentary the next day, many weren't able to stem their tears. They knew the man, and they knew what Bonen had written was true. By midmorning, Bonen had heard from scores of traders who wanted dozens of copies of the Charlie D tribute. They called from London, Toronto, Tokyo, and Sydney.

Later that day one trader who was not necessarily a close friend of Charlie D's confided to Bonen that he had to leave the bond pit because he was so overcome by the man's absence. Another big hitter on the floor later admitted to running into the men's room stall as he sobbed uncontrollably. They were all touched by Bonen's words, but more important, they all realized that they had been touched by the presence of a true trading genius on the floor—the Sultan of Scalp.

"I sat there wondering if Charlie's kids would ever really know the magnitude of their Dad," said Bonen. "How could they ever know what Charlie meant to the 'game' he loved so passionately? How could they even know why so many strangers at the Board would truly miss their father? How could they understand, years later, what their Dad did to affect so many other lives at the exchange? It was the easiest piece I'd ever written."

Bonen, now a sports writer for a daily newspaper on the south side of Chicago, stands behind his words today. He is convinced that, like many unique athletes, Charlie D had a way of making those around him better people, better at what they were doing. While he traded, whenever he traded, Bonen says Charlie D set the tone for the pit and the traders within it. Charlie D would stretch their role in the market's overall efficiency to important new levels. Who could say with certainty, but maybe this partly explains why Bassett's fishing expedition in the pit was not so successful.

Bonen is not alone in his belief that Charlie was a paragon in the pit. His sentiments are common to a number of locals and brokers who worked at the Chicago Board of Trade when Charlie D was still standing on the top step. One trader who witnessed the fearless risk-taking that Bonen eulogized was Johnny Musso, once runner-up for the Heisman Trophy, awarded annually to college football's outstanding player. A small running back who relied on speed and quickness for a national collegiate championship team, and a running back whose skills made him "the greatest football player at Alabama ever," according to the legendary coach Paul "Bear" Bryant, Musso wound up at the Board of Trade after a short pro career with the Chicago Bears. Musso regularly stood within shouting distance of Charlie D when activity in the bond futures pit was breaking volume records, often monthly and sometimes weekly or even daily, during the go-go 1980s.

Musso recalls Charlie D's trading style and integrity as being like no one else's for a number of reasons. Unlike many other big traders at that time, Charlie D was known for trading size at any tick in the market, not only when it promised to make him money. "It was a pride thing with him," he says. "It was like nobody was going to back him down; nobody was going to scare him. I don't even think Charlie was money-oriented. Certainly, it was a way of keeping score in the pit, but I don't think it was his *primary* way of keeping score.

"He was so honest," adds Musso. "He had more integrity than anybody I ever knew. And his integrity had a cost to it. When he was on the Board of Trade's floor committee that decided what quotes counted and what the opening ranges were, he had to make decisions that affected other people in the pit. He would always do the right thing. And if traders had to suffer because they made mistakes, usually they had to eat the mistake, and he would often eat it for them. Traders would say, 'I can't do that.' And he would say, 'How much is it going to cost you?' Well, he'd eat it. He'd do the right thing regardless of what the cost was to himself."

Charlie D moved through the symbolic hierarchy of the pit in quieter ways. Tom Gallagher, a former lineman for the Miami Dolphins, remembers the time Charlie D spent with him discussing trading. He met Charlie through Ann, who was waitressing at Harry's Café on Bellevue and Rush. Charlie and Ann had been married for about a year.

Gallagher recalled one day when Charlie sold a futures contract to him and then bought it back five minutes later at four ticks higher to give him a profit of $126 on his one-lot trade. Charlie D had given up the edge to Gallagher as he went in and out of the trade, something he sincerely explained to Gallagher he would never do again, once the closing bell had rung and they were riding in the elevators. "Next time I'll beat your ass," he would say.

Gallagher was so happy to come out of this day of trading a winner that, after going out with Charlie and Ann for dinner one evening, he sent Charlie $100 worth of his favorite steaks to acknowledge his help and support over a few crazy days on the floor. In time, he would survive the pit's trial by fire and become a successful trader in his own right, though never on the scale of Charlie D.

"To this day, I think that gesture meant more to him than anything I ever did," said Gallagher. "But the next day, after I brought him the steaks, he joked with all the other guys in the pit, 'This is the guy who sent me $100 of steaks on a $30 trade. What a fucking idiot.' Later I would hear him explain the market many times," Gallagher adds, "and I had no clue what he was talking about—even after trading down here for many years. I get emotional every time I think of him. Charlie traded bonds like nobody else."

The difference between Charlie D and other big traders on the floor had to do with an ability to handle risk. According to Gallagher, even in their prime, more than a few big dogs in the bond pit have lucked into some of their best days of trading. "When Charlie was cold, he wasn't waiting for luck to get him back into the game," he explains. "One of the biggest traders down here, Steve Lawrence, had one of his best days when he had his shoulder operated on. I know that for a fact. No disrespect to Steve, because he is a great trader, but he was on the operating table with an open position when the government released an important number in the morning. When he woke up from the surgery, everyone said you just made $3 million while you were asleep. Charlie never had to depend on that sort of luck."

What impact did Charlie D have on the market? Of course, it would be almost impossible to estimate his contribution in relation to other big traders on the floor whose large positions give the market its ultimate liquidity. Big dogs, as they are known in the bond pit, can trade up to 500 lots at a crack, the notional equivalent of $50 million worth of Treasury bonds. A one-tick change in price for that quantity of futures contracts can either make or cost the trader $15,750 in less time than it takes to bat an eye.

In addition to Charlie D, competing traders are quick to praise a handful of traders who provided 50- to 100-lot liquidity in the market up until 1982, when such size was still considered a huge trade. Those traders included Terry Cullerton, Frank Doherty, Chris Hehmeyer, Larry Turner, Dick Pfeil, Jeff Abrams, R. Jeffs Kollar, and Jim Heinz. They also tip their hats to a new group of traders who became the liquidity providers in the bond pit after its location was moved to the Board of Trade's North Room in 1982, trading 200 to 500 lots at a crack when they were rolling. In addition to Kollar and Pfeil, added to the list were Tom Baldwin, Steve Lawrence, and Rob and John Moore. But none of them, although big and enormously profitable traders, played the constant role of a market maker that Charlie D did through the 1980s.

This fact is borne out by Mike Manning, who once served as director of risk management for LIT America, the successor firm to Goldberg Brothers, and who is now the executive vice president of Rand Financial Services and a member of the board of directors at the Chicago Board of Trade. At one time or another, Manning says Goldberg Brothers and later LIT cleared most of the biggest floor traders on the Board of Trade. Included in his list are brothers Rob, John, Mike, and Art Moore, Dick Pfeil, Steve Lawrence, R. Jeffs Kollar, Tom Baldwin, Kevin Dowdle, Tom Gallagher, Jon Tubbs, and Charlie D.

"All of these traders are successful," he explains. "However, during a period from 1982 until about a year before Charlie passed away, he was far and away the most voluminous trader on the floor. None of the others matched him for sheer activity. He consistently traded amounts in excess of 10,000 round turns daily, at a time when that was unprecedented. It would not surprise me if Tom Baldwin now trades that kind of size, but there were days when Charlie's activity was in excess of 18,000 round turns. None of the other traders I have named, although large and successful in their own right, had the real, perceived, or psychological impact Charlie had on the market during this era. The only one who might be comparable today is Tom Baldwin."

Others saw this phenomenon from the pit itself. In virtually no time Charlie D had become one of the pit's largest traders. According to fellow competitor and friend Mark Droegemueller, a large bond trader affiliated with LIT Clearing Services, Charlie D traded 100 contracts at a clip when the bond pit was trading only around 25,000 bonds per day. On average, he estimates that Charlie D traded 2500 to 3000 contracts a day when the bond pit was still a relatively new game at the Chicago Board of Trade in the early 1980s. Such trading volume could represent 10 percent or more of the daily volume at that time.

"Charlie's deal was high volume," says Droegemueller. "He always believed that the more you traded the more you made. From day one until the day he died, he was probably the highest volume trader in the pit. When he got up in the morning and shaved, he felt he had a job to do—and that was to offer liquidity to the market and to make money as a result. More than any other trader who's ever been down here, he was a true market maker."

Former chairman of the Board of Trade in 1985 and legendary trader Bobby Goldberg, one of the clearing partners who set up the unit called "B&D" to handle only the trades of megatraders Rob Moore and Charlie D, concurs: "His volume just kept increasing as time went by and I remember saying to myself, 'This guy was once a banker?' He was a risk taker with great ability and his risk taking far exceeded the parameters that most traders would even consider. I'm telling you—I couldn't even hold Charlie's jock."

It was not just his volume, however, that mattered to other traders who competed against Charlie D in the pit. A successful pit trader in the 1980s who has since sold his seat, Musso saw a side to Charlie that often brought back memories of Alabama football coaching legend, Paul "Bear" Bryant, when surrounded by the market's swirling chaos. "Charlie was the best friend you could have," he says. "He was probably the best friend to a dozen other people. Was he competitive with me? No. Because I wasn't in his league. He simply challenged you—to do it bigger, to do it better, to do it right. He was a coach at heart. He'd make fun of you if he thought you were being a weak hand on a trade. If he saw you get a trade that you mishandled, he'd just smirk or shake his head. If he saw you turn down a trade because it was too big for you—they showed you 200, and you waved it off and then took 50—he'd go 'buck buck bah buck buck bah,' like a chicken. It was nothing other than a coach trying to get everything out of you. Only the people who were his equal in trading size were his real competition because he always wanted to be the biggest and the best."

Ann Cavanaugh, one of the few women traders in the bond pit during the 1980s and later a senior vice president of the Asia Division at Dean Witter Futures in Chicago, observed the qualities that Bonen first praised. "I can't tell you about the moles," she says. "But as far as

Charlie's integrity is concerned from a trader's perspective, you normally hear rumors around the floor, whether someone is dirty or clean. Once you dirty your reputation, everyone knows. No matter how much you try to make it good, everyone in the pit knows. And you can never go back and clean it. I can tell you that I never ever heard anyone saying anything like that about Charlie. Never. When you trade with someone, you learn a lot about what they are like inside. And he made money the way you are supposed to make money. He saw a market movement, a pricing relationship that was out of whack, a weakness in the market, and he jumped on it."

When Charlie D did so, however, he wasn't bloodthirsty. "It's a tough business," says one trader who requested anonymity. "Sometimes you will literally step on someone just to force him out because you have a position on the other side. You can't think about that person being a nice guy, his kids' college money, you can't think of it that way. All you can think of is your survival versus his. It's very much a dog-eat-dog situation, but Charlie never relished hurting other locals. And that's not always the case in these pits. All you would ever get from him, whether it was a good trade or bad, was that Mona Lisa smile."

The mystery behind that Mona Lisa smile meant something different to Charlie D's biggest competitors, traders who were his most direct adversaries in making a market and trading against outside order flows. None of his largest competitors in the bond pit who still trade would publicly comment about him. What they saw, some of them say, was nothing less than an ego that never wanted to play second-string when it came to trading bonds. At least one of his biggest competitors in the bond pit is rumored to have said that he would be happy to see Charlie D die so that there would be more room on the top step. A bit of black humor tends to swirl in the rumor mill of the pit, but it might just as easily be read as a testament to Charlie D's presence in the pit.

Noel Moore, owner of Sangamon Trading, a successful commodity trading advisor in Chicago, witnessed Charlie D's competitive fire when observing him from the trading desks surrounding the bond pit as former first vice president of sales for Dean Witter Reynolds. Moore saw the man as "daring and unflappable," and observed, "Some of Charlie's limitations as a risk manager were deeply tied to his greatest strengths as a market maker. He made a commitment to make the big trades with the big houses—the equivalent of a market maker's Hippocratic oath. He pursued this role, sometimes to extremes, just as he tested his limits in gambling or sports. He chose to trade in a charismatic style. A trader wouldn't behave this way if making money was the only goal. I can remember when Dave Ryan, the bond pit's largest broker, quickly traded the equivalent of $300 million in bonds with Charlie. Despite his losses, Charlie didn't flinch. He was someone who wanted to lead the parade, not follow it.

"When Charlie was sick with cancer, as well as the period after his death, no one tried to stand in his place in the pit. Partly this was due to the respect Charlie earned as the room's most aggressive trader. But I think there was something more. We were all grateful to Charlie because his integrity and passion for his profession elevated all of us."

Whether Charlie D's story should be sprinkled with some sort of macho pixie dust depends on your point of view, whether you dared trade against the confidence he exuded, whether you won or lost in the pit's battle of wills and financial staying power, or whether Charlie D let you in or out of a trade. But during Charlie D's tenure at the Chicago Board of Trade, it is clear that the U.S. Treasury bond futures market flourished like few markets ever have. In 1978, the market traded 555,350 contracts, ranking it the 22nd largest futures contract in the United States with less than a 1 percent market share. At the time, the Chicago Board of Trade alone had six other futures contracts trading larger volumes, including soybean futures, the number one ranking contract in 1978. In 1980, the year Charlie D started trading, the bond contract was the fourth largest contract with a volume of almost 6 million contracts, still behind corn and soybean futures contracts at the Chicago Board of Trade, which both traded over 11.7 million contracts each. But in 1981, the bond futures contract became the world's largest, trading 13.9 million contracts. It retained the number one ranking in 1990, the last full year that Charlie traded, trading 75.5 million contracts, or 27.3 percent of the total volume of 51 futures contracts with volume over 100,000 contracts. In addition, it held the position as the number one futures contract for the entire decade through 1990. In 1995, the Board of Trade's interest rate complex became the exchange's economic engine, accounting for

160 million of 210 million total futures and option contracts traded at the world's largest futures and option exchange.

Of course, it would be erroneous to give the credit for such performance to one individual, since Board of Trade membership more than doubled from 1784 members in 1980 to 3642 by 1990. No doubt there were other big dogs in the pit then, and even bigger big dogs now than Charlie D ever was. Credit for the success of futures contracts on U.S. debt instruments is certainly theirs as well. But it is also clear that if Manning's estimate of Charlie D's trading volume in his prime is correct, he traded millions of contracts annually for much of the decade. Perhaps that is why some traders and market experts, Bonen included, believe that it was Charlie D who assumed a leadership position in the bond pit for the 1980s. They argue that he was as responsible as anyone for making the large local trader a key ingredient in priming the liquidity pump each and every day for the Board of Trade's success in bonds. Once bonds became number one at the Board of Trade, a meteoric rise in the exchange's whole complex of interest rate futures and option contracts followed in its wake.

"Charlie D was one of the best traders ever at the Chicago Board of Trade," adds Goldberg. "He was definitely the best at his type of trading, which was spreading. He traded on both sides of the market, which meant double the volume. He was in and out of the market every tick, which kept his risk [relatively] low as he traded huge volume. He took little blips out with enormous size, and that adds up to a lot of money. In contrast, Tom Baldwin's style was to be a tremendously successful daytrader. So comparing them is a bit like comparing apples and oranges, or asking who was the best baseball player of all time. They both were."

Rereading an old xeroxed copy of Bonen's newsletter, I can hear Bonen pecking away on his back porch in the not-so-distant past, writing about a day and time that hardly registers in the Board of Trade's 150-year history. "Two weeks ago, Charlie D appeared on the floor for the last time of his incredible career. The cancer had taken its toll. Charlie snuck out of his hospital room at noon and took a cab over to the CBOT to trade the final 90 minutes of his career as the primary dealers were submitting their 'bids' on the 30-year bond auction in the May refunding."

It is somewhere about this point that I pause, realizing that all of Bonen's praise wouldn't matter, of course, if Charlie D hadn't made money in the process. After all, money is the way that economic animals in the bond pit keep score. Charlie D kept score avidly—often taking out annual trading profits well into the seven figures from 1983 onward. Of course, his life inside and outside of the bond pit had many adventurous and some unfortunate turns along the way, some of which took much of his money and all of his health, but never his spirit.

It wasn't exclusively Charlie D's financial success as a trader that pushed Bonen to sit at his word processor. An inspired witness writing to a market of traders who are typically very young and full of big dreams, and often thinking more about their future than someone else's past, he saw Charlie with the hindsight of over a decade of history. Another rain, as Bonen predicted in his eulogy, began to fall the following morning, and a change of prices in one of the craziest and most thrilling of marketplaces would perhaps wash a few of these youngsters into other less-risky careers.

Bonen sat there composing his tribute, wanting to add his own downpour to what he had seen fall from the billowing weight of the clouds on a workaday Thursday morning. In his backyard, curiously, the sun was shining after the earlier burst of rain.

"It is fair to say that they must have broken the mold that was used to make Charlie D, because there will never be another one just like him. He was known for his generosity and fairness. He was known for his commitment to making markets at all costs to himself. He was known for his love as a trader."

lotto | 4

On Friday, February 7, 1986, a crowd of young traders rambunctiously rode the escalators that lowered them into the Board of Trade lobby. For anyone who hasn't jumped these escalators, they move at a double-time clip that would fray the nerves of any senior citizen who dared make the brave steps on and off. Elevator carloads of people were also flooding the lobby. This river of humanity flowed down from the Board of Trade's trading floor every day after the close, but today the torrent moved faster than normal. It was Friday, and the bond market had just closed 25 ticks higher for the day, buoyed by the Dow breaking above 1600 for the first time. These were fast times in even faster markets. A skinny trader with a spiked haircut and rat tail in back already had struck a match to light a Marlboro, while his friend went straight from the escalator into a beckoning cloud of perfume wafting delicately from some dolled-up young ladies in search of a party. Still others in a wolf pack of broad-shouldered men, with hoarse voices from yelling in the pits all day, rushed off to the Board of Trade's main entrance at the corner of LaSalle and Jackson. They would cool their raspy throats that evening with a few pitchers of beer. "Rush Street," one of them said, as he jumped into a yellow cab with two of his buddies.

Amid this logjam of people, one trader descended after first taking a quick shower in his 12th-floor office. The shower had been specially installed at his request, for he was known for working up a sweat as he traded, his hair sometimes sticking to his forehead on sweltering summer days in the bond pit, despite the air conditioning. But today, while he looked fresh and clean, he felt more exhausted than usual. It had been a good week for this seemingly nondescript 34-year-old, two $100,000 days under his belt and smaller profits on the other three. Spreading bonds against the stock market's movements and against a surge in the price of oil, he was more than satisfied with his trading for the week.

Charlie D was moving at the same pace as the Friday CBOT crowd, almost invisible really, pausing to greet a few friends in the Board of Trade lobby, before darting off to the left to make a quick stop at LaSalle News, a newspaper and candy shop in the Board of Trade's main lobby. His usual purchases included a box of Milk Duds for some quick energy, a copy of *Golf* magazine, and the *Chicago Tribune.* His right side was bothering him, underneath the armpit, though he didn't know why. Perhaps he had strained a rib muscle with his arms raised trading for much of the day. All he knew was that he was looking forward to a trip to the Desert Inn in Las Vegas to swing his new medal woods and to gamble. It was a golden boy face accented by thin lips that grimaced as he tried to raise his arm above his shoulder from beneath a cardigan sweater. That motion made his shoulder tingly, but he seemed to have no idea or time to wonder why. Perhaps his football days were catching up with him.

The two brothers, George and Archie, who owned the newsstand, recognized him by reputation. Although they didn't know Charlie D by name, they knew he was one of the bond pit's fabled leprechauns, a trader with a knack for finding a rainbow of price volatility on most days and riding it to an enormous pot of gold before the closing bell rang. It was a golden goose fairytale image on the trading floor that followed Charlie D wherever he went in the Board of Trade and had been passed by word of mouth from other traders as they lined up shoulder to shoulder in the pit. From this newsstand, these traders bought price charts or newspapers in the morning, candy for breakfast and energy during the day, and sometimes an issue of *Sports Illustrated* or *Playboy* when the trading pits were really slow in the late morning or during lunch. Nothing traveled faster than information in the futures market, except rumors and hearsay about who was making the most money and making it most often. Charlie D's name was always in such conversations. It was a Midas-touch reputation that was passed from fellow trader to broker to market price reporter to security guard, and sometimes around the horn the other way. It came silently and sometimes off the cuff, sometimes over beers at the Brokers Inn or the Sign of the Trader, two trader watering holes. Such rumors came and went as frequently as traders traveled in and out of the trading pits.

Probably one of the few people around the Chicago Board of Trade newsstand totally unfamiliar with Charlie D's reputation was a 55-year-old black LaSalle News employee named Ellis Penix, who had been hired to stock the magazine, snack, and candy racks. Penix was barely able to read much better than a child or to add and subtract when he first started at the newsstand. Aided by some on-the-job tutoring from the newsstand's owners, Penix learned enough to get by. He was now capable of manning the cash register and giving customers accurate change. Provided he was frugal, he could squeak by on his hourly wage.

A meager salary, however, hadn't stopped the seemingly diffident Penix from gaining a reputation of recklessness among the Board of Trade locals and security guards for playing the Illinois Lotto with all the devotion of a High Priest of Long Odds. And he regularly paid alms to the Goddess of Chance for his faith-is-blind devotion. A chunk of his pay was plunked down every day to play the Little Lotto and Grand Prize Lotto at the end of the week and sometimes on other games of chance. It had gotten to the point where the owners of the store had privately discussed with Penix the possibility of rationing his salary throughout the week. They were tired of the problems his "gambling" led to when Penix requested an advance against his wages. It was a fine line he often crossed with impunity.

On this day, Penix and the LaSalle News brothers battled in muted but direct tones in the little shop in the center of the Board of Trade's lobby. No one in particular was listening or really cared about this owner-employee heart-to-heart conversation, except a trader at the newsstand in search of a copy of *Golf* magazine. He couldn't help but overhear, even if all he heard was in some sense partially imagined. The owner was threatening to ration his employee's wages, unless the employee could find a way to budget himself. The trader grabbed a box of Milk Duds and the magazine, paying with a $100 bill. He contemplated how he could solve Penix's and the owner's financial conflict and came up with an answer as apparently spontaneous as any of his decisions in the trading pit. The man named Ellis Penix had loaded the snack racks and was sweeping up some paper scraps, his back turned to the owner of the store, half out of anger and half out of embarrassment. George and Archie may have a point. Why did he blow all his hard-earned money playing the lottery, anyway? The red-faced owner was closing out his register, perturbed himself, but also polite and caring. He was asking himself the very same question about Ellis. Why?

Charlie got the man's attention by walking directly toward his dustpan, his shiny brown loafers within viewing range of the man's downtrodden eyes. The man glanced up from the shoes.

"Excuse me, partner," Charlie D stated, looking directly into Penix's eyes. "Thanks for being so helpful in finding me the magazine I was looking for. Here's a little something for your trouble. Keep your chin up. Things always look better after a relaxing weekend."

The owner heard the compliment. Perhaps Penix wasn't such a bad employee in all respects. But what the owner hadn't seen was the $100 the trader had folded in half and wedged between the man's thumb and index finger clinging to his pint-sized broom. The trader patted the man on the right arm like an old friend, someone he looked forward to seeing every week, and slipped him the money. It seemed as if they knew each other, or so even Penix and the owner thought for a brief moment. But that wasn't the case.

"Remember, it always pays to use the right side of your brain when you work or trade. Have a great weekend, my friend. Take it easy."

Before the man could respond Charlie D was down the hall. It appeared the owner-employee argument at the newsstand had blown over. Penix lifted his broom a couple of feet off the ground in some abstract salute, and finished off his daily chores.

Indeed, it was a good weekend, though hardly a relaxing one as the unknown trader had proffered. As the Lotto bubbles tumbled on air in a clear plastic box on TV and then were sucked one by one randomly into a vacuum tube that Saturday at 5:00 P.M., the winning numbers emerged for what was a $5 million jackpot. 21-24-28-29-37-41 was the magical number series for which only one mad genius of randomness had the answer. On Sunday, these numbers were published as they always were in the *Chicago Sun-Times* on page 2, wedged between the late TV listings and local weather.

That same day, in his Southside apartment near Cottage Grove Avenue, Penix sat alone, staring at one ticket in particular and that very same newspaper. The rest of his tickets were scattered on the floor beside him. He seemed dazed. Every hour, he removed this one ticket from his pocket and took a look at it again, comparing it to what he had seen on TV and in the paper. He felt silly doing so, but he felt his eyes must be playing tricks on him. But there he stood as the man with the correct answer to the mystical series of six random numbers. How had he solved the equation? And how was he going to explain to the brothers who owned LaSalle News that he had won the very Lotto that they had advised him to stop playing so frequently so he had enough money during the week to make ends meet? Laughter burst forth from him as though from some inner wellspring. They just might fire him, but who really cared? The verb "to fire" was a word in his vocabulary that had no real meaning. The emotion welling up inside him almost made him cry. Living in a rough neighborhood, he checked the locks on his doors that night in between peeks at the ticket placed in a secret place in his wallet. That two-by-three inch of paper was as good as solid gold.

A front-page article in the *Chicago Sun-Times* that Sunday, entitled DO RICHES CHANGE LOTTERY WINNERS? would have had special meaning to Penix if he read it. "People who win big in state lotteries usually keep working anyway, go on spending sprees, stay happily married and give generously to relatives—but not much to charity," noted reporter Jim Ritter in the story's lead sentence. Ritter was reporting on the survey work of Roy Kaplan, a sociologist at the Florida Institute of Technology. "It's true that money doesn't buy happiness. But it's a very important ingredient in the recipe," he told Ritter. Sudden wealth, he added, "removes a tremendous emotional and psychological burden" by giving a Lotto winner a sense of security.

On Sunday evening, the bespectacled and gentle-looking George, co-owner of LaSalle News, received a call from his employee, Ellis Penix, telling him that he was sick and not coming to work on Monday. Given the newsstand conversation on Friday, George suspected something other than illness was keeping Ellis from work. He asked Ellis to be straight with him. If he wasn't going to be truthful, George couldn't depend on him and allow him to keep his job. Just at the point that George started scolding Ellis for playing games with him on the phone, Penix was left with no choice but to throw up his arms and explain the real reason he couldn't come to work Monday morning. He had won the lottery and didn't want any of his gang-banging neighbors to know. He planned to turn the ticket in before anyone found out and attempted to steal it from him. George had heard everything now. Whether Penix was sick or a lottery winner or had lost all his money or marbles over the weekend, he doubted he would ever see Penix again. However, that afternoon, Penix showed up at the newsstand, his ticket safe in the hands of the executives of the Illinois State Lottery. He apologized to George for the strange phone conversation and proceeded to explain why he no longer intended to work another day in his life. George suggested that his son, who was an attorney, might be of some assistance. Penix took him up on the offer. Later that day, Penix crossed paths with Charlie D and euphorically offered to buy him a new car for all his good karma. Charlie D thanked him for the offer, explaining that wasn't necessary. He shook Penix's hand and then deadpanned about his understudy's recent financial success: "Ever think about trading bonds?"

That was that: a Miracle on LaSalle Street. The two risk takers never saw each other again, or so the story goes, passed by word of mouth from trader to trader.

Still don't believe it? I'm not sure I do either. But that is one of the Charlie D legends I have heard through the white noise of history in the Board of Trade lobby—the tale told to me piecemeal again and again by traders who knew Charlie D. Initially I couldn't make the leap of faith either. Tom Gallagher and Mark Droegemueller first told me parts of the story while shuffling a deck of cards and watching a quote machine terminal in their office on the 19th floor of the Board of Trade. The Animal House ambiance of their office, which included a couch for napping, a broken snare drum, and a hockey stick in the corner, hurt their credibility. So too did the gaping holes in their Charlie D–Ellis P fairytale, which was a little thin on hard facts. This legend seemed no more than a classic Liar's Poker bluff that could quickly be discounted if I dogged a few leads. But then Charlie D's close friend Johnny Musso confirmed that he had heard the same story as did a few others. Musso admitted that he couldn't say it was a true story for sure, but he didn't think it had been something Charlie D made up either, even though he was known for playing tricks and stretching facts in the interest of fun. None of his jokes or tales was as elaborate as this and he always came clean after a prank. And if it wasn't a true story, why had the legend been preserved in the erratic brain synapses of a few of Charlie D's closest trading buddies?

This seemed a good question to ask the Board of Trade's only Lotto winner if I could identify and track him down. George's brother Archie told me that one of their employees, a man named Ellis, had hit the jackpot for $5 million playing the Lotto five or six years earlier. He suggested that George, who generally worked mornings, might know more of the Lotto story. I also contacted Mike Lang, director of communications at the Illinois State Lottery, to seek his help in locating a man I only knew as Ellis. A guarded Lang seemed to half-believe my tale, and asked me to put my information request to the Illinois State Lottery in writing. In a few days, he provided me with the full name of the Lotto winner, the size of the Lotto pot he had won, and the date he had won it. Lang refused to arrange an interview with Mr. Penix or contact him directly on my behalf. It was a matter of Lotto policy to respect each winner's privacy. It was not easy to verify one of the more sensational of the Charlie D legends.

Ultimately, I tracked down Penix through a byzantine search. I first discovered through a local operator that his phone number was unpublished, which meant he lived in the city. I still might find him. I then attempted to round up his address and phone number through the last resorts available to any reporter: Voter Registration Records and Driver's License Records at the Illinois Department of Motor Vehicles. The latter avenue cost me $8 and I came up empty. It didn't seem that Mr. Penix could legally drive a car. On June 4, 1996, the Board of Election Commissioners office in Chicago sent me the publicly available information I had requested. "We have checked our current active and inactive registrations and found an active registration on Ellis Penis at . . ." The rest of the message included his address and birthdate, August 29, 1919. It ended: "Thank you. Sincerely yours, Verne Apke." Lotto winners may not drive, but they do vote.

Apke's reply only added to my confusion. The birth date, if correct, turned this Lotto winner 66, not 55 as reported in the *Chicago Sun-Times.* Was this a typo or was Penix fudging a little on his age, instant wealth both a fountain of youth and father-time reminder that life is short and sometimes cruel. Your guess is as good as mine. And was I looking for Mr. Penix, or as Apke's reply suggested, Mr. Penis? I was not sure which man I was after, though the latter was perhaps the better name for a man whose Lotto ticket had just gone *schwing!* However, I wasn't so sure I was comfortable knocking on the door of a Mr. Penix and asking if I could speak with a Mr. Penis. The reverse, asking a Mr. Penis if I could speak to Mr. Penix, likewise seemed equally as disrespectful. I had no choice but to reach the very dark conclusion that Charlie D was playing a dirty and evil trick on me. Charlie D had never consented to interviews, and I was almost certain that something mischievous was paying me back for all my troubles. But what the hell? The Board of Elections had taken me this far. Another typo and I might meet a man named Elvis, so what was to fear? It was off to Apartment 3309.

After preparing a letter requesting an interview with Mr. Penix (I trusted Lang and the *Sun-Times'* spelling more than I did that of a Board of Elections paper-shuffler unearthing an official voter registration record), I jumped on the Jeffrey No. 6 Express bus to go visit the Lotto winner. I typed a formal interview request the night before that explained my strange obsession with the bond trading legend nicknamed Charlie D.

Penix's address turned out to be part of an apartment complex known as Regents Park, which I recognized from my days as a U of C undergraduate as having an upper-middle-class clientele. I entered the Regents Park revolving door, announcing myself to a security guard who seemed to be a clone of boxing promoter Don King. This man wore a snappy green uniform and sat behind a walnut reception area equipped with phones and mini-TVs for surveillance. I told the guard, whose hair towered upward into black and white afro-flames, that I had a package I would like to hand-deliver to Mr. Penix. He didn't give me a second look, dialing from the lobby for Mr. Penix.

"Hello, Mrs. Penix, I have a package to be delivered from a Mr. Bill Fal-on. A messenger in the lobby would like to hand-deliver it to your husband this morning. Great. Thank you. I'll send him up."

The Don King look-alike buzzed the glass security door on my right.

"33rd Floor of the south tower. Go through the glass door and the elevators are down the hall and to your right, just before the health club. Mrs. Penix said it's OK for you to go on up."

There was no time to waste. I scooted along to beat the buzzer that unlocked the door to the south tower, rode an elevator up, and hoped for the best. The apartment number I had was 3309 south. As I looked for Penix's apartment, moving 30 yards down the hall, a voice interrupted my search before I had even had a chance to knock on any apartment door.

"Who is it?"

The voice came not from behind the door of Apartment 3309, at which I stared, but from a door to Apartment 3307, directly behind me. I turned around and lifted up my envelope so that it could be clearly seen through the peephole. It didn't help that no one popped open a door to greet me, our meeting unfortunately an unplanned surprise for us both. The door stayed locked. My words flowed rapid-fire.

"Sir, I have a package to drop off for Mr. Penix, if that's you. The package includes a letter that requests an interview with you concerning a gentleman named Charles P. DiFrancesca. Mrs. Penix sent me up. Mr. DiFrancesca was a well-known bond futures trader who I was told you encountered just before you won the Lottery. Mr. DiFrancesca died in 1991 of cancer, and Mr. Falloon, who is actually me, is preparing a book about his life. If you do remember him, I was hoping that you would be willing to read the enclosed letter and description about my book. I would like to verify the story I have about you and Mr. DiFrancesca."

"Who?" the door said to me.

I heard the sound of two or three dead bolt locks turning. One yellow and bloodshot eye looked directly at me from just above two chain locks that allowed the door to crack open only three or four inches. The eye seem to be attempting to place me somewhere in time, perhaps in the Board of Trade lobby over 10 years ago, perhaps somewhere else. The cyclopic human hiding behind the door decided he had never seen me before. I just continued my plea.

"Charles DiFrancesca, a bond trader at the Board of Trade they called Charlie D. I was told he gave you $100 on the Friday before you won the lottery, and that you used that money to buy your winning ticket. I thought it was an interesting story that you could help me with. Someone told me that Charlie saw you having a bad day with your boss, so he gave you some money to brighten it up. I heard your boss was giving you a hard time and Charlie saw it happening. He gave you the money and told you to keep your chin up, something like that. I've heard many versions of the story, and don't know which one is true. I thought it was worth telling—assuming it's true—and I would like to tell as much of it as I can in my book. If you have anything to add about the story, I'd appreciate it if you would read the letter I've written and talk with me later. If it's not a true story, I don't really want to write about it. It's all there in this envelope, including my phone number. If you'd rather, you can read it and give me a call. I really don't mean to bother you, sir. But your phone number is unlisted, so I could only contact you by coming here directly. The letter explains how I tracked you down. I'd appreciate any help you can give me."

"Slide your envelope to me through the door. I will read it and call you."

"Thank you, Mr. Penix. I appreciate the help. Here it is."

The same two fingers that supposedly held the broom came out from somewhere behind the door and reached out two or three inches to pinch the envelope like a pair of extremely dull scissors. I lifted the letter-sized envelope and placed it in his hand, just above the chain lock. Although it was roughly 11:00 A.M., I could see the sleeve of Mr. Penix's blue pajamas, half a disheveled face, and half a head of salt-and-pepper hair, but none of the face's life over the last 10 years. Researching Charlie D's life often meant that facts came to me in a twisted and contorted manner, as they might appear if seen through a funny mirror at the circus. A man named Penix was no exception to this rule.

"I'll give you a call" was the last I heard from him. The Cyclops pulled his hand inside the door. I heard the sounds of deadbolt locks being turned once again.

"Thanks again, Mr. Penix, for your help," I said to the door. "My number is at the bottom of my letter. Talk to you soon."

Months have since passed and I still have not heard from him. I attempted to drop off a rough draft of a portion of this chapter to Penix to verify its accuracy but to no avail.

Not even a couple of encounters with George at LaSalle News helped me confirm anything more about this strange tale. All George could tell me was that he couldn't add anything more to the story. It was too far back to remember. He did attempt to call Ellis Penix on my behalf a couple of times without success, using the number Penix had given to him after he quit. As Penix's phone rang endlessly in the backoffice storage area at LaSalle News, all George could do was try to explain his absence.

"He's probably in Las Vegas or on some riverboat casino right now. He loves to make those kinds of trips. I'm sorry I haven't been able to get in touch with him for you. But I can't give you his number. I told him I wouldn't give it to anyone."

It hardly seemed worth it to continue, since I had given Mr. Penix my number and address twice.

From Penix's 33rd floor view of Regents Park, he could no doubt see the myriad colors of Lake Michigan and the Lake Shore skyline, a view even Monet would find inspiring. He might also choose to walk in the park just south of his window, where trees are home to a flock of Hyde Park's most famous avian citizens, "Harold's Birds." The story is told that two bright green parakeets from the Andes in South America had once escaped from a bird cage in the neighborhood and survived a couple of Chicago winters by eating bread crumbs and seed alongside the city pigeons. When Chicago turned to ice in the winter, these Andes-born birds were not at all fazed by the harsh weather. They quickly adapted and multiplied in their new environment. The birds' enormous houses of twigs and mud resembled a wild sort of globular adobe apartment complex, just across from the Hampton House where Chicago mayor Harold Washington once lived on 53rd Street. The police protection that the mayor received when he lived there kept the trees safe for the parakeets. Perhaps the power of the mayor or the oddballs who fed those birds and the pigeons in the dead of winter, if Penix thought about it, might remind him of his encounter with Charlie D. Maybe someday those birds will prove to be a blessing for a commodities trader, as one of their kind had been for Mr. Penix. Another colony of the parakeets has migrated to a perch near St. Thomas' Church, and some say they will keep moving south in greater numbers over time. I could hardly wish that on Illinois farmers, since these birds have a reputation for being destructive and raucous. Some environmentalists argue that the birds should be captured before they multiply further, ravage a corn field or two, and no longer become a novelty. If that ever happened, these birds could prove to be a commodities trader's best friend, my friends in Hyde Park often joke.

I don't know what to think anymore about this legend, though I no longer doubt its veracity. My only hope is that Charlie D meant something to Penix. The miraculousness of all these strange birds, if I had my wish, should remind all of us of another deceased "relative" of high odds. Maybe worries about too much money are the same as worries about having too little, and what matters is somewhere in between. I'm sure by now that I must seem as pesky and determined to Penix as those green birds to dare tell this story, but life's crumbs—particularly Charlie D's—are often a tasty meal.

If my belief about the veracity of this story isn't correct, I beg the forgiveness of anyone who reads it. Perhaps it was Charlie D's stellar ability in the bond pit that made the story seem true to those who first heard it. I suppose in some sense it is just as much a symbol of Charlie D's strange powers when it came to trading, much in the same way that Babe Ruth's "called shot" is still a fable attached to his home run prowess. Babe Ruth always denied ever calling that homer, but plain as day he did seem to point his bat in the replays I've seen. Perhaps Penix knows if Charlie D conjured up any right-field bleachers to point to that day they supposedly met in the Board of Trade lobby. Charlie was never afraid to take his cuts at the plate or help others to try.

Then again, Charlie D might enjoy the Lotto legend even more if there were no truth to it at all—if it were a myth he planted simply to spread a little bit of optimism to lives faced with long odds. As Charlie D knew, life doesn't get any better than contemplating the hidden powers of some very strange birds. His spirit was without question a shade of green and, if you ask me, sometimes could fly.

caddyshack | 5

The stories I've collected of Charlie D's life are chronicled in six large three-ring binders, stacked in a row like cinder blocks, down in my basement. The binders are a repository of jigsaw-puzzle pieces of a man's life and death that will never fit together cleanly and completely. To be honest, I am resigned to the fact that what I write is only the filtered narration of family, friends and acquaintances, a few photos, newspaper and magazine clippings, and home videos—hardly the collected first-person papers and diaries that most biographers might have at their fingertips.

What a shame, I often think when frustrated by the missing pieces of the puzzle, that I was never able to challenge Charlie D to a round of golf. After all, it was just after a trip around the fairways of the Wigwam Resort that Charlie D first came into view, and it is no coincidence that many of the odd-shaped pieces of his life in my notebooks are set on plush fairways. One puzzle piece appears to me this morning from one of the largest notebooks. It is Charlie's obituary from the *Chicago Tribune*, surrounded by no other tightly interlocking pieces.

His passions included poker and golf, which he sometimes played with Chicago Bulls star Michael Jordan.

"I'll never forget the first time he met Jordan," said Fitzgerald, who introduced the two. "He says to Michael, 'Do you know Dave Corzine? Think you could get his autograph for me?' Michael turns to me and says, 'Who is this guy?'"

My question, exactly.

It is that quote from His Airness and all that it says about Charlie D that demands golf be part of my incomplete biographical sketch. No doubt Charlie D will forever be remembered by his friends, Michael Jordan included, for his comical and competitive ways on the fairways. If I could ever play golf with Michael, Tiger, or Charlie, I'm unashamed to say that the proud inventor of Double-Redouble (an interesting variation on the standard golf game, described in detail later), not these sports superstars, is the first guy I'd like to have in my foursome. His golf game pops out of my three-ring binders with more competitive verve than Tiger's clenched fist after a final putt at the Masters, and with more comedy than all the Looney-Tunes combined who kidnapped a retired MJ from the golf course in *Space Jam*.

Along with Michael Jordan, the men who witnessed the golfing looney named Charlie D include Board of Trade trader Tom Fitzgerald and trader Tom Gallagher, who persuaded Charlie to join Evanston Country Club so that he could hack it around with them. His golfing partners also include J. B. Dougherty, Johnny Musso, Tom DeMark, John and Vince, Ann, and one-time tour player and head professional at Point O' Woods, Fred Reeder. The list could continue forever really; no doubt Charlie loved to play golf whenever he had the chance. It is through some of these fairways tales that Charlie's life takes on an intimacy that can be achieved only through time spent together riding in golf carts.

"Do I have lots of Charlie D golf stories?" asks Fitz, as if that's a sure sign that I never knew the guy. "I remember one time going with him to Puerto Rico. The golf course was 45 minutes from our hotel, and we were bussed there every day to play. Charlie's sick as a dog. My brother's a golf pro, and Charlie would take lessons from just about anybody. So he takes me to the driving range. The guy there says we're closed. 'What?' Charlie says, with a pocketful of hundreds to this Puerto Rican kid. '*Bucketos grandes, por favor!*' 'Charlie,' I say. 'It's dark. We can't see the ball.'"

" 'I only have five more years to learn this game, Fitz,' he says. 'You've got all the time in the world.'

"So he gets this kid to pull up his car, a 1962 Pinto, all rusted out. 'Over here,' Charlie says. 'Turn on the headlights, *por favor.*'

"He must have hit over 300 balls in the dark. He hits this one shot probably 50 yards to the right.

" 'What am I doing, Fitz?' he says.

" 'Move it back 2 inches.' Well, he nearly hits the stick, somewhere out there in the Pinto's headlights. He smiles at me. 'Hey partner,' he says, 'you should've told me that on the golf course.' We're standing there laughing. The bus is long gone. I'm thinking, what the hell are we going to do? It's pitch black out there and we don't have a ride. Charlie's just laughing. He tells the kid to put the spare tire somewhere to make some room. I'm thinking now we're going to get mugged. But Charlie's positive that way, always. He's sicker than a billy goat on that trip, but upbeat. He gets the kid to pull into a McDonald's and orders us milkshakes, fries, and cheeseburgers. The kid then takes us back to our hotel."

Fred Reeder at Point O' Woods is also happy to add to the library of golfing tales. As head pro at the Robert Trent Jones–designed gem of a golf course in Benton Harbor, Michigan, and host to the prestigious Western Amateur every summer, he describes the course as one of Charlie's favorites. The subject of my question for Fred, or indirectly for Charlie through Fred, is Charlie D's favorite game on the golf course, Double-Redouble. Charlie D's son Jake has told me about his father's habit of sometimes stuffing greenbacks in the bottom of the putting green cup to focus better his playing partner's body and soul. Through Fred, as with Fitz, I can hear Charlie's voice in the background, coming from the notebooks. In my imagination, I'm riding in a golf cart next to Charlie and Fitz, or Charlie and Fred, somewhere between Puerto Rico and Michigan. Johnny Musso is also with this group, and so is Tom Gallagher. A golfing voyeur of the worst kind, I am delegated the job of retrieving Charlie D's lost ball in some ominous-looking trees. When it comes to golfing with Charlie, there are just stories—no defined places or dates that are all that precise. I bring up the game of Double-Redouble with Fred.

"Charlie was a great guy," he says. "As far as his golf betting, it was just for fun. Charlie got his jollies from seeing if you could handle the pressure. He came up with this game on the course, Double-Redouble. He just loved his cottage up in Michigan and used to come by at night to play a few holes. When he'd stop into the clubhouse, he'd say to any of us still in the pro shop, 'Hey, what rhymes with trouble?' We all knew what that meant and we'd be out the door. He'd play a two-ball scramble, two balls against your ball. So if he had a three-foot putt, he'd miss it once and get to putt it again."

" 'Double,' he says.

"He'd still miss it. He was this piece of work, let me tell you. Double-Redouble was a game that always was evolving. It became more elaborate every time we played. He came up with this special rule he called the Air Press. That meant he could double the bet while the ball was in the air. So you're in the middle of your backswing and he says, 'Air Press.' "

The term Air Press, for obvious reasons, is one that prompts me to bring up with Fred the Michael Jordan story in the obituary. He doesn't tell me one way or the other whether Charlie ever used it to rattle Michael in the middle of a backswing, or if their games were what inspired its creation. Golf as a metaphor for Charlie D's life is far more interesting than talking about any skins games Charlie may have played with Michael. Golf to him was a game of friendly competition, even with Michael. No more, no less, regardless of the size of the wager.

"By the end he was bald," Fred continues, remembering the last holes Charlie ever played at Point O' Woods. "He looked like Telly Savalas when he didn't have his hair. But it never got him down. He comes into the pro shop like always.

" 'Who loves you, baby?' he says. That was Charlie.

" 'Well, Fred, this is it. This is my big dress rehearsal.'

" 'What are you talking about, Charlie?

" 'This is it.' "

Not much else needed to be said.

"I knew what he meant and we just went out and played five or six holes. I never saw him again after that."

"What about the skill factor in his golf game, Fred? Or was there any?" I wanted to know.

"He didn't have a real bad swing," Fred answers. "It was up and out. He came back from out there somewhere, but he knew how to play it. He was a 10 or 13, depending on the day. A pretty good putter, I'd say. He liked to challenge you even when he knew he didn't have a chance. One time I was five under, going into 12. We had a fair amount going. It didn't take long in Double-Redouble with all those Air Presses. 'Never do this with a member,' he joked. Then he doubled the bet on the green. I made the putt. Johnny Musso was following us.

" 'Fred's got brass balls,' " Fred adds, quoting Charlie on the putting green, to capture the moment completely.

"And Fred, could Charlie break par?"

"Never. Never. Maybe a 78 or 79 on a good day, but there weren't many of those. He did have his streaks, though. I remember one time he holed a sand wedge on number 2, a par five. He absolutely blades it but the ball hits the pin. Kerplunk, it's down.

" 'Finally got you,' Charlie says, smiling that smile. So then we're standing on the 11th hole, this par three. '10,000 bucks if you knock it in,' he says. I hit a five-iron that stops half an inch in front of the cup.

" 'Pretty stout,' he says, 'but well short of the cup.' We're just standing there on the tee woofing about it. Those were some games we used to play."

Johnny Musso jumps out of the three-ring binder and into our group at that moment, joining the fun and relishing the opportunity to seek revenge for all the golf equipment and balls Charlie once charged to his country-club tab at Point O' Woods as a joke. Charlie later covered the expense of the prank himself. As I pull Johnny's quote from the binder, I can still see him shaking his head when he tried to explain what playing golf with Charlie was like. A caddyshack golfer decked out in new golf apparel with shiny golf equipment at Point O' Woods never disappeared from Musso's personal collection of memories.

"Golf killed Charlie," Johnny says, a wry smile emerging despite his best efforts to hold it back, now that Charlie's image on the course is sharply in focus. "It *killed* him. He was not a good golfer. He wasted so much money on it. He'd go to these golf schools, buy new clubs. It was just an unbelievable endeavor to watch him learn to play golf, because he was terrible. He was a 20, maybe a 16, but it was an ego handicap. He was a 35 if you ask me. When he got into an arena where he couldn't compete, it just killed him. He would always put more time and effort into it to try to compete.

"The only way he could compete in golf was to bet, because if he got the bet up big enough, everyone would suddenly play down to his level. He could handicap anything. It made whoever he played against so nervous, because he could seem to care less about the money. He was having fun. He loved to play against the pros. He'd play a scramble, two shots to their one. Then the betting would equalize it for him. That was his arena, figuring out a way to win. We had some woof games, for sure, and he often found a way to have the last laugh."

That Charlie played by his own rules on the golf course was never more obvious than when he competed with Tom Gallagher in the Butterfield Invitational, a serious two-man team event using handicaps to allow golfers of all skill levels to compete. Playing in one of the tournament's lower flights, Charlie put his team down two holes in match play by missing his tee time by 20 minutes. Where was he? "Trading the opening in the bond pit," says Gallagher. "I told him he'd never make it back in time. But he said he'd be there. And there he was, waiting for us on one of the tee boxes somewhere in the round."

Gallagher played the first few holes by himself, and Team Gallagher-DiFrancesca was one down at the turn. Their team came back later in the match, potentially closing out the match by the 14th hole. Charlie, however, would intentionally miss some putts to keep the match alive so that he could enjoy playing a few more competitive holes before returning to the clubhouse. After Gallagher explained the difference between a real tournament and Charlie's version of competitive golf to his partner, Charlie straightened his visor and stopped missing short putts—at least, that is, for fun. The competition in the tournament later stiffened, but the two men won their flight.

It is stories like these, along with tales of Charlie D in pro-ams in Las Vegas or Florida, that bring to mind George Plimpton's *The Bogey Man*, an irreverent account of Plimpton's real but tragically comical experiences playing in tournaments with PGA tour players. Plimpton played the game for the comic relief of golfers everywhere, and so too did Charlie. The thoughts that went through Charlie's mind whenever he would address the ball could also have filled a book.

The game itself may have extracted final revenge. The ultimate torment for any serious golfer may be to hit a hole in one without his heckling golfing buddies as witnesses. And that is exactly the rub-of-the-green miracle that Charlie performed one day playing with his wife, Ann, not even one spanking dollar skin riding on the hole. *Did a tree actually fall in the forest if no one heard it fall? Did the ball really go down?* Charlie heard the ribbing from friends later, and knew it would come in time the moment he pulled his ball out from the bottom of the cup and kissed it. "Cinderella story" was a phrase made famous by the insane greenskeeper played by Bill Murray in *Caddyshack,* and those words no doubt fit Charlie's shot like a glove. At least on one shot in his life, his iron had nipped the flower from the stem cleanly and won *the Masters.*

All these stories, when I think about it, might in some way account for a dream I had one night about Charlie D on the golf course. On the blue fairways of this dream, I am trapped. I am being forced to ask Charlie D serious questions about Ben Hogan's *Five Lessons: The Modern Fundamentals of Golf* to test his true working knowledge of the mechanics of the golf swing. Every answer he gives to my impromptu quiz sounds correct—that is, until he attempts to demonstrate the proper swing by going through those peculiar motions of his. It is in this dream that Charlie agrees to be interviewed about his trading, on the condition that I agree to point out the common ground between how Hogan learned to play golf and how he learned to trade. Did Charlie D ever read this extremely thin paperback written by the Master of the Perfect Golf Swing, I ponder on the billowy blue fairways of sleep? I'll never know.

At this point in my dream, I don't know what to think. I first become frightened when Charlie notices the jigsaw puzzle that I'm working on in the clubhouse and doesn't seem amused. I have no idea what he'll say until he confronts me, his spikes scratching a cart path as he walks toward me, like chalk against a blackboard.

Like most idiots down on the floor, says a Mona Lisa–type beast holding a metal wood, *you haven't a clue about how to trade. I tell you how difficult it is: One of the most successful traders down in the bond pit, Steve Lawrence, pulled millions out of the pit. Then one day he gets stopped in his car by some policeman who asks him why he is speeding. By this time, Steve's driving a pretty nice car. But he says he is going to work at Jewel where he is the produce manager. The cop takes one look at his car and writes him a ticket, pissed off. But the funny thing is Steve wasn't lying. It was true—Steve Lawrence was a produce manager at a grocery store, even when he was a millionaire bond trader. It took him the longest time before he could quit that job even when he was a successful trader. The good traders like Steve always remember that, without discipline, you end up bagging someone else's groceries. That story, by the way, may also explain why Steve tipped so poorly.*

Who is this guy? It is at that point that I pick up my dog-eared paperback copy of Hogan's book, now dangerously close to my Charlie D three-ring notebooks, sitting beside me in a golf cart. The words from Hogan's book seem to walk like ants toward the notebooks, and I am helpless to stop them. As they enter one of the notebooks about golf, the words become audible, the first two spoken with the same Telly Savalas inflection that Charlie sometimes used on Fred: *Air Press, baby.* We are somewhere on the course, and I'm not sure my pocketbook can handle another Air Press. I somehow scrape it onto the green.

The next words heard in my dream seem delusional but comical, as if spoken by a high-handicap golfer who believes that he is the Master of a game that could even make Hogan yip a putt. In the middle of lining up a three-foot putt, I hear a voice out of the corner of my ear, whispering and mimicking the Texas drawl of the Master of the Golf Swing himself. Is it just Charlie or Benny D?

As I see it, some measures long esteemed to be of paramount importance in Double-Redouble are really not important at all. On the other hand, certain other measures that have been considered of secondary importance (or of no importance at all) strike me as being invaluable—to be, in fact, the true fundamentals of the game. Another thing. I am an advocate of the kind of teaching that stresses the exact nature and feel of the movements a golfer makes to achieve the results he wants. If you were teaching a child how to open a door, you wouldn't open the door for him and then describe at length how the door looked when it was open. No, you would teach him how to turn the doorknob so he could open the door him-self. . . . For all the personal touches and mannerisms which are part of the great golfers' individual styles, I have never seen a great golfer whose method did not include the essential fundamental known as an Air Press. Otherwise—it is as simple as that—the golfer could not be a great one.

I do some Double-Redouble calculations on a $1 bet over 18 holes, assuming my shank stays with me the whole round. $1. $2. $4. $8. $16. $32. $64. $128. $256. $512. $1024. $2048. $4096. $8192. $16,384. $32,768. $65,536. $131,072. Just before I hit the putt, my forearms tighten and try to conceal my twitch. *How much are we playing for? someone asks.*

I wake up, uncertain whether I made or missed the putt. There are many other Charlie D golf stories in my notebooks—but none any more dramatic than my puzzling dream—which somehow seems to fit. As a frustrated biographer, notebooks before me, I realize I can dream on for only a few swings with Charlie D in the darkness, anywhere between Michigan and Puerto Rico, a red flag and range balls encircled by the converging tunnels of two Ford Pinto headlights.

god doesn't trade bonds | 6

March 22, 1989. A brisk, crystal clear Wednesday afternoon in Chicago. Large popcorn-shaped clouds above the Chicago Board of Trade drift slowly behind a faceless statue of Ceres, the Goddess of Wheat, atop the limestone monolith known as the world's oldest and largest futures exchange. Walking through the building's art deco entrance hall—a towering space with protruding columns of black and gray marble that makes any visitor feel as though Jay Gatsby's blood is flowing through his veins—is a trader wearing a sky blue jacket. He exits the revolving front door, in a hurry, running.

His glasses seem to catch fire as the sunlight reflects off the lens. A small stack of notecards stuffed in his left pocket, just above the 666, bulge out. Nothing noteworthy stands out about him other than he isn't dressed properly for a brisk spring day in Chicago with the temperature in the mid-20s. Everyone else on the street is wearing a coat. He joins the swarming convergence around the awkward T that forms the intersection at LaSalle and Jackson, not waiting for the pedestrian crossing lights. As anonymously as Clark Kent in Metropolis, he walks one block north on LaSalle, left on Adams, into another revolving turnstile front door into the Midland Hotel. He is five minutes early, a rarity, according to friends.

He proceeds to a room packed with 200 traders. They quiet as he enters. A navy blue and silver patch on the right side of his trader's jacket that indicates his clearing firm—GB for Goldberg Brothers—is a little misleading. The informal seminar is actually being sponsored by LIT America, a futures commission merchant that just purchased Dave and Bobby Goldberg's firm. These Goldberg brothers are a Chicago Board of Trade landmark themselves by reputation as well-known traders in the grain pit and as respected clearing members.

The audience well knows that the man about to lecture them on the nuances of pit trading is the most feared and revered in the bond futures market when the opening bell rings in the morning. Always positioned on the top step on the west side of the octagonal pit, his bass-baritone voice can travel above all the shouting and panic of a fast market to the bond pit's farthest corners. Such conviction is projected by his voice to the point that it takes nerves of steel for less-confident traders to challenge it. His sight lines are unobstructed on the top step: No one can avoid his piercing stare.

While Charlie D refuses all interviews from the press, he isn't averse to teaching fellow traders about how to survive in the pits. After all, he remembers his early days as a trader, starting in May 1980, with enough money to lease a seat for three months and not much pocket money for margin, maybe $3000. Most of that was earned in a condo conversion with Balcor friend, Tony Manno, after borrowing $1 million from downtown banker Buddy Cohen to make the conversion. They had completed the deal not a moment too soon; the real estate market in Chicago was going softer by the minute.

Unfortunately for Chuck, as he was then known, he was losing as much as he was winning. During his first two-and-a-half months in the pits, he sometimes executed a one-lot day trade, each price change of 1/32nd of a point (one tick) worth $31.25. He agonized each time he shouted out in the pit, the market seemingly always the winner. Even when he won, he didn't really know why. To make matters worse, he was petrified of his own voice, which frequently cut off involuntarily midsentence when he thought about pulling the trigger. He wanted to scribble a trade on a chip or bullet, as a local trader's cards are referred to on the floor, but had nothing to write. "Are you bidding or offering?" seasoned red-faced traders complained in the heat of battle. The uncertainty and his fickle voice made him feel like a pigeon in this rough-and-tumble, harsh economic jungle. He wasn't going to last.

More frightening than his meek and panicked voice was an obsessive fear of money. The fear of losing it and returning to an apartment on Belmont with no furniture other than one desk and a mattress depressed him. At 28, he had already been divorced once, from Sally, whom he met at Colorado State University. The thought of what his girlfriend Ann would think, or his father Vince, who had remortgaged his house to add to his son's seed money, caused his palms to sweat profusely. He had played football at Wisconsin and Colorado State before huge crowds, but the noise of the trading pits was different. He had trouble concentrating, hearing himself think, reacting. These had never been problems for him as a player—all-state in Waukesha, Wisconsin, as a gifted high school quarterback—between the gridiron's neatly painted white lines.

"There was nothing about him that stood out," says Mike Manning, former director of operations and risk management for Goldberg Brothers. "Sure, Chuck was a nice young kid, but there are a lot of nice young kids that come down to the Board to Trade. I can't say he caught my attention then. He was spinning his wheels."

Two-and-a-half months into this nightmare, Goldberg Brothers' partner John Ruth, whom he had befriended when they both worked at Harris Bank, paid the neophyte trader a visit on the fringes of the pit.

"Chuck, you've only made six trades since you started. Is something wrong?" asked Ruth.

Chuck wouldn't answer. He seemed to listen closely to the elder statesman of the futures industry, thank Ruth for the advice, and retreat silently up to the members' gallery to watch the action in the bond pit in the Board of Trade's south room. He hoped that no one had heard their conversation. Time was running out. He had been making the trek upstairs for weeks, studying the floor the way a coach in the press box studies player positions in the field and their motions, making mental notes, paper trading. When a big dog, as he referred to the biggest hitters in the pit, would look at the green and red price screens the size of Super Bowl scoreboards and make a move, he followed their gaze to see what they saw. So that's how he bids and offers with conviction? Interesting.

Another paper trade. The thick pane of glass provided solace—a chance to be a student of the market, to organize the madness, to plan.

One day in early August 1980, something clicked. Ten paper trades, four winners, one loser, five scratches. Though he found it difficult to explain, he finally understood what Bobby Goldberg and other old grain traders had meant by spreading—spreading against the yen, the Dow, a commodity basket, another bond futures contract expiring at a later date. He descended to the floor, his mind clear, and traded 265 futures contracts in the last hour, spread himself silly, and made $5000. His voice, his nerves, his confidence changed. After a similar day a few weeks later, he called his brother—an $11,000-per-year elementary schoolteacher in the suburbs—and told him the good news. "John, you need to get down here," he said over the phone.

Two weeks later, his girlfriend Ann and her parents came to meet him on the floor. He greeted them with an enigmatic smile that trading buddies sometimes saw at the end of a good night of poker. "I just made $19,000," he whispered to Ann, a biologist who worked in a lab during the day and Harry's Café on Rush at night to support her two young children from a previous marriage. Out of earshot, Ann's parents stood dazed and oblivious their first time on the trading floor, happy because their daughter apparently understood the madness and was in love.

A $100,000 day in the pit came shortly after Charlie and Ann were married in September 1980. When traders more senior offered tips at the East Bank Club, the Chuck in Charlie listened, never telling them what Charlie D himself already knew—his P&L was better than theirs. He would be the biggest trader the pit had ever seen, he told his wife. That was his dream. By the time of this lecture in 1989, he was just that, estimated to be worth $40 million by those who tried to guesstimate. Whatever the number, it had all been taken out of the bond pit school of hard knocks. Traders in the audience—even though they didn't know— knew this: The only thing that travels faster than money made or lost in the pits is reputation. The nickname that stuck on the trading floor, Charlie D, came after he had made a small fortune and, for a jock like Chuck, meant just as much as the money. Why? Because a nickname among competing players, many of them also ex-jocks, showed respect for his mental toughness and smooth trading style. A 100-lot trade now felt smaller than one of the six 1-lots he had traded before talking with Ruth, each tick now worth $3125. On a typical day in his prime in the 1980s, he took a stack of cards 18 inches thick to his clearing firm, often representing as much as 20,000 trades on each side of the market in a single day. "He was huge," says Manning, "bigger himself than most firms. At his peak, he was definitely the largest trader on the floor—and we cleared them all: Dick Pfeil, Jeff Kollar, Steve Lawrence, and Tom Baldwin."

Charlie D's lecture was another example of a personal desire to return what he had received—help from the pros. And, a second recurrence of his cancer in August 1988 had made him only too aware of the seriousness of his illness. The choices he pondered in the medical realm were more difficult than what he faced in the pit. Though his full head of hair seemed to suggest the appearance of a healthy individual, doctors had warned Charlie that his lymphoma may not have disappeared completely. The second recurrence was a telltale sign that his continued good health was in question. To stay alive meant even more aggressive and experimental treatments, including a possible bone marrow transplant and more highly toxic chemotherapy. The future for him, though not obvious to a room full of men who judged his health by physical looks, was uncertain. A decision to try a bone marrow transplant, as his doctors suggested, might generate fatal toxicity levels that could kill him before the cancer did. There were no easy answers.

It hadn't been a good week for many traders leading up to this speech. His brother John put Charlie's emotions into some perspective: "I know him too well. In that video, he was corked." Perhaps with good reason. After the producer price figures were released the previous Friday morning, his fellow-trader Tom Baldwin reportedly lost $5 million on March 17, 1989, in a matter of 25 minutes. Long 6000 contracts, bond prices tanked. That loss was later described in a profile article on Baldwin by William B. Crawford, Jr., appearing in the *Chicago Tribune* on November 28, 1993. "I remember that day well," said Baldwin to Crawford. "One does not easily forget such events."

Baldwin certainly wasn't alone. But despite a bad week, personally and professionally, Charlie hadn't lost his sense of humor completely. The room that day was tightly packed, like a locker room before a championship game. In retrospect, there couldn't have been a more surreal setting for the lecture. A video camera had been set directly in front of him, a mirrored wall behind him as a backdrop. Watching the tape of Charlie's lecture, over and over, it's as if the reflection of Charlie D, like Miles Davis with a trumpet, is giving us all he can with his back to his audience. The camera is set on automatic; we see his face as it might appear through water, sometimes breaking through the surface for air, sometimes fuzzily submerged.

This was the man about whom I had heard so much market folklore, in the flesh. His head appears cast, almost Spartan, as if it has been poured into and later removed from a football helmet–shaped mold. His straight hair is parted toward his left shoulder, cut halfway down the ear and just above the collar in back. His skin is smooth, almost tender and rosy, like the macho guys in Gillette shaving cream commercials after a clean shave. He wears glasses, clear tortoise shell frames, more businesslike than professorial, slightly masking prominent eyebrows and the sharpness of his eyes. As he speaks, his lips appear thin, almost angry, like a coach's after a loss. He rocks from foot to foot, pacing four aggressive steps forward, five slower steps backward, incessantly, for 2 hours 12 minutes and 17 seconds. He begins with a joke about his four-day losing streak, the first in six years, threatening not to entertain any questions or repeat himself to torture his audience as he was tortured. The audience laughs at this self-mocking attitude, and he smiles. But it is only a brief moment before his lips thin out again. He has obviously read the major newspaper headlines of the last week, particularly the ones where some politicians attending the Futures Industry Association annual meeting in Boca Raton had remarked that the FBI sting operation of Chicago futures exchanges had ushered in a different era for futures trading. There was talk about eliminating dual trading, which allows brokers on the floor to execute trades for both customers and their own accounts. All the bad press about his business made him doubly unhappy.

"I took a shower before I came up here, and cried a little bit. I started thinking: Do I want to be a good loser? Just as an aside, one thing I don't want to be is a good loser. I don't think anybody in this room wants to be a good loser. And I don't think anyone who trades in the pit wants to be a good loser. There's no value in walking down the hall and having guys look at you and say, 'That son of a bitch, he's a good loser. He doesn't get upset. He smiles when he loses. He's a good loser.' That's the Alpha School of Trading, and I don't buy it. Nobody wants to be a good loser. But there's a difference between being a rotten loser and being mean to your dog and kids when you lose, and being dishonorable when you are losing. Particularly in these times, I hope everyone in this room makes a commitment: Please, please, please, don't be a goddamn thief. There's plenty of money to go around. It's the best business in the world. Brokers in the U.S. Treasury bond pit make more money with less risk than anyone except those guys in Florida with the cigarette boats. I don't think anybody in here has to be dishonorable when they trade."

Capturing the image of the man—visual and audible—his love of life, his humor in the face of death, and trading wisdom cannot be replicated easily on the printed page. His comments are germane particularly to traders but perhaps even for those who don't trade. We all take risks of some form and compete with others in the daily hustle to make a living. The suggestion by Charlie D to make decisions based on information you observe at the moment, not based on an expectation of what you fear might happen, is a valuable lesson universally. So, too, are his specific ideas on self-reliance amidst apparent chaos, positioning yourself for success, managing losses and making them work in your favor, and adding to winners in a manner that demonstrates you are capable, unlike most traders, of having the discipline to resist human nature. Charlie was known to say, "if a monkey could talk, he could trade." Given his belief that trading was not "rocket science," it makes sense that position, tenacity, and size would be important factors in a winning strategy— almost a "brawn, not brain" approach.

While Charlie D's words no doubt have helped some traders make more money than they thought possible, or lose less than they might have, all of us can benefit from and enjoy his speech. With that in mind, I have organized his speech to make it more reader-friendly, only altering his words when logic or repetitive patterns of speech so dictated that some editing was in order. When his speech borders on stream of consciousness, I have added italicized print to capture at least part of his inflection—particularly when it seems he has a foot firmly planted in the trading pit. And, finally, I have added some helpful footnotes for those unfamiliar with a pit trader's jargon. While Charlie was known for helping others, he forever remained opaque about his specific trading methodologies. His video is full of valuable information, but his speech is not always easy to grasp. Of equal import is what he does not say. Whether the tape offers moneymaking tips or not, it does offer us Charlie's voice, spirit and tenacity—equally as important to his trading success.

If you are fanatically enthusiastic about futures trading, Charlie D's advice should improve your efficiency and profitability. His words certainly give us greater insights into who he was and also an appreciation for the role that market makers like him on exchange floors play in the overall global economy. The clip at which his brilliant trading mind moved in the pit, as embodied by his speech, is breathtaking. At some points in the speech, his voice—crescendoing and falling at every turn—was almost impossible to capture. Like the motions of a great athlete who reacts rather than thinks when he is "in the zone," his actions in the pit—which he tries to describe—perhaps defy complete explanation.

Of course, it is far from certain that those who jump into a trading pit will ever make enough money to survive. Perhaps not so surprisingly, the difficulty of doing battle in the trading pits successfully prompted the U.S. Marines to send special forces into trading pits in order to gain valuable decision-making experience among a less-fatal form of chaos. Lt. Gen. Paul K. Van Riper, who launched this joint program between the Marines and the New York Mercantile Exchange, explained why the insights of a trader such as Charlie D may have broader applications for those who are willing to go to the trading pits and attempt to understand his daily exercise. In a December 16, 1996, article in the *Wall Street Journal* entitled MARINES LAND ON MERC TRADING FLOOR TO SWAP TIPS ON WORKING UNDER FIRE, Lt. Gen. Van Riper noted: "There seems to be a natural empathy or bonding between our two groups. We're both required to make quick decisions with limited information."

My only regret is that so little of Charlie D's gift as a trader survives him. As the Marines so aptly pointed out based on their trading pit experiences, what makes traders like Charlie D seem so remarkable is the ability to win in combat against the market's efficiency. That their trading brethren could move so fast and intelligently against an "enemy" with less-than-perfect "battle" information was something that made even the Marine commanders scratch their heads in amazement. Perhaps there were some valuable lessons in military strategy to be learned. It is that skill as one of the trading pit's finest that defined the clairvoyance, integrity, and courage of Charlie D. Here's Charlie . . .

I would like to talk to you in-depth about trading, trading in the pit rather than trading off of the computer screen from off the floor. I have four basic fundamentals to talk about. If you understand these four fundamentals and apply them with discipline, you can be a successful market maker and futures trader in any trading pit.

Let's start from the beginning. The first thing to remember is, despite what you've heard, futures trading is not a zero-sum-total game.* For every winner there isn't a loser, from the perspective of a market maker† on the floor. There are professional hedgers who use futures markets and their numbers continue to grow, and it is their order flow that gives you an opportunity as a trader in the pit. But there's only so much that you can take out of every trading pit as market makers and facilitators for this order flow, and you must divide that opportunity to make money by the number of locals‡ in the pit. The more locals in the pit, the more that opportunity pie has to be divided up.

---

* The popular notion in futures markets is there's a loser for every winner in the pit. As strange as it sounds, Charlie's point is this simply isn't the case from the perspective of a trader on the floor. Consider the selling of a house. If you sell a house for $100,000 that you bought for $90,000, and then the individual who bought it from you sells it for $110,000 down the road, is there a loser? No, both of you have profited. The same is true in the pit. More than one pit trader can make money against the flow of orders coming into the pit, and the opposite is also true.

† A market maker is a trader in the pit who is prepared to trade both sides of the market at any point in time, profiting from the small edge that others may give up in return for accessing the market maker's liquidity. Charlie also refers to these individuals as scalpers or scalp-beggars in his lecture.

‡ Locals are traders in the pit of any exchange. There are two types: A floor trader executes trades for his or her own account; a floor broker executes trades for customers and accepts a fee in return for each contract transacted on behalf of a customer.

While it's baloney that it's a zero-sum-total game down there in the pit, it's true that the opportunity pie has to be divided up among market makers in each pit. Not every market maker is guaranteed a living. In that sense, when you go into a pit, you're potentially taking money out of the mouths of the traders who stand next to you. So, you have to understand why the guy next to you doesn't necessarily tell you it's nice to see you and thank you for coming. To a certain extent, you're costing that guy his Mercedes.

I've had success over my career in the bond pit by following four fundamentals that potentially helped maximize my slice of the opportunity pie: (1) choosing the right pit; (2) getting trades; (3) taking a loss (the fundamental that most risk managers consider the most important); and (4) taking a profit, something I always like to talk about.

The value of one tick* on a Treasury bond futures contract, which represents 1/32nd of a point in the incremental price change of the contract, is $31.25. When I trade 500 bonds, I'm trading a position whose change in value approximates $16,000 for each tick in the change of price. If you have limited success in any pit, and I've always had limited success, my limited success has always been more profitable for me in bonds compared to trading beans in the grain room, which I also did for a spell.

Trading size comes with time and experience. You can only get to that point by serving time in the pit with positions on. Now, as a rhetorical question, I ask you: Who's a better trader? The 1-lot trader who trades 100 lots (futures contracts) a day and makes 30 ticks, or a 10-lot trader

---

* What is a tick? Traders go long (buy) or short (sell) T-bond futures to take delivery or make delivery of $100,000 face value of cash Treasury bonds. All contracts are quoted in percentage of par in minimum increments of (1/32nd) of 1 percent. A tick, the minimum unit of price fluctuation, equals $31.25 (1/32nd of 1 percent of $100,000). If the market is 90-06, this is equivalent to 90 and 6/32nds of $100,000. The front part of the price handle—90 in my example—is assumed as a given for notation purposes by a trader shouting to buy and sell in the pit. If the price changes to 90-07, a trader who bought (long) 500 bonds, or $5 million in face value of cash Treasury bonds, has gained $15,625 on this one-tick move. The trader who sold (short) the same position has lost the same amount of money.

who trades 10 times a day and makes 30 ticks.* The 1-lot trader is the better trader.

Probably the best "small" trader in the world is sitting in this room. His name is Johnny Musso. If I had my wish, he wouldn't be a smaller lot trader. He'd be a 20-lot trader or a 50-lot trader. The principles of trading are the same if you're trading 10, 20, 50, or 100 contracts at a time, or if you're simply trading one. But it takes less time to make more money when you're a larger trader. I'm perhaps the only trader who's going to say this, and the clearing firms are going to hate it, but I believe with all my heart and soul that bigger is better in the futures business. The larger you trade, the better it is for you and the more profitable you are. When you trade a 1-lot, no matter how loud you are when trading, your pit is only a certain size. It will never grow. When you trade a 10-lot, your pit gets bigger. When you do a 50-lot and you're loud and know what you're doing, and you can do the job with confidence and handle it, your pit is huge. When you trade a 100-lot or a 500-lot, the market comes to you. You can go to the bathroom, and other traders will be sitting there with you. Your pit gets huge.

When it comes down to the percent of trades that are profitable, if I'm a 50-lot trader with the same discipline as a smaller trader (and I probably lose on 20 percent of my trades, make money on 30 percent of my trades, and scratch† 50 percent of the time), think how much more money I make than if I'm a 1-lot trader always living in fear of losing money. And more important, think how many more good trades I get if I'm a larger trader because I'm selling 20. That guy across from me in the pit is *7 bid! 7 for 275!* He's going to hit my offer for 20 because he's a broker, and it's easy for him to be out of balance with all the orders in his deck. I repeat: I get better trades when I trade larger. If he's *7 for 100!* and you sell him one, he's not going to buy 99 more from you at 8. It just doesn't

---

* A 1-lot trader has price exposure of \$31.25 per tick, while the 10-lot trader's price exposure is 10 times that, or \$312.50. The latter is trading 10 T-bond futures; the former, one.

† To scratch a trade simply means to buy and sell, or sell and buy, at exactly the same price. The only loss incurred by a trader such as Charlie is the fee paid per trade to his clearing firm, a small amount.

happen. The larger you trade and the quicker you can get your size up, the better you are. And remember this too: If you're a scalper, what does it really mean to be one? All a scalper is is somebody who stands next to brokers and says, "OK, you're a nice guy and you're a nice guy and you're brokers. But guess what? I can fill your orders better than you. Over the course of the year, I'm going to make a whole lot of money because I fill your orders better than you fill them."

Assume you're a scalper in the bond pit. The market is 6 bid at 7.* This broker in the pit buys 50 from you at 7 because he had an order to buy 50. A little while later, you buy 50 at 6. Now, if the broker had nothing else to worry about but that one 50-lot order and knew the market as well as you did, he wouldn't perhaps have paid 7. He would have squeezed it a little and paid 6. But you just went in there and filled his orders better and faster than he can. The bond pit, more than any other pit in history of the futures market, has brokers with huge decks[†] that have incredible size to them. Don't misunderstand me on this point: They give customers good fills like they are supposed to, and a lot of times they give them better fills than that, but they have so much to do that they can't squeeze every order. So they buy 10 at 7, and suddenly in the pit it's big 7 sellers, big 7 sellers.[‡] The local in the pit goes a tick lower and buys 10 at 6. It's a skill that doesn't seem like much, but on a 100-lot, that's over $3000. It doesn't sound like much, but in return for being more efficient and liquid than the market, and for being prepared to assume that position, you can see what that would add up to over a year. It's over $700,000. The question is: Can you

---

* 6 bid at 7. Throughout Charlie's lecture, always remember B is for "bid" and "buy." Thus, a market that is 6 bid at 7 means that locals are willing to buy T-bond futures at 6/32nds and sell (offer at) 7/32nds. So 6 bid at 7 literally translates to 6 bid (buy) at 7 offer (sell). If a traders says 6 for 50, he is stating price first and quantity second, so he is willing to buy 50 bond futures at 6/32nds. If a trader says 50 at 6, he's a seller because he stated quantity first and price second. Charlie uses slight variations on this floor lingo throughout his speech, but this will help you follow along.

† A deck is simply the stack of orders (paper) that a broker controls in the pit. If a broker's deck is huge, it suggests there are many orders to fill.

‡ Big 7 sellers, big 7 sellers. A lot of traders in the pit want to sell bond futures at 7, or 7/32nds, suggesting selling pressure at that particular price.

be more efficient than the market? Most traders cannot. But perhaps these fundamentals will put new traders and smaller traders one step closer to their ultimate goal: to join an elite group of traders that always occupy the top step of any trading pit. As a market maker, always challenge yourself to do it bigger and better and with more size.

lesson 1: choosing the right pit

How do you choose the right pit? The first thing you have to zero in on is open interest—the outstanding open long or short positions in any futures contract. Exchanges publish this number daily. Large open interest* is a sign that there are a lot of players in the market, and there's room for you to go in that pit and make a living. When there's a large open interest, something dramatic happens, and the market rallies; the shorts will cover and the longs will buy. Things happen. If the market breaks, the shorts will price it and longs will get out. Things happen, as long as there's open interest.

In addition to a pit where there's healthy open interest, make sure that you go into a pit where there's price volatility. Volatility is critical. You can be the nicest guy in the world, bidding and offering all day long, but if you aren't getting trades, you aren't going to make a living. And if the pit isn't moving, if the bid isn't changing and the offer isn't changing, you aren't going to get trades, in my opinion.

Another important consideration, in choosing a pit in which to trade, is availability of a reasonable position for you to stand. The bond pit at the Board of Trade, speaking frankly, is a little bit like a Monopoly board. Some of the positions in there are Boardwalk and Park Place. Some of them are greens like Pacific Avenue and yellows like Marvin Gardens. And the spots down in the middle of the octagonal pit, for the guys who don't spread and try to bid the front months, are a little bit like standing on Baltic or Mediterranean Avenue. I'm a firm believer that the spot makes a man rather than a man makes the spot. We've got all kinds of

---

* Open interest is the number of futures contracts outstanding at any point in time. Daily trading volume, in contrast, is the total number of futures contracts changing hands in a day. A buy position not offset by a sale and vice versa add up to total open interest.

players who want to get into the bond pit, all kinds of houses, all kinds of cash arbitrage guys, all kinds of spec houses, all kinds of investors and hedgers. There's plenty of paper* coming into the pit from all angles. If you stand in a good spot, if you're a 1-lot trader and can get over the bumps and the grinds of your early experiences in the pit, you will very quickly become a 50-lot trader.

It's terribly important to find a pit where you can get a position that's meaningful. If you're down in front in the center of the trading pit, down in the shit hole as I like to call it, it's hard to get trades. And it's hard for people to see you. The reason for this is limited sight angles.† Brokers in the Chicago Board of Trade's old grain room when I traded there used to say, "You know, we used to bring the orders down to the middle of the bean pit, and you could stand down there in the middle of that pit and get all of the paper you wanted, and you could trade like crazy." Well, I traded in the middle of the bean pit and I was an idiot. If any bean trader or any grain trader tells you that you don't need to stand on the top step to be a good trader, the answer to that is *bullshit*. You have to stand on the top step, or as close to the top of the pit as you can get.

Why? As I said: sight angles. As traders on the top step, we can probably understand what goes on in an area which encompasses a field of about 180 degrees. If I can rotate my head in the pit with clear sight angles on the top step, I can see the whole pit. Now as we talk about trading today, you're going to understand that one of the most important things in the pit is to know what's going on all around you. You can't be an idiot. You can't be there in the pit—offering 5s, offering 5s, offering 5s, offering 5s—and not see all the locals on the other side getting loaded up on 5s, ready to go *5 bid!, 6 bid!, 7 bid!* You have to know what's going on. One of the ways we know what's going on in the pit is by following an open outcry system.‡ We're supposed to know what trades,

---

* Paper. The buy and sell orders coming into the pit.

† A quarterback who doesn't have good sight angles and throwing lanes is dead in the pocket, and so too is the market maker facing similar problems.

‡ Open outcry pit. An open auction environment where a number of traders voice their bids and offers continuously.

no matter what our location in the pit. And don't ever be afraid to ask anybody in the pit: What in the world traded up there? What traded? In an open outcry pit, they're supposed to tell you. It's not a secret. But this is not a business for weak people, and you have to be able to yell and shout. Don't be afraid to ask what went on.

So here I am on the top step. I can see a field of about 180 degrees. I can see most of what goes on in this pit. I basically know what's happening—what's happening with the spreaders,* in the back months,† and I can even see a little bit into the other trading pits to know what's going on there. If you take another guy and move him down four steps, his field of vision just shrank considerably. Everything that transpires behind him he can't see, and he can't see what's happening in the corners of the pit. So here I am trying to be a scalper, trying to follow all the scalper's trading rules, going *6 bid at 7! 6 bid at 7! 6 bid 7! I'll do anything you want.* I'm basically trading with the attitude of a scalper that I'll sell 7s and scratch them forever if I have to avoid a loss or need to avoid holding that position for too long.

There's just one problem with this philosophy in the trading pit. If I go to Jewel to buy groceries, the store owner doesn't want to hear that I can't pay for my groceries because I scratched all my trades. You've got to be able to see that pit. You've got to be able to go into a pit where you can see.

Now, along those same lines, when you walk into a pit, where's a good place to stand? A good place to stand is that area where the locals that drive the nicest cars and make the most money stand. One thing you'll find out the longer you're in this business: Nobody, *nobody* comes up with anything new. Everything that's been done by you as a trader and everything that's been done by the trader who started six months earlier has been done

---

* Spreaders. Traders who take two positions—one long and one short—to profit from a change in the difference between the two futures prices, or prices of the same futures contract expiring in different months. A spread is considered less risky than just a pure long or short position, since prices in different expiration months (a calendar spread) tend to go up and down together. This tends to lessen some of the price volatility to which a trader is exposed.

† Back months. Futures contracts that mature later in time, as opposed to the front-month contract, which is nearest to maturity or expiration, and also the most liquid.

a thousand times before. There really aren't too many new twists to making money when you're in a pit. It's kind of a cop-out for me to say this, but the best way for anybody to become a good trader is to become a copycat. You watch good traders. And you copy what they do. You don't necessarily dress the way they dress or talk the way they talk, but you stand in a position as close to the position they stand. You watch them when they sell it and bid for it right away. A big trader sold it and covered,* *why?* He sold it and offered more, *why?* He sold at 5 and offered 4s, *why?* If it was me, and I just lost money for four days in a row, it's because I was long at 7.

When you go into a new pit, when you choose a pit, make sure you can get a position in that pit that closely approximates the positions of big dogs.† The reason is simple: Nobody reinvents the wheel on a regular basis. We're pit scalpers, or scalp-beggars, in that pit. Most of the time, it's *6 Lord, please; sell it at 7, please!* OK? There's not much you can do to maximize your income other than stand in the right spot and be disciplined. In my opinion, without giving away any secrets because everybody knows this, you can walk around the trading floor and there are certain pits where it is easier for you to get a position to stand that approximates the locations in which big money makers stand.

I started down here in 1980. At that time, we traded 10,000 to 12,000 bonds a day, and there were maybe 60 locals. I can remember the first day we traded 25,000 contracts in a day, and we all threw our trading cards in the air. That was a big deal back then. Our open interest didn't come anywhere close to the open interest you now see in many trading pits, so I don't think the opportunity for making it as a trader at the Chicago Board of Trade is gone.

Once again, choose the right pit. Make sure you can get into a spot where you can trade. There just isn't any advantage to being down in the hole. When I last looked at the meal pit and the oil pit, you could go into the pit and stand right next to the most successful trader in there, Dennis Flynn. You'd probably get hit in the ribs about five times if you

---

* Covered. Closing a trading position by taking the opposite position. A short position covers a long position of the same quantity, and vice versa.

† A term many traders use to describe the large traders in any pit.

tried, but you could do it. You could stand right next to him. Theoretically, that means you're starting on an even keel, with the exception of your capitalization.

It's a Monopoly board down in the trading pit—and the man doesn't make the spot, the spot makes the man. So pick the right spot. Incidentally, when we started down in the first bond pit in the Board of Trade's South Room, some of us as traders were bright enough, I guess, to figure out it really made a difference as to which spot you stood in the pit. Guys like myself—and I was not alone—came down for 18 to 19 months in a row in those days at 2 o'clock in the morning just so we could get the right spot in the bond pit. My brother John came down at midnight for six months because he was in a time war with another guy for a particular spot in the pit. Eventually traders started sleeping in the hallways and everyone would rush in when they opened up the gates. I just mention this to show there's always been a premium on spots and most probably always will be.

lesson 2: getting trades

Getting trades in the pit may seem easy to someone from the visitor's gallery looking in, but it isn't—particularly for a less experienced trader. The fact is you can never take a profit if you can't get a trade. For the first two-and-a-half months that I was down at the Board of Trade, I didn't do anything in the pit. I used to wear three-piece suits to Harris Bank, and when I came down to the pit, I wore the same three-piece suits, just taking off my suit jacket to trade. I had my vest on, buttoned my trader's jacket like this over it, and I stood in the pit with my arms crossed. And the traders in the pit would go *6 bid!* And I said, *Yep, 6 bid. 7 sellers!* they'd shout. *Yep, 7 sellers.* And about once a week, I couldn't stand it anymore. I would buy one contract, keep it for a day, and then get out of it. At the end of about two-and-a-half months, I still found the concept of scalping incredibly tough. I didn't understand why you had to sell them when you bought 6s because I could remember days when it was 6 bid for 500 and 10 were offered at 7, and all of a sudden the 5s would come in and sell 1000 at 6, 500 at 5, 500 at 4. The 1-lot that I bought at 6, which I thought was the greatest deal, was suddenly a 3-tick loser. The opposite also happened: I would sell 1 at 7 and there would be

500 bid, and before you knew it, I had a profit on my 1-lot. That bugged the hell out of me. So, I became a spreader in the trading pit. This was back at a time when tax laws were different and there was an incentive for people to use contracts that were in the front months. I don't think we will ever see those types of opportunities again, but my notions about spreading never really changed. Later, as a scalper in the pit, I remained a spreader at heart, just a spreader of a different sort.

The reason for this is simple: Over the history of the Board of Trade, there's only been one group of traders that has consistently made money, and those are spreaders. Up until the creation of the bond pit, there was no such thing as a scalper who made money. Johnny Musso knows this and I know this because we also traded in the bean pit. When you were in the bean pit, and when you were *6 for 100!* and another trader sold you 100 at 6, everybody in the pit tested you. They made it 6 sellers. If you were 5½ bid for a 100, it maybe went back to 6 bid. There was no such thing as a pit being a clearly defined 6 bid at 6½, or 6 bid at 7.

In the bond pit, it's clearly defined as everybody knows. It's *6 bid at 7.** In the bean pit, and basically every other pit within the history of the Board of Trade, there was no such thing as a clear edge. There was no such thing as a scalper, or scalp-beggar, as I sometimes say. Everybody was a mini-speculator and a mini-daytrader in every pit. And for the most part, those guys went bust. The people who made money on a continual basis down here were spreaders. They spread and they spread and they spread. That's how I got my start.

Once I understood the concept of spreading and figured it out in the cafeteria, I became a 50-lot trader the next day instead of a 1-lot trader. People who spread mature faster as traders and, at least in the old days, had an opportunity to make a lot of money. Now because tax laws are different there's no such thing as a spread like this. Of course, there are guys in the middle of the bond pit who make money spreading. And if you are a note over bonds (NOB) spreader,† you're a pure spreader.

---

* A one-tick spread between the bid and offer.

†NOB spreader. A trader taking advantage of either a parallel or a nonparallel shift in the yield curve, between intermediate-term Treasury notes and long-term Treasury notes.

When I use the word scalper, by the way, I use the term in kind of a loose sense, not in an Everett Klipp kind of way. Everett Klipp is the guy who runs Alpha Trading, and he's probably one of the best guys at the Board of Trade teaching new traders how to trade and trade with discipline. Everett is from the school of *6 bid at 7*. In his world, if I buy at 6, it's one-thousand-one, one-thousand-two, one-thousand-three, I'm out. It's time to go on to the next trade. Everett has a whole bunch of Alpha traders who have come down to the Board of Trade and made a lot of money. But Everett doesn't have any Alpha traders who have come down to the Board of Trade recently and made any money. Despite that, Everett's the guy who taught everybody what it really meant to be a scalper. If any of you ever had an occasion to visit Dave Goldberg, which I did in the morning on occasion when I first became a trader, we talked about the old guys up there scalping in the trading pits. Dave used to say, "Every day is a new day at bat. Every day is a new inning. . . ." I could give you that speech from Dave, but I won't. I simply bring it up as a reminder to any new trader of the discipline it takes to become a successful trader.

For the most part, traders in the financial instruments at the Board of Trade who stand in those particular pits are not spreaders, but they *are*. That's where my thinking differs from Everett's. To get trades you have to adapt the mentality of a spreader. What are you talking about, Charlie? I'm saying you may be a scalper in the bond pit or any pit for that matter, but you have to think like a spreader. Everybody who trades bonds from the outside spreads. Everybody who's trading in the bond pit spreads. And every order that comes in to the bond pit is basically a function of a spread. I guess I shouldn't say *everybody* or *every* order, but probably 65 percent of the people who send orders into the front month contract* are trading against another cash instrument for the most part.

What does that mean if you are standing in the pit? It means that we are spreaders in the bond pit, pure and simple. We're trading bonds but really we're trading bonds against some other commodity. Everybody's trading price relationships. I can still remember how frustrated I was

---

* The futures contract nearest to its expiration date.

when I started out trading in the bond pit. I'd be *6 bid at 7.* I'd say to myself: Why do I want to buy 6s? Because everybody else in the pit does? If that's true, what's the probability that I'm going to get a 6? Zero. Then I'd say to myself: I want to sell at 7 when everybody else wants to, so what's the probability that I was going to get 7s? Again, the answer is zero.

The only way to solve this herd problem is to be a spreader at heart. Let's take the bond pit as an example. What do I want to spread against? I want to spread against outside markets. But before I go into that, I want you to understand one thing right now: If it's a big 6 bid in the pit, you want to buy 6s; if it's big 7 sellers, you want to sell 7s. If you don't remember anything else, remember that when you go to the floor and trade. That will save you from a lot of trouble early on.

How do you get 6s or 7s? How do you get 6s when they are not quite as attractive as they were when 500 other people were trying to buy them? And how did you get 7s when they weren't quite as attractive and 500 other people wanted to sell them? You want to offer or bid against another market. I personally follow other markets when I'm in the bond pit and I'm no different than other successful traders at the Board of Trade, past and present. As you know, there are a whole bunch of guys trading bonds who follow the yen. When the yen ticks up, they're aggressive sellers; when the yen ticks down, they're aggressive buyers. On another day in the pit it may be different. If we're watching the Dow one day and the Dow breaks, I may be an aggressive seller or an aggressive buyer, depending on how much it has broken. Today, for example, we watched oil at the end of the day. When oil broke, we were aggressive buyers. When it rallied, we became aggressive sellers.

As you can see, I'm not an advocate of stepping out when you're trading. That's not a spreader's mentality. If another market participant wants to trade and *it's 6 bid at 7,* I don't believe you should buy 10 at 7 and be happy to have a trade on. That's not the way to do it, and let me explain why. Brokers want to trade with locals, but they don't want to trade with you unless you're an aggressive bid or an aggressive offer. Unfortunately, the hardest thing in the world for the relatively new trader is to step into a pit and be an aggressive 6 bid or 7 offer when that person does not have a position on. The bottom line is that you just don't know that much about what's going on. You have to have a reason for what you're doing.

You may think to yourself: Why do I not want to buy 6s, why do I not want to sell 7s?

When I was a spreader early in my career, I spread the middle month against the top [front] month. If I offered the middle month, I might offer at 20. Someone in the pit would shout, "How many do you have at 20?" I would look how many they offered at 16 [in the front month], which is what I wanted to buy. I'd yell, "I've got 400 at 20." No one would have given a damn if I had 400 at 20 and wanted to buy a spread. But I was offering with confidence, so when a broker had an order, he came to me just like that. "I'll buy a 100." It was done because the broker knew I wanted to sell at 20.

There's nothing worse than a new trader in the pit who sounds like Dopey in *Snow White* and says, *Well, uh, 6 bid at 7, 6 bid at 7. Uh, I really don't know what I want to do—to buy 6s or sell 7s, but, uh, 6 bid at 7.*

Say a broker in the pit feels sorry for you or guilty—they all feel guilty because they make so much money—and he says to you in the pit, *What are you doing?* He wants to do you a favor and trade with you. This time you're worse than Dopey, you're Bashful, and say, *6-7*, in a real quiet voice. You may forget to say 6 because you're so shy, and the broker's going to find himself with a 6 that is like gold to him. That's not the way to trade. Don't be one of those "7" dwarfs in the pit. Offer 7s with a reason and offer them with confidence. You can do that easily with some practice. You do it against another market by thinking like a spreader.

Let's all imagine for a second that we've just jumped into the trading pit and the market's live. I'm going to buy 6s. I have decided to do so because I'm spreading against the yen because that's what makes sense at that point in time. The yen breaks, weakening relative to the U.S. dollar, so bonds are more attractive. The pit is *6 bid at 7*. I'm shouting at a broker, *6 for 10! 6 for 10!* The broker wants to help me if he has the opportunity to do so, particularly if other traders around me don't seem to be demonstrating the same level of confidence in what they want to do.

One day I may follow yen, doing bonds against the yen. The next day it may change. But I'm a spreader at heart—all the time watching what's going on in the pit. I shout *6 for 10! 6 for 10!* The broker will say, *God, that guy's 6 for 10!* He may want to help you. The new trader in the pit knows how ridiculous it sounds in the pit when you yell *6 for 10! Sell 10 at 7!* You can hear your own voice, and you feel embarrassed and all the other stuff. I don't get embarrassed anymore, but I did when I first started trading. Everybody then thought I was bidding when the number in the pit was 6 because I would shout *6!*—swallowing the 6 at the same time I swallowed my tongue. I was that bad. My own voice in the pit made me nervous. Then I would get up my nerve and throw in a 7, but that number would come out of my mouth a decibel higher because I was so embarrassed to hear my own voice. When you have a reason for doing what you're doing in the pit, it's so much easier to be loud and that enlarges your pit size.

Don't ever forget that enlarging your pit size is a critical part of getting trades. Don't be like I was and stand there like an idiot going *6 bid at 7!* Come up with reasons for bidding and offering. If you're shouting *20 at 7!,* you have a better chance to get a trade off with another trader who says *6 for 10!* and wants to sell. Spreading against another market is the easiest way to do it, short of knowing a lot about everybody's position in the pit.

If you can follow my example of spreading against the yen, you can become an aggressive bidder when the yen breaks. Shout *6 for 10! 6 for 20! 6 for 30!,* whatever your trading unit size. Boom, you'll get a trade. You may want to get rid of it immediately by scratching,* but at least you've gotten into the trade—and you've got a reason for doing so. That's three-quarters of the battle, not half the battle, let me tell you. You don't always have to spread against the yen. You may want to spread against the front month. You may want to look at the big dogs up there on the top step and spread against them. Say I see a big dog like up there, for example. He's selling: *100 at 5, 100 at 5, 100 at 5!* Just like that, in less than a snap of my fingers, my attention may change to something else that I can spread against. Watching the big dog may tell me it might just be a matter of time before the market's going to go 5 sellers. So where am I? At the very least, that information may make me an aggressive 6 seller. Now, I'm spreading on many levels. I'm spreading the front month, I'm spreading my bid against his bid, and I'm offering 6s because he's selling

---

* Making the opposite open outcry trade at the same price.

5s. Now the market is *5 bid at 6.* But I'm offering 6s and I'm offering them aggressively.

Boom!—let's look at that scenario for a second. You're an aggressive seller and brokers know what you want to do. I've got 20 to buy. *Sold!,* someone shouts, putting you in the market. Perhaps the brokers don't know what the market is or they're doing you a favor. Now I've got 20 at 6 and there are all those 5s out there in the pit. The 5s are bidding, bidding for more, but you know it's all a bunch of bullshit. I've got 20 at 6 and wait for it to go 5 sellers. Guess what? Now I'm an aggressive *5 bid, 5 bid, 5 bid.* The broker who wants to help you knows you want to do something because you're shouting *5 bid at 6!* The broker has 10 to buy. He doesn't want to stick you or hurt you. He doesn't want to buy 10 from you if you don't know how to handle it, and he doesn't want to buy 10 from you if you don't want to sell it. But you're telling him by your actions that you can. You saw something transpire on the top step, or you saw something transpire in the middle month, or in an outside market, so you have become an aggressive offer or an aggressive bid.

From experience in the pit, I know brokers don't want to trade with losers. Everybody who has ever processed paper or brokered paper knows that you don't like to stick a guy when you're in that position. If you're *6 bid at 7! 6 bid at 7!,* and all of a sudden it goes 6 sellers and you breathe like the wind is sucked out of you, the brokers won't want to trade with you anymore. They don't want to trade with you anymore because they don't want to be responsible for your loss. For that reason, in the pit, you've got to convince them that you want those 6s or want to sell those 7s. If it's me, I want to sell 7s not because I'm a genius who knows bonds are going down 2 ticks, but because I saw something transpire in another market that's going to weaken the price in the bond pit. That's when I become an aggressive seller.

It could be I'm following a change in the price of yen, or oil, or a commodities basket, or the Dow, or the noise level from guys screaming in the Treasury note pit, or that something transpired on the top step, in the middle or back month contracts. And it may not be something I have to live with if I get the trade I think I want, but I bid and offer with meaning and vigor on that basis.

Remember, if a big dog is loaded up with a position, he may want to shut you up. If you offer *20 at 7!*, he may want to buy your 7s just to shut you up, even if he's long at 6. Some traders have made a lot of money simply by being shut up by big dogs on a regular basis in the bond pit. If you are a loud and confident trader, everybody has to trade with you if you want to trade.

Another concept: personal pit size. It's a critical part of getting trades. My pit size when I'm a meek *6 bid at 7, 6 bid at 7* is puny. Somebody says *Sell 2 at 6!* and you buy them. You put your broker's house down on your trading card and feel good that you got off a trade. I'm telling you, that's how you lose. After you write it down on the card, say the market goes 6 sellers. You have to get out. *Sold!* you shout, giving 1-lots to the friendly guys next to you on your left and right. *Whew, I'm out!* I sold you one and you one. The problem with that is your pit size has shrunk and so has your opportunity. You haven't done anything to enhance your pit size trading that way. If you want to make more money, you trade in a larger pit.

How large a pit can you trade in? You trade in a pit that goes completely around all eight corners of the octagonal pit. You don't necessarily become obnoxious, but you do get loud. *6 for 10! 6 for 10! 6 for 10!* If you don't enhance your pit size, you're an asshole only shooting yourself in the foot. God forbid it goes 6 sellers and you didn't get a chance to get out. Now, it's 5 bid for 150. But all of a sudden, it's 6 offer. It's time for you to take your loss, but your pit size is small. You've got 10 at 6, but you've just lost $312.50 because this guy on your right loves you and this guy on your left loves you because you gave them a shot to make a little money.

I'll show you why not to do that. Say you've bought 10 at 6 and it's 6 sellers. It's time to sell. You pick somebody and sell them 10, and you do it loud. And you pick somebody out that can help you. You don't sell it to the guy next to you. You look around the pit. And here's a broker with 50, let's say, from Refco. *Sell you 10 at 5!* you shout. You sell him 10 at 5. You put your name on the card. Who is that guy, you think? I only trade with my friends. You've just enlarged your pit size. Something right happens. He's got discretion. He's a broker. He's an idiot. He's bought 10 at

5. *I'll sell 40 at 6!* he shouts. Now he's showing 40 at 6. You're 500 up at 6. Now you are at *5 for 40, 5 for 40.* Now you've just increased your pit size. The 5 bid grows, the 6 offer gets smaller, and you are short 40 at 6, and it's time to cover. You look around the pit when you've got time, and you say, *Who can I buy the 6s from? Who can I give the edge up to that will come back and make it worth my while? Justin! Justin Nolan, I'll buy 40 at 6!* Justin Nolan looks at you, *Sold!* Later in the day, after you bought those 40 at 6, it went 5 sellers, 4 sellers, 3 sellers, 2 sellers. Justin Nolan thought you were taking a loss but were nice enough to look him up and give him the 40 ticks. But later in the day, it's *2 bid at 3.* Everybody in the world wants to buy 2s. You want to buy 2s because the yen is breaking. *2 for 10! 2 for 10!* You hear someone say, *Hey, sell you 50!* Thank you, Justin. He came back to help you. Because you enlarged your pit size. I can't emphasize this enough. Don't, don't, *don't* be a myopic trader who has a small group of friends who commiserate after work and say, *God, we're not getting any trades.* And whenever you get a 2-lot, don't say he deserves one and he deserves one. Don't do that. It's not fair to him, and it's not fair to you.

This is the most important part of the futures business for traders. When you get a trade and you have to get out, and everybody has to get out of that trade sometime, take advantage of it. Give it to somebody who can come back and help you. Now, say I'm a broker. This is an open out-cry pit and I have 100 to sell. There are 50 guys who want to buy 5s, and there are 50 guys who want to sell 6s. By the rules, I have 100 to sell, but I don't have to say, *Sell 100 at 5!*, and the first guy who says *Sold!* gets them. Remember I'm a broker, and I know that's not fair to people. So I say, *Sell you 20. Sell you 20. Sell you 20. Sell you 20. Sell you 20.* The customer gets the fill that he deserves, and the broker has done his job. But the broker has exercised his judgment. The broker has decided to split the order with somebody. At some point in time, when that trader has a big position on and this broker goes sellers, and his house expects it, the broker expects that guy to come back to him and take him out—when that guy has an opportunity to take out anybody in the place. It goes both ways. But you never have those types of opportunities unless you have enlarged your pit size by taking advantage of your position.

The Alpha School of Trading guys do a tremendous job of getting out in the bond pit. If the Alpha guys buy 5s, it's one-thousand-one, one-thousand-two, one-thousand-three, and they are ready to get out at 5. They let everyone know. *Sell 10 at 5! Sell 10 at 5!* They do a great job of enlarging their pit size, and always have 75 other traders ready to tear their faces off when they trade. In the long run, enlarging their pit size helps them enormously.

Getting trades becomes even more of an art form once you get comfortable with another notion in the trading pit—transition trading. You get trades by being a spreader, but you also get them by being a transition trader. You get trades by assuming a spreader's mentality and by enlarging your pit when you don't have a position on. But let's assume you've got a position on now and are trying to take advantage of it. Remember, for all the time you spend in that pit, there are probably six nanoseconds a day when you have a position on when you first start out. But good traders have a position on from the time the bell rings until the end of the day, although there are some of us who are idiots and even carry positions past the last bell.

Why is having a position on all day a good idea? If I have a position on, and if I'm long 100 at 5 and you're flat, who's going to get to a broker first when he says *6 for 10!* Who's going to win, you or me? I'll beat your ass because I have a position on and know exactly what I want to do. I want to sell 6s. More realistically, if I'm short at 4 and the broker says *6 for 10*, I'll beat you to the punch again because I don't want you to get short at 6 and try to buy 5s. Traders with positions on get very fast, faster than you can believe. And they get smarter.

New traders and less successful traders, unfortunately, have a position on about six nanoseconds a day. You hear an interchange between them and other traders go something like this: *6 for 1! Sold! Sell 1 at 6! My God, that was close!* In the back of their minds they're thinking about all the stuff that could have happened but didn't. The president could die. The Japanese could decide to sell their entire U.S. bond portfolio. All that kind of stuff is in the trader's mind. Three-and-a-half hours later, just like when I was a new trader, you see these traders do the same thing again: *2 for 1! Sold! Sell 1 at 2! I'm out! Oh my God, I could have lost everything again!* Don't do that! Have a position on all day long, bid and offer with authority, and enlarge the size of your pit by becoming what I call a transition trader.

A transition trader is a nice way to describe a trader who *steals* trades. Am I advocating stealing for a living? Absolutely not. What I mean by a transition trader is a trader who *steals* a trade in a sense because he is more efficient than the rest of the market in providing liquidity. He does this by being absolutely involved in whatever happens in the trading pit.

Let's walk through an example of this, imagining ourselves in the pit for a moment. If it's *6 bid at 7* in that pit, and it goes 6 sellers, my mind goes ding-ding-ding, here's an opportunity for profit. At 6 bid at 7, 99 out of 100 times you aren't going to make a damn nickel by buying 6s and selling 7s. Take my word for it. Nobody is going to sell you 6s and buy 7s because you are good-looking and you're a new trader. It just doesn't happen. If you want to play in a trading pit, you've got to get into the market any way that you can. Let me explain how you become a transition trader. If it's *6 bid at 7*, a big dog says *Sell 500 at 6!*, you say *Sell you 10!* There were 10 bid right there, and you sold him 10 at 6 because he wanted to sell 500. Did he get filled? Absolutely. That's your 10. Now it's 6 sellers. You are short 10 at 6 but you are in the market. Congratulations, you are in the market; you are finally playing. When you're in the market, you have an opportunity to make money. When you're not in the market, you don't do anything.

Transition trading* is a very, very, *very* touchy subject. I'm not telling you to go out and steal a trade. But listen—this is the way the world is: *6 bid at 7!* One of the big dogs says *Sell 200 at 6!* You like it and think it's a good idea and he's bidding for 25. *Sold!* Did he get his? He sure did. These are yours. Did he not get his? *Hey, I'll buy 25!* Boom. An honest guy. Somebody like me appreciates that. And believe me, they remember it forever. *Sell 25! I'll bid 25. That's my market! Hey, I'm off. Fuck you!* A little later in the day, big shot says sell 200 at 6. *Sell you 25! Hey, that's my market. Well, you were off last time. Remember that?* What's fair is fair. It's a hard, hard life. It's a tough world out there. You want to be in

---

* Transition trading. The market goes from one bid-ask price to another, and you are there with it as it makes the "transition" in the pit just as it is turning over to a new price level.

the market when the bid changes and the offer changes. That's when the opportunity for making money happens, particularly when you know what you want to do.

Another situation: You see 6s trading. You're an aggressive 7 seller. But, by God, you are ready to go to 6. Anything will trip your wire. Somebody says *Sell it at 6!* because he wants to sweep the market. Well, you've just helped him sweep the market.* You sell him his 25 because he deserves it because he was sweeping the market. Guess what? Later in the day, later in the week, later in the month, that money will come back to you. And it will come back tenfold to you. More important, since that particular notion is so esoteric to understand unless you've been in the pit and seen it happen, remember if he doesn't want it or he gets filled, that's your trade anyway.

Now, here's another situation for the transition trader. *5 bid at 6! Sell 10 at 5! Sell 500 at 5!* The big dog tries to walk over you, but he can't. *Heh, I never got my 10!* The guy buys 25 at 5—it's his market. *I'll buy 10.* You sell 25. Did he get filled? The other guy never got filled. He says, *It's my market! I offered 500 at 5!* Bullshit. He was first. He offered 10 at 5. It was your market and you're in. You're short 15 at 5 and you want to be short. Because the big dog wants to sell them. You've just become a transition trader—that's how you get trades. You don't steal trades, you don't steal them. But when the market changes, you be part of the action.

Let's take another scenario: I've got *6 bid at 7.* Who's the 6 bid? How far is he from you? Ideally, you are close enough in the pit to this guy where, if it goes 6 sellers, you can get these. Ideally. Remember that's got to do with pit position, too. Remember, if you're a broker, and I'm here, and he's standing next to you, and I know you're bidding for 25, and all of sudden a big dog says *Buy 500 at 6!* Sell you 25. By the time I do that, the guy next to me has already grabbed me and yelled *Sold!* So proximity in a pit means something and is one reason that your position in the pit is important. The closer you are to a broker or a large trader, the easier it is to trade.

---

* Sweep the market. A power play by a big trader, who literally sweeps up the positions of other traders, just as the wooden arm at the craps table in Las Vegas sweeps up all the chips. Exchanges hate analogies to Vegas, but there you have it.

Now, understand also what the positions are of the locals around you. Say here's John Doe in the pit. He's short 10 at 7. You are an aggressive seller. And he's a lucky dog. He's short 10 at 7 and you're an aggressive 7 seller. Boom. The market goes 6 sellers. You're offering him 6s because chances are he's going to take his profit. You're in the market. You're a transition trader. If he's short 10 and it goes 6 sellers. *Sell at 6! Sell 500 at 6!* And he doesn't, so I'll buy 10. He's *5 for 10, 5 for 10*. And then he goes *6 for 10*. It's your market. It's anybody's market at that point in time. Do you understand me on that point?

Now these are tough questions to deal with in the pit. I think that the guys in the bond pit know that I feel pretty strongly about people who steal trades. Sometimes I get vocal about it. And I don't like it. I don't like people who steal trades. I think if you make a market, you ought to get filled up. And I think there are a couple guys in the bond pit who say *Sell at 6* and that means if you bid, or you're thinking about bidding for it, or your mother wants them, buy it from me. There are an awful lot of guys in the bond pit when they make a market who go, *Sell it at 6!* Boom. You are trying to buy 500 from them and they say, "Uh-oh," and then whisper, *Sell 50.* Those are the guys you make a living on if and when they become transition traders, or if and when you get the opportunity to become a transition trader.

As a transition trader, you want to get into the market and you want to be long at the bid or short at the offer. How do you do it? You are standing in the pit. Somebody says *Sell it at 6! Sell 300 at 6.* It's Justin Nolan, the broker. And it's a 125 bid, OK. You sell Justin his 25. I promise you. I promise you it will come back to you, OK? Not only that, but you've done a trade. There are a lot of people in a lot of pits who lose money. And there are a lot of people who try to turn sellers when they're never going to turn sellers. They are trying to turn a big one, but they're never going to turn a big one. So don't get in a position where somebody says *Sell 100 at 6!* and you know everybody else has sold 7s. Just because they're doing that, don't say, *Sell you 25.* Don't do that. When you're a transition trader, you're a transition trader because you're saying *I want to be a 7 seller.* When the opportunity presents itself, I'll be a 6 seller because I'll still be short at 6. I can't tell you how important that is. And I can't tell you how it changes your life when you're a new trader. Before that, you're standing in the pit and don't have a position on. You're looking at the tiles on the ceiling. You're like me when I started out. *My God, I used to think, they've got microphones in the ceiling!* And I would stand there and look at them, saying, *That's ridiculous! The guy next to me is 6 for 100! Sell 100 at 7!*, but I wouldn't even know what he's talking about and wouldn't even care. Instead, I'm looking at the people in the visitor's gallery from the pit, thinking, *My God, they're Amish!* I used to do that a lot. Either the staring or the Amish people cost me a lot of money, I'm not sure which. Transition trading is a way to keep your interest at its peak at all times in the pit.

lesson 3: taking a loss

I could mark this lesson up with a few of my own scars, believe me. Knowing when to take a loss is extremely important. It's very simple: If you don't take your losses in the trading pit, you can't play with us in the pit for very long. We will chew you up, spit you out, and get rid of you.

Before I get into the specifics of taking a loss, let's go back to the concept of enlarging your pit. When you take a loss, it hurts. And it should. I say it once: Nobody, *nobody* should be a good loser. Don't be a good loser. It doesn't fit right with you. It doesn't look good on you. And it isn't good for the people you love. But when you have to take a loss, take it like a man. A real trader knows that you can take advantage of that loss by making sure it comes back to help you out later in a different situation.

Say, for a moment, that I'm long 10 at 6, and it goes 6 sellers. It's probably time for me to get out because I'm not going to sell 6s. Now I'm long 10 at 6 and it's 5 *bid at 6* and I'm an aggressive 6 seller and everybody who knows me in the pit knows I want to sell 6s. They can hear it in my voice and know damn well that I'll sell 6s.

Take somebody out, if you have to, a piece at a time, and take advantage of your position. Use that loss by selling to people who will come back to you. There are locals in our bond pit, there are locals in the bean pit, and there are locals in almost every pit who are locals but really aren't locals to a certain extent. They just act like locals. I remember the first time I ever talked with anybody at Goldberg Brothers. I'd been in the business for four years, and I gave some lectures on spreading, and

somebody said, *Why are you talking about spreading?* They actually
thought I was a broker. They did, they thought I was a broker. And a lot
of people said I could become a broker because I gave up the edge too
much. But, that means if you want to get out, you probably want to go to a
local like me that will come back to you. And when I say me, I'm not saying me. Go to a local trading size who can help you at some point in time.
People scratch other people's backs. Say it's *5 bid at 6,* you're long 6,
you've got to sell 10 at 5. Take advantage of it. Sell it to somebody who
will come back and help you at a later date because, by God, a one-tick
loss on a 10-lot is $312.50 and it's gone forever—unless I plant a seed.
So I plant a seed. I enlarge my pit size and I sell that 10-lot to somebody
who can help. When you're standing in a pit, and you're long at 6, and
you're stomach's tight, and it's *5 bid at 6,* and it's not fun, get out! Get out
of the trade. Do something else. Go to another trade.

Sometimes, when you're long at 6 and it's trading 6, but you want to
hang on to this one, there may be somebody you want to sell it to so that
it will be to your advantage. There may be a broker with discretion on an
order. Let me give you an example. Has everyone seen someone at the
outside desks look at a broker and pull an ear lobe? It means the broker
is being given one-tick discretion. So he has 6 for 50, but can go up to 7.
All right. Say I'm a broker. I've got 50 to buy. Somebody sells me 10 at 6.
I go to 7. By the rules, I don't have to go back to him. But, as a matter of
etiquette, who do I go back to? The guy who sold me 6s. OK, now, say
you want to be long at 6. The world wants to sell it at 7. You sell 10 at 6
because you were long there. Now you are short 40 at 7. That's the greatest trade you ever made. OK. Keep that in mind. Discretion helps. Go to
people who can exercise discretion on your trades when you're taking a
loss. The name of this game in pit trading, no matter how badly I did
today, was that I took my losses in a manner that was good enough so that
I can come back tomorrow.

As a rule of thumb, I always believed that you had to make 4000 to
5000 trades before you had faced everything you might see in the pit.
Now being faced with everything means you are long at 6, and it's max
sellers before you know it; it means you're long at 6; Greenspan says
something, and it's 12 bid. Now you know what to do with a 6-tick profit
because you just experienced one. It means that a broker sells you 10 at

6, sells you 10 at 5, sells you 10 at 4, sells 50 at 3, and before you know it, you don't want that much and have to puke your position all over your shoes. That's a new experience, OK. It means a broker buys 200 from you right out of the blue, and you have to scratch and take a loss. That's a new experience.

Now once you've experienced everything, you're able to handle it in the pit. But in the interim, you have to build up your time served with positions on. That's what trading is all about. The longer time you serve in a pit, with a position on, the more you know about yourself and the more you know about trading. If I'm long 10 at 6, sell them at 6 a second later, and I get my next trade later that day or early the next day, I haven't learned much. You were long at 6 and got out at 6. Why did you get out at 6? *Because it was 6 bid and I didn't want to take a loss.* When you get to a point where you have a position on and can actually say—*I'm long at 6, who's bidding, who's offering, what's it trading? Do I want to get long at 6? What are the outside markets doing?*—and you know your mind, and your mind works quite quickly when you're long at 6, and when you can understand the 17 variables involved in trading or the 20 variables involved in trading, then you're OK. Serve time with positions on. It's the only way to get to that point. I can't tell you how personalities change when you are in the pit. You can be a Phi Beta Kappa, but unless you've served that time, you can just forget absolutely everything you've ever learned about trading—unless you put yourself under fire enough times and learn from it.

One of the most important things you learn with positions on is how to get out of a trade. It's one thing when the price in the market stays the same for 10 minutes. And it's quite another thing when you're long 10 at 6, and someone says, *You want 300 to eat? You want 525? You want to look at 620?* That's a whole lot different, and you have to handle it differently. You're going to learn a lot about yourself and about trading, and you learn how to move faster than I can clap my hands. And one of the most important things you learn when you're moving that fast is how to exit a trade.

How do I get out? There are many ways. Here's one way to get out. I can yell in a panic, *Sell 10 at 4, sell 10 at 3, sell 10 at 2, sell 10 at 1!* That's one way to get out—the expensive way. But there's another way to get out. At all times, know who the brokers and who the locals are and what their positions are. You can't know what a broker's position or orders are going to be. But you can know where to go. When it's time for you to get out, when you don't give a shit and you want to get out, when your voice gets a little screechy, don't offer it to the microphone in the ceiling or the visitor's gallery. The Amish people up there and the microphones don't care what you're doing.

Believe me, I've tried to sell a loser to the visitor's gallery. The people up there don't want them. Nobody wants them. Don't offer it to the ceiling of the trading floor. *Don't.* Offer it to specific people with specific locations within the pit. Say I'm long 10 at 6, and it's time to get out. I shout *Sell 10 at 4!* Don't say that without any eye contact, no nothing. *Who's he talking to?* If I sell 4s or I sell 5s, another trader may think *I'll come back and get it later.* But if you say *Sell 10 at 4!*, and he locks eyes, he thinks, *Man, I know I can't sell 4s because he offered me 10 at 4.* OK? That's the way to get out of the ballgame. And if you're a big trader, you might just want to buy 10 at 4, all right. Or if you're a broker, you may have 10 to buy. Or you may find a trader who points in the pit to show you where it's happening. But you have to make eye contact. And you make eye contact with as many people as you can, as quickly as you can. When it's time to get out and get out fast, know where you're going. Know where the paper is, the brokers with the big decks. Big locals are likely candidates.

Always remember that people who survive at the Board of Trade have a low puke point. Does everybody know what a high puke point is? Does everybody know? That means: *I'm long at 4, I'm long at 2, I'm long at even, I'm long at 30, I'm long at 28,* and I'm not even thinking about getting out because I don't have a low puke point. *I can stay with this stuff forever!* Well, it doesn't come back. I figured that out early on. There were a number of times I was in the pit and I would be long, and the market would be breaking, and I'd say, *God, please make the market come back!* I did. I said that. And I think a lot of people have said that. You know, it took me nine years to figure out that the reason why God never let bonds come back sometimes was because there were people in the pit who were as good as I am, who were saying, *God, please let it break!* I can remember a guy in our office, who did the best deal ever when he was short 10 and the market was a point against him. He said, *God. Please do this for me, God. If you let it come back, I'll get out of the business!* Well, the market never came back, and he stayed in the business that day.

Don't forget your puke point, because God doesn't trade bonds. I guarantee it. He doesn't care what you're going to name your next kid; he doesn't trade bonds. He doesn't care what kind of trouble you're in; he doesn't trade bonds. You want to throw those futures contracts up all over your shoes. You better make sure there's something inside that's always clicking, because that's your self-defense mechanism. In the pit, there has to be a feeling inside of you that won't let you stay with something too long.

Part of taking a loss is being able to determine at the time you have position on—*Are you short with all the other idiots in the pit? Or are you long with all the other idiots in the pit? How do you know if the other idiots in the pit are long?* Think about it. Say we seven traders in the front row here are all in the pit. You're a local and long 10 at 6. So are you. You're another local and you're long 10 at 7. You're long 10 at 5, you're long 10 at 7. You're long 10 at 3, and you're long 10 at 10. That adds up to 70 lots between us. We have a book of orders just like brokers; we are supposed to sell those 70 lots best-can.* Say all of a sudden you realize that all these guys are long about 700 contracts between them. How do you know when you're long and the rest of the pit is long? The easiest way is to be in a position where your sight angle is such that you can see what's going on.

We had a surprise today, for example. Somebody in one of the corners, in the northeast corner, came out. *6 bid! 6 bid!* You remember? We didn't know what was going on. There were 500 offered at 6. *6 bid!* he shouted. He's a large trader. And then, all the other Balfour brokers came out. Even bid. Balfour was starting 2000. And they sold it at 01 and 31 and they started in that corner of the pit. When this big dog came out bidding, we knew all the other idiots were short, along with us. How did we know? We knew, number one, because nobody was putting the high ball out.

---

* Best-can means to transact at the best price you can find at that moment. Charlie's brother John says worst-can, in contrast, means to puke a position loudly in the pit, or possibly even to bluff (even more loudly!) that you are puking to sucker other traders in order to do the exact opposite later on.

Does everybody know what a low ball and high ball are?* Say I'm trading at home off the screen. I see on my screen 2 bid at 3, 2 bid at 3, flashing. Well, it's 300 offered at 3. OK, and let's say I'm short. They take the 3s out of my computer and print a 4, bing! A high ball! Is it real? No. The *Tribune* would disagree with this, but I'm telling you the truth. A high ball does not define stops. A high ball is to paint a picture for screen traders. It paints a picture. You want a 4 pulled out so the guys who are short are queasy. And they got that feeling in their stomachs like the traders who trade with the screen. They see that 4 out there, and it's *3 bid at 4, 3 bid at 4.* It's *3 for 10, 500 offered at 4!* You're a pit trader when you have access to that information. But you're still picking that screen. *4 for 1, 4 for 1, 4 for 1.* Because you want to paint that screen, OK! Now, the pit's short, and it's 2 bid at 3, and it goes 3 bid, where's that 4? Where's that 4? Well, I know I'm not going to put a 4 out if I'm short and all these guys are short, and they aren't putting it out, so no 4 comes out. One way to know if you're short with all the other idiots is to ask: *Are any high balls coming out?* OK. If you're long with all the other idiots, and the market is breaking, you see that low ball coming out. High balls and low balls can tell you when you're in the wrong chute as a trader.

Don't be in a position where you're long and everyone in the pit is too. It just doesn't work out. It just never works out because when those people get out, they're going to try to get through that same door at that same time, and it just isn't big enough. As an example, take last Friday. I would guess between 87-25 and 87-20, on the way down, the pit collectively was probably long—and these are not speculators; these are day traders, and scalpers—probably long 5000 bonds. And everybody

---

* Low balls and high balls. According to Charlie's brother John, a high ball can be explained by a real estate analogy. You own 100 condos, each worth $60,000. You put a high ball out at $70,000 and find someone who buys one of your 100. Are all the condos now worth $70,000? Probably not, unless that one smaller trade bumps up the price by attracting other buyers. On the trading floor, if Charlie's long 1000 at 6 and the market goes 7 bid, he may instanly go 8 bid, says John. For the trader off the floor looking at his computer (screen trader), it looks as if the market just went 8 bid on his computer screen. Will Charlie attract buyers? Maybe. A high ball is put out by a trader like Charlie in an attempt to get prices to move higher, perhaps creating room for him to get out a 7. A low ball is simply the mirror opposite scenario.

looked at everybody else in that pit and said it's time to get out. We all got out alright, a point lower.* It cost people money.

Like I said, you want to make eye contact. The bigger the trader you make eye contact with, the more he feels responsible for taking you out of this trade. I can't explain it to you; all I can tell you is that it's true. If you make eye contact with a big trader in the pit and you're stuck, and you want to sell it to him, make eye contact. Alright? Something good will happen in terms of getting out of that trade.

lesson 4: taking a profit (something i like to talk about)

You know you're a good trader when you can stand in that pit and feel like you're the eye of the hurricane. That's everyone's goal and it certainly was mine: to be the eye of the hurricane.

Say you're standing in the commodities pit and it's a hurricane, like it is most days. It's all around you and you are right in the middle of it, but you are calm. You say, *I want to sell those at 7. I want to buy those at 5 from that other guy. I want to sell 200 at 6.* That's everybody's goal—to be the center of calm. The only way you develop that is with time spent in a pit with positions on. And nothing, nothing breeds success like success. Nothing does away with panic like having enough success when you know, even if I have a bad trade and stumble out of this trade, I know that's not the end my week. I know I'll have another opportunity.

The only way you get to that point is by being able to analyze every trade in the pit on its own merits. *I'm long at 6. I'm long 10 at 6.* You have to analyze that trade at each point in time continuously as a man who is thinking yes or no at the same time he is periodically clapping his hands over short intervals of time. *Clap. Do I want to be long 10 at 6? Or not?* OK. Theoretically, if I say I don't want to be long 10 at 6, I'm out. *Clap.* Now I can't get out at 6. Now I'm long 10 at 6 and it's 5 bid at 6. I want to analyze the trade. *Clap.* It's 5 bid at 6. Forget about the 10 I'm long at 6. Do I want to be long at 5 or do I want be short at 6? *Clap.* You're saying to yourself: *I'm long 10 at 6, but by God, if I could get 10 at 5, I've got a damn good chance of selling 6s and making a profit out of*

---

* A point lower. A bond futures market that drops a point has fallen 32 ticks.

this one. Clap. So you buy your 10 at 5; now you're only going to get 10 at 5 if everybody thinks you are wrong, OK. Or somebody else thinks you are wrong, OK. So you have to start questioning yourself then. If you're long 10 at 6 and 10 at 5 and if your puke mechanism hasn't come into effect, then it better be in effect. *Clap.* You better say to yourself: *I'm going to sell 4s unless Alan Greenspan's nephew walks into the pit and starts buying 5s and 6s.* You were wrong on that one. Those days become good days for you in a sense as a trader because you have minimized your losses, but done so by analyzing each situation independently at different points in time.

So how do you know when you're a good trader—who knows when to take a profit within the hurricane around you? Here's how you know you're a good trader. You buy 10 at 6. *Clap.* You're long 10 at 6. *Clap.* It goes 6 sellers, 5 bid, you are ready to sell the 5s, but boom, 6 bid. *Clap.* I'm long at 6; do I want to be long at 6? There's 500 bid. The locals are short. The brokers are buying it. The outside market price of the yen or another key variable is supporting my position and decision. *Clap.* I'm long 10 at 6. What do I do? Do I stand there as the lone wolf? Do I sell 10 because I haven't had a profit in four days? Do you shout *Sell 10 at 7! Sell 10 at 7! Sell 10 at 7!* and become the only idiot who wants to sell 10 at 7. *Clap.* Or do I step back and say: *Here's the market. You know what, I'd like to be long 10 at 6. All I want to do is buy 6s. 6 for 20! 6 for 20! Boom—7 bid.* Instead of puking a quick profit, you take a look at the market. All this has to happen fast, and the longer you have a position on in the pit, the faster it happens. *Clap.* Now you're long and the market is at 7. *Clap.* Do I want to sell 10 at 8 and get out of my position? Or do I want to buy 10 at 7? *Clap.* Well, guess what, you bid 10 at 7! And now you have 10 at 6 and 20 at 7. You just added to a winner. What a feeling that is. That's the best feeling in the world. Now you're long 30! *8 bid!* Now it's 8 bid because there are 500 offered at 9. So, the first thing you do is: Sell 30 at 8 to a broker. You sell him 30 at 8 and have a profit.

The time you know you've become a good trader is that first day you were able to win by holding and adding to a winning position. Let me tell you: There are a lot of guys who have traded for a long time who have never added to a winner.

Unfortunately, it's only human nature to want to cut your winnings. Everett Klipp taught me that. I'm long at 6 and I have an opportunity to sell 7s, *so get me out!* That's human nature. Human nature also says ride your losses. I'm long at 6. Should I sell those 5s? Well, if I sell those 5s on a 10-lot, I've lost $312.50. What can I do with $312.50? $312.50 can pay my rent. I can't sell 5s. *Sell it at 4!* someone in the pit shouts. Now that's $625. I can't do that. That's rent for two months! Human nature says ride those losses. I'm stuck. Don't sell. But when you're a good futures trader, everything you do hurts. The Amish people are up in the visitor's gallery saying *Sell it at 1! Sell it at 1!* And you're long at even. Now it's 1 bid. Let it run. You want to sell it at 2. You've already spent the money. You've allocated the money! It's in the Christmas fund. *Sell you 3s!* someone shouts. Don't do it. You've got to fight it unless there's a reason to take a profit based on what you see in the market. You've got to have a reason for everything you do. If you're standing in the pit—and I will reemphasize this—if you're standing in the pit like a nail, you don't have reason for anything. You've got to say, why do I want to be long?

Now we will try to list the reasons why you want to be long and why you want to be short: Outside market action. Position of the locals. Which way is the paper going? Is a big dog hot or a big dog cold? Am I fading a big dog?* What do the guys around me want to do? Pit noise. That might give it away. Where's the pit noise? Keep all that stuff in your mind. You've got to have a reason for doing what you're doing. That's when you rely on your outside crutches as a scalper who spreads price relationships and imbalances that you see developing inside and outside the pit. You have to have an outside crutch. That crutch will help you bid and offer with restraint. Sometimes that outside crutch might be something like, *Oh, the yen broke five ticks, so I'll be an aggressive bid in bonds.* Nobody in the world knows where the market is going, so you must have that sort of crutch to lean on when you go into the pit.

---

* Fading a big dog. Any trader who goes the opposite way of a large trader in the pit is "fading" him.

super bowl mvps | 7

Never underestimate the significance of a gesture. In January 1988, 18 months after he learned he had cancer, Charlie D decided he was going to do something special for his former high school football coaches. Perhaps he thought of it as a form of payback—it was under their tutelage, after all, that Chuck had first taken the field on a crisp Autumn night under the lights of a windswept Wisconsin sky. He was young. He was the starting quarterback. People cheered. Quite possibly it was the first time in his life he ever felt the undisputed master of his destiny. More likely, at that moment, all he knew was that life was unmistakably fun. Such glistening memories should be repaid in kind.

Approximately 10 days before the Washington Redskins and Denver Broncos played Super Bowl XXII, Ken Hollub answered the phone late on a Thursday night. It was one of his former players, and he knew exactly which one.

"Hello."

"Hey Coach, how are you doing?"

"Fine, Chuck."

"Great. Great. Listen, Coach. How would you like to go to the Super Bowl with me, Mike Haas, and Coach Graf?"

"The Super Bowl?"

"Listen, get time off at the high school because we're going in 10 days. I'm making plans."

"That sounds like a dream, Chuck. But I don't think I can afford to do it. And are you even sure you can get tickets?"

"I'm sure. Don't worry about a thing. You and Coach Graf are my guests. Just ask your wife."

"Have you told Harley? He's not going to believe it."

"Bring a nice suit and a couple of nice shirts. I'll take care of the rest. We'll play around in Las Vegas for two days, if that's OK."

A pause.

"Chuck, are you serious?"

"Yeah, it's for the team, remember? I've got to call Coach Graf before it gets too late. Talk to him tomorrow."

"Chuck, is this some joke you've got going with Harley?"

"No, Coach. We'll be on a plane in 10 days. Bye, Coach."

Before Coach Hollub could answer, Chuck was gone. His good-bye trailed off, trapped in the tunnel of optic wires stretched between Waukesha and Chicago. Or was that something else buzzing in his ear?

"Ken, are you OK? Did someone just die or something?" asked his wife.

"No, I'm fine, honey. Just a call from one of my former players who wants to . . . who wants to take me to the Super Bowl."

His wife looked puzzled. Coach Hollub didn't believe it either. He would call Harley tomorrow. No, tonight. As he rose from the chair in the kitchen, a surge of adrenaline rushed from his feet up through his body. Not certain what to do with himself, he tried to clean up the living room for 10 minutes, and then rushed out of the room, tripping on the leg of a dining room chair. He hadn't tripped on anything in his house in 20 years.

Elsewhere, Coach Graf was in a foul mood. His job with the Waukesha School District wasn't going as well. In charge of the district's physical education programs, the teachers that week had ticked him off, calling for more meetings. His plate was full already, and he wasn't looking forward to a fight in the staff lounge tomorrow. He rubbed his eyes, and sunk deeper into the cushions of his favorite recliner, watching a little evening sports news on TV. The phone rang.

"Coach, Chuck. How are things going?"

"Just great. Great. Chuck, why are you calling?"

"Good news. Look, we're going to the Super Bowl. Get time off. Coach Hollub is in, and Mike Haas is too. The team needs another gamer. Are you in? . . ."

The Super Bowl?

". . . Better start packing, Coach. My assistant Susie is making the arrangements. She'll give you a call in a week, OK? Talk to Coach Hollub tomorrow."

"Chuck, you're playing games."

"Nope, it's for the team. Expect to hear from Susie."

And he was gone. A few minutes later the phone rang again. He picked it up halfway through the first ring.

"Harley, did you get a call from Chuck?"

"Ken, is your quarterback serious?"

They still didn't believe it. But just in case, they had to make some emergency plans for their first major road trip in eons. They talked about how much cash they could scrape together in 10 days. Coach Graf talked with his wife that night about the 1968 championship team and some wild and crazy bond trader named Chuck DiFrancesca. She remembered skinny number 10, the coach's son. He never seemed that wild and crazy to her. But she could not refuse every football coach's dream.

It wasn't until the two coaches talked next that the guilt of freeloading on a former student set in. Chuck pay?

"We're supposed to hear from his secretary in about a week. I don't know, I guess I'll take about $400."

"I can take $500. We should be alright with $900 between us, don't you think, Harley?"

They had no idea. The thought made their stomachs sink a bit. On high school teacher wages, both feared they might well run out of money and end up riding a Greyhound bus back from Nevada, even if they were guests.

"Vegas. Who knows what that will cost us? All he told me was to bring a good suit along, Ken. Is he serious?"

On Monday evening, Coach Graf called Chuck back. He still wondered if it was a prank. He told Chuck they had gotten the time off, just to test the waters.

"Great, my secretary will send you plane tickets in a week."

Chuck still showed no signs he was bluffing, but Coach Graf remained skeptical. Just in case, he and Coach Hollub had spoken to the superintendent of the Waukesha School District. Teachers don't customarily take time off during a school year, but who was the superintendent to stop a minor miracle for two high school football coaches, if a minor miracle was indeed in the making? Coach Graf searched for an explanation that sounded somewhat plausible.

"You're not going to believe this, but a former student—remember Chuck DiFrancesca, Ken's former quarterback?—he wants to take us to the Super Bowl."

The superintendent was amazed. And he did remember the name— Chuck DiFrancesca—because Chuck's father Vince had coached at Carroll College.

"Look, you guys have done a lot of volunteering," the superintendent finally said. "Take the time off and make it up when you come back."

But the two coaches didn't hear from Chuck's assistant that week. They were borderline manic, sitting on their hands, trying to teach. Three days before they were supposed to leave, Coach Hollub called Chuck at his home—a call he dreaded—and reached his wife Ann.

"What?" said Ann. "You haven't heard from Charlie? I'll see to it that his secretary sends you plane tickets through overnight mail. They'll arrive in the morning."

On Thursday, January 28, 1988, Coach Hollub's daughter Kelly drove the two Super Bowl agnostics from Waukesha into Milwaukee to catch a Greyhound bus to Chicago's O'Hare Airport. The tickets cost $18 each, bringing their pooled $900 bankroll down to $864. They hoped their money would last the trip. They brought their own snacks. Sitting at the front of the bus, hyper as small children, they small-talked with the bus driver.

They arrived at O'Hare early. Charlie had instructed them to meet him at the American Airlines check-in counter at 5:15 P.M. At 5:05 P.M. Coach Graf sat on top of his slightly worn Samsonite luggage in American Airlines' terminal C, antsy. So was Coach Hollub, but he had the better poker face. Hollub, silent, looked at his friend, and felt his

A day in the pits—Charlie alongside other top dogs, including Steve Lawrence (to left).

Busy buying T-bonds—Charlie with a classic "MJ" tongue.

Charlie D and Maggie
at Lake Michigan.

Charlie and Jake playing football, 1978.

Charlie, Jake, Maggie, and Laura.
Ann and Charlie's wedding, 1980.

Ann's 40th birthday party. The Plaza Hotel, 1986.

Charlie D—selling T-bonds on the top step, 1986.

Charlie and Coach Hollub.

"Bomb's Away".

Charlie, John and Janet
DiFrancesca (Parshall).

Charlie playing golf—Tiger Woods *not*.

Golf photos courtesy of Ann DiFrancesca

Charlie and Johnny Musso.

Courtesy of Harley Graf

Super Bowl surprise.

John's wedding, 1986. The cancer brothers point to each other's "problems."

Charlie, Craig "the Walrus" Stadler (1982 Masters Champion), and personal friend J. B. Dougherty.

Charlie, Ann, and Nancy and Tom DeMark. Bally's, Las Vegas, 1990.

Cancer research benefit. Charlie buys bozo bonds for cancer research, February 1991.

Charlie and Maggie.

gaze drawn ever more frequently to the airport clock. Both coaches sat, nervously fingering their luggage handles, full of visions of their money burning faster than jet fuel.

American Airlines flight 637 to Las Vegas was scheduled for takeoff at 6:34 P.M.

At 5:12 P.M., they both picked up their luggage and started walking. As they turned the corner, coming through the turnstile door was Chuck. Dressed in a blue sports jacket, brown slacks, and penny loafers, he walked up to them carrying an enormous army duffel bag he had bought at a thrift store at Colorado State University in Fort Collins. He may have looked like a casual-day Santa, but there was no mistaking the twinkle in his eye.

"Great, great," he deadpanned. "Look at that. Didn't think you two were going to show up."

All Coach Graf could do was shake his head in disbelief at his quarterback's showboating.

"We're going to the Big Show!" said Charlie, suddenly all high fives and fired up.

And so two small town phys ed teachers became special guests on Charlie D's Super Bowl extravaganza, whisked away to Las Vegas, Beverly Hills, and then on to San Diego's Jack Murphy Stadium. To this day, Wisconsin college and high school coaches still ask Ken and Harley if it *really* happened. *Your quarterback, he did that for you?*

The party from Waukesha South High School was among the last, and loudest, to board the plane. As a former signal-caller and man who earned his living yelling, Charlie D's voice dominated the first-class cabin. In no time, the jokes were rolling from seats 4A, E, and F (the two coaches, hardly the nostalgic types, saved their itineraries and airplane and Super Bowl ticket stubs in scrap books). A man in a business suit in 3E dropped his paper below nose level to see what the commotion was all about and futilely resumed reading. After overhearing a few one-liners he gave up; after several more he too was laughing, won over by the rah-rah enthusiasm of the three men.

At that point, a stunning blonde stewardess in a sharp blue uniform entered the first-class cabin, silencing the Waukesha entourage. Charlie

D winked at his colleagues and stole a glimpse at the stewardess, who was stuffing pillows in a storage bin above another man's seat.

"Excuse me, ma'am, can you tell me: Is there a movie on this flight?" a man well behind them in the aisle asked, puppy-eyed, ambiguously flirting or perhaps posing an innocent question with all the earnestness of a first-time Las Vegas tourist.

After a long day of flying, the stewardess was much too busy and too bothered to care. She answered without a glance at the passenger. "Oh no, I'm really sorry, sir, it's much too short a flight."

Displaying a bit of a comedian's deft sense of timing, Charlie D paused for a beat, then repeated the question word-for-word, but with exaggerated boyish innocence. Like with comedian Bill Murray, it was all in the delivery.

"Excuse me, is there a movie on this flight?"

She smiled, looking directly at him.

"Yes, sir, it's a real short one," she replied, offering him a pillow. "It's the story of your life."

Charlie D feigned taking a bullet to the heart, killed instantaneously by the stewardess's not-so-friendly fire. The coaches felt their hearts sink for a second, realizing that the stewardess knew nothing of their quarterback's quiet battle with cancer. But Charlie D winked again, still holding his arm across his wounded chest.

The stewardess returned on another trip down the aisle. The Mona Lisa of the trading floor again interrupted her.

"Excuse me, miss. I'd like to order a Black Russian."

"Sorry, sir, we don't have the alcohol for that drink on the plane."

"OK, then how about a margarita or a Long Island ice tea?"

"Can't make either of those, sir. I'm sorry."

Charlie feigned defeat, but then reverted once again to his sheepdog grin. Not many can pull this off—the pestering boyish charm best used by actor Bill Murray to wear down opponents into liking him—but Charlie could pull it off, and he was a man on a mission.

"Well, then a Coke with a slice of lime would be just fine. A round of those for all my friends on the plane, whenever you have a second. Oh yes, and can you bring me a larger glass than the rest . . . you know, with a little extra room for the two of us and my nose."

You love me, don't you, you know you do. Who's your pal? Who's your buddy?

The stewardess laughed; the ice finally cracked through a bad day of obnoxious airline passengers. *Yes, I do.* Who was this guy with the lampoon swagger? Maybe it was time for her to have a little fun.

She made direct eye contact.

"I'll be back to you in just a second, sir, with those drinks. Once we are in the air. I'm sorry, but we are about to take off."

The whole first-class cabin—at least those who had just witnessed the fun—were laughing at what was brewing. Charlie D chuckled along with them, at himself, even at the ironies of his own life that the stewardess had so directly pointed out to him, unbeknownst to her. The stewardess's voice, almost sultry, emerged from behind one of the plane's dividing curtains near the flight crew's cabin, in view of Charlie D's coaches, to give the customary preflight instructions.

"Good evening, ladies and gentlemen, my name is Elena Ruth. Welcome to American Airlines flight 637 to Las Vegas. Your crew today is Captain Danny Williams and first flight captain George Brennan. If you would please, pull the safety instruction card from the seat in front of you and follow along with my safety instructions. The cabin is equipped with four safety exits highlighted by the signs, two near the wings of the aircraft, and one in the rear and front of the cabin. Please locate the one nearest you. For those of you traveling with small children, *or near anyone near an aisle seat acting like a small child,* please make sure his seat belt is *tightly* fastened for his safety."

You love me, don't you? I do.

The passenger cabin erupted, drowning out the remainder of the preflight instructions on the airplane's speaker system. Charlie hoisted an imaginary glass of champagne and toasted his worthy adversary, and then the coaches. They too clinked their imaginary glasses. Time flew on what was now anything but a routine 3½-hour flight.

"Chuck was on the left and we were on the right," says Coach Graf, "so we could see both him and the stewardess when she was behind the curtain. It was hilarious. He cracked even more jokes and one-liners the rest of the way until there was this whole commotion on the plane in the air. He had this charisma, and he could get by with it—without that stewardess ever knowing what was really going on in his life. He was just like a young kid that trip, walking six feet off the ground. He was going to make our trip a seventh heaven."

Coach Hollub still chuckles about the game of one-upmanship with the stewardess.

"The strongest thing we had to drink on the plane was Coke and orange juice. But Chuck sure seemed to know how to order his exotic drinks."

American flight 637 landed in Las Vegas at roughly 8:30 P.M., the runway and airport terminal lights making it difficult to see the desert. In the terminal, Charlie and the coaches hooked up with Mike Haas, Charlie's favorite target in high school as wide receiver. Haas, a financial planner, had come in from Dallas to join them at Charlie D's invitation. He met them at the luggage gate. A blue limousine, compliments of the Desert Inn, was waiting for the most unforeseen of foursomes at the curb. The Waukesha Blackshirts, the Wisconsin Suburban Conference Champions in 1968, were about to live the highlife in Las Vegas on their way to the Super Bowl.

As was customary in Las Vegas for high rollers, Charlie D's foursome stayed in the penthouse suite reportedly used by the late Howard Hughes. This 7th-floor suite overlooked the swimming pool and golf course at the Desert Inn. After a whirlwind tour by limo of the glittering Las Vegas strip, the Blackshirts settled into this suite, uncomfortable with all the space.

"They checked our luggage and took us up to this enormous room," recalls Coach Graf. "This suite had three bedrooms, a living room, a dining room. There were fresh flowers on the table. The square footage of the bedroom Ken and I slept in seemed bigger than my house. Anytime we went anywhere, a guy from the Desert Inn was there to take care of us. I was still on Waukesha time, so I was wide awake just waiting for something to happen."

At about 10:00 that night, the team ordered room service before paying their first visit to the casino floor. They started with a game called baccarat that first became famous among the gaming crowds in Monaco's Monte Carlo. A gambler playing baccarat could wager either on his cards or those dealt to the casino's bank. Both the player and the bank are dealt two cards and, under rigid baccarat rules, a third card may be dealt. The hand achieving a total of 9, or the next highest number, wins. All picture cards count 10, and all other cards are counted at their face value. An ace is counted as one. As Charlie D briefly tried to explain to his team, the last digit of the sum determines the value of the hand. For example, 8 and 8 total 16. The hand value would be 6. A 5 percent commission on all money won on the cards held by the Desert Inn's "bank" was charged, and a number of rules that only Charlie D and the dealer knew stipulated when a third card would be dealt.

Confused? So were the coaches, suffering from the hazing process that often overwhelms many Las Vegas tourist-gamblers. But Charlie D escorted his team to the baccarat table, sat them down in a line of chairs, and called a Desert Inn employee over to sign for $15,000 worth of chips. At the table, he gave each of his team members their own stack of poker chips from his draw and humunah-humunahed the rules. His last bit of advice was easier to understand in the loose huddle around the table: Just do what I do.

"He came over and gave us these piles of chips, always calling us Coach," remembers Coach Hollub. "I went through mine so doggone fast because it was a $100 minimum table. All I remember was three cards out of a shoot. I didn't know what I was betting on or anything. All I remember after that is, after about an hour, he called a gal back and tore up the slip. I had lost; he had won. After she left, he grinned at us and said, 'Now, Coach, we're going to play with the house's money.'"

In the words of Coach Graf, the next stop was a room in Caesar's Palace "where you can bet on any sporting event anywhere posted on the big screen." Charlie gave them a tour of the sports betting room and later the rest of Caesar's Palace, pointing to all the possible Super Bowl bets that they should consider. After all, that part of the trip was only a few days away, he reminded them, throwing an imaginary football at the board of lights.

Returning to the Desert Inn later, the Waukesha Blackshirts revisited the craps table for another gambling spectacle. The size of the team's bets, with Charlie D quarterbacking the wagers, drew an audience of smaller bettors closer to their table.

"That's where I threw the dice one time for him and it didn't even get to the end of the table," chuckles Coach Graf. "All I remember is that I hit something else other than the craps table wall and all these chips just went flying. Charlie grabs and raises my hand and says to the crowd, 'Look at this folks. We've got a limp wrist at the table.' The crowd just howled."

Between baccarat, craps, and a few hands of blackjack, the team amassed enough chips that night that they had doubled the coaches' concealed bankroll many times over. They returned to their room early Friday morning, sometime after midnight. Coach Hollub was the first to hit the sack, while the other three stayed up to talk, still buzzing. Coach Graf mentioned that a retirement party for Coach Hollub was being scheduled in Waukesha in a couple of months, and that he hoped that both Chuck and Mike might be able to make it.

"We were just sitting there, reminiscing, and we all were talking about the banquet coming up because we had formed this committee. And Charlie said, 'Well, what are you going to get him for his retirement gift?' I said that we are getting all his former players to pitch in to see if we could get him a camper for his retirement. I told him I knew that's what Coach Hollub wanted because I had already gone along with him and his son a couple of times to look around. Charlie just said, 'Whatever you don't collect for Coach, I'll make up the difference.' I wasn't sure if he was serious or not."

The team went to bed that night, rising early that Friday morning. Charlie was the first one up, already having mapped out the day's events. When none of his company knew quite what to do with themselves that morning in the expanse of such a large suite, he suggested that the coaches call their wives and kids. Knowing that Coach Graf liked to play golf, he offered to buy him a new set of golf clubs. After showers and a late breakfast, he gave each of his team members two pink Desert Inn chips, worth $1000 in total.

"Charlie," Coach Graf joked, with a puzzled look on his face. "I haven't even been able to use up the chips that you gave me last night."

Charlie's money continued to burn a hole in everyone's pocket all the way through Friday night. That evening Charlie took the team over to see Siegfried and Roy, the internationally renowned magicians who regularly did shows at the Frontier Hotel in 1988, just across from the Desert Inn on Las Vegas Boulevard. Since taking their marquee act to the Mirage, this duo drew applause by making white tigers disappear in ways that left the audience questioning the boundaries between hocus-pocus and reality. Charlie D was making them question the same boundaries, but such was life on the Las Vegas strip. That evening, Crystal Gayle was booked at the Crystal Room at the Desert Inn, and the Blackshirts went to hear her sing as the day's encore.

The team relaxed after the shows by playing a little keno, the only game you can play anywhere on the casino floor. It was a chance for the team to regroup after the first-half whirlwind performance of the Blackshirts' quarterback and time to play the game in Las Vegas that offered the best odds. To play keno, all the team needed to do—with the possibility of winning $50,000—was to pick numbers 1 through 80 in varied combinations for different price amounts. Picking six matching numbers, for a $1 ticket paid $18; seven paid $130; eight $960; and nine $3800. A keno runner came by every few minutes to get the team into another game. The preferred drink for these high rollers continued to be either Coke or orange juice.

The team ordered a round of refreshments at a side table where they could play keno and talk about old high school football games, retirement, kids, jobs. Conversation was interrupted only by another keno bet. During these games, Coach Hollub watched Charlie slip a $100 chip as a tip to a waitress with a polite thank-you. The waitress nearly fumbled the chip off her tray, in Coach Hollub's words, "after nearly having a stroke."

"I can't take this from you, sir," she said.

"No, it's yours," Charlie said. "Take your boyfriend out somewhere fun and have a good time. Enjoy it. Really."

The team played more craps and a few hands of blackjack, perhaps the only game each of the Blackshirts felt confident playing on their own. On the way over to the craps table, the group caught a glimpse of a knockout in a skintight miniskirt and a few friends of Charlie D's in the distance, some of whom were also Board of Trade traders or Las Vegas acquaintances. Before they knew it, Charlie was on the floor, DOA of an apparent heart attack, all the time staring at what everyone else had seen but wouldn't say they had. Those in the casino who watched roared with laughter, except for one older woman, who abandoned her slot machine (no ordinary event in Vegas) to come to Charlie D's aid.

"Young man, are you OK?" she asked, obviously concerned about his health.

"Yes, I'm fine, ma'am," said Charlie D, opening his eyes and rising from the dead. "I'm just relaxing down here, trying to look up that woman's skirt."

The grandmother glanced at the women in red near the craps table, well in the distance. Both she and Charlie D howled out loud at the rare birds seen in Las Vegas.

Charlie's luck changed that night as his pile of chips started to shrink. The tension among the Blackshirts and dealer who watched grew, as it sometimes would during a close football game. Without any warning, Charlie surprised the coaches by spontaneously increasing his bet to $1000 at a $5 table. No one knew quite what to think of this apparent audible at the line of scrimmage.

"I'm sorry, sir, I can't cover that," said the dealer, who waved over a pit boss.

"Why can't you cover it?" Charlie asked politely.

"What's the problem here?" said the pit boss. The dealer and pit boss had a private discussion behind the table. The pit boss kept glancing over at Charlie as he talked.

"Mr. D wants to bet $1000," said the pit boss, waiving the table's bet size for Charlie. "So he is welcome to bet."

Charlie D won on that hand with 16, just as he sometimes lost. But there was no gambler's touchdown dance or change in emotion after his on-the-spot audible. He tipped the dealer a $100 chip and left, the size of his pile of chips slightly higher than it once was. Everyone was having a good time; Charlie called to have their flight the next morning pushed up to noon, rather than 9:30 A.M. That evening, preparing for the Saturday flight to Los Angeles, the Blackshirts emptied out their pockets on a table in Howard Hughes' suite after a final good night of gambling.

"Charlie, here's your money back," Coach Graf said, speaking for the team. "Thanks for all the fun."

"No, you won it. It's yours," Charlie said. "You'll need it for the Super Bowl bets tomorrow. Hang on to it."

The spoils from two successful days at the Desert Inn for Charlie was $38,000. Coach Hollub had winnings of $2800 and Coach Graf left with $2300. Mike Haas left Las Vegas with something over $1000. "We had close to $45,000," estimates Graf.

After a team photo in front of the limousine taking them to the airport, the pace of their trip quickened. Charlie jumped in the front seat and directed the driver to stop at the Barbary Coast before heading to the airport, tipping him $100 in advance. The engine running, the Blackshirts made their way to the Barbary's betting area. Charlie explained that this place offered better odds on Super Bowl bets than Caesar's Palace or Bally's. On behalf of the team, he placed bets on total numbers of fumbles and interceptions and a bet that seemed to all of the Blackshirts to be showing very good odds. Would Doug Williams, the first black quarterback ever to start in the Super Bowl, score a running touchdown? Why not, thought Charlie. It was a favorite play of his.

"We all felt if he was close to the goal line, he might try the sneak," said Coach Hollub. "Chuck used to call that play himself. We also felt it was going to be an air show with Elway and Williams, so we figured there would definitely be more than four interceptions for the game. Chuck put a bet down for us on that as well, and one on Washington to win the game and beat the spread."

The second half of the team's Super Bowl trip began with a smooth flight through L.A. smog, after crossing a ridge of mountains dividing Nevada from California. The smog improved only slightly on the weekends. Upon landing, Charlie D offered to help a senior citizen behind him off of the plane. He grabbed her purse in the process, and threw it over his shoulder. Outside the passenger runway, he squeezed the lady's hand good-bye and began walking off with her purse, the more spontaneous the punch line the better.

"Young man, my purse!"

Me? Run away with the purse? He looked back at the lady in feigned embarrassment, apologized, without anyone else but the team knowing that he was still racking up comedy points, even in airports, even with old ladies, wherever he had a chance. The lady later discovered he had dropped some money into the purse, not taken any out.

Charlie D rented a white Cadillac and drove his team to their next stop—the Biltmore Hotel. In the car, Coach Hollub welcomed the somewhat familiar and quieter surroundings. As a serviceman in the Navy, he had been stationed in Los Angeles. He told his friends he looked forward to visiting Pershing Park on the drive to the Biltmore Hotel, and recollected the park's beautiful palm trees, waterfalls, and fountains. Charlie D looked forward to the Biltmore Hotel, a place he had never stayed before. "My assistant Susie tells me even I haven't lived this great," he said as he drove. "She says there are even butlers in the rooms to take care of us."

"We came around this corner in the road," recalled Coach Hollub, "and here was this big brass sign: Pershing Park. I couldn't believe what I saw. There was no grass at all, and it was filled with homeless people wandering around, sleeping all over it. When I was in the service, it had been a beautiful park in downtown L.A. It had statues and flower gardens." Coach Hollub could say only one thing that popped out unconsciously: "My God."

If Pershing Park proved to be a bad omen, the main floor of the Biltmore proved equally disappointing to Charlie. The entire lounge was covered with plastic seat covers and the whole hotel seemed to be under construction repair. "The poor bellboy kept saying we can take care of you," says Coach Graf, "but about that time, I hear Charlie say, 'This is bullshit. We are out of here. Take our stuff back to the car.' "

Obviously embarrassed about this roadtrip blip on the way to the Super Bowl, Charlie was not happy. He called the Beverly Hills' 20th Century Plaza Towers, right across from 20th Century Plaza. His guests stood dazed, not so displeased as he was with the hotel, even if it were undergoing repairs. After all, it seemed a little closer to what they were used to. Charlie picked up the public phone in the lobby.

"Do you have two rooms for Saturday and Sunday night? Put us down. We need room for two fathers and two sons. What? Just put us down as A, B, C, and D. We're coming right over."

At that point, the odds of getting into 20th Century Plaza Towers, a hotel for presidents and Hollywood stars, did not look good for the Waukesha Blackshirts. But off Charlie D drove in the white Cadillac to a hotel that Coach Graf said "was so hoity-toity that we felt more like ducks out of water than we did in Las Vegas." At the check-in counter, the hotel staff indicated that one room may be available, if a guest did not arrive very soon. No one heard what was said, but in a few minutes, the high rollers from Las Vegas were unloading their newfound wealth in a secure room of safety vaults for jewelry and other valuables.

The 15th-floor room at 20th Century Plaza Towers overlooked 20th Century Studios. The coaches took one bedroom and Charlie D claimed he would sleep tilted upright on the couch, in a position that he said was more comfortable for him. Mike Haas took the second bedroom. However, just as they unpacked their luggage, water poured from the bathroom ceiling. Charlie phoned the hotel receptionist and asked them to send someone up to fix it, miffed once again, and then called his wife.

"The hotel manager comes in to our room to inspect the trouble," says Coach Graf. "She was a nice-looking lady, but she was also a little bit on the heavy side. Despite the trouble with the hotel, Charlie's having a great old time talking to his wife Ann on the phone about how our trip to the Biltmore had ended up in this place. He says to her, 'Heh, Ann, they just sent up the hookers to compensate us for all the water trouble, so we've got to go take some showers.' Well, the manager in the bathroom heard this, so she comes up with the best one-liner of the whole trip. She sticks her head out of the bathroom, and says, 'You mean I'm supposed to do all four of you guys?' The place was up for grabs after that. You talk about things meshing together. Everything was just flowing. To this day, I'll bet there have never been two high school coaches treated as well as we were on that trip."

That evening, Charlie had a Lincoln Continental luxury limousine drive them around Sunset Boulevard. He took the coaches to see the sites at Hollywood and Vine, and later to La Scala Restaurant in Beverly Hills. After the meal, Charlie instructed the limousine driver to come back an hour later than the scheduled pickup time so that he could reminisce a little longer with his team.

"When this limo came back to pick us up," jokes Coach Graf, "all these celebrity watchers were hanging around to see who was going to jump in it. So who comes out the door: two high school coaches and two former players, A, B, C, and D."

The next day, Charlie D's white Cadillac pulled out of 20th Century Plaza Towers at 10:00 A.M. for a 4:00 P.M. game. Charlie set it on cruise control at 80 mph so that the coaches would have a chance to get into the VIP area of the Super Bowl, courtesy of Charlie's Wilmette neighbor, J. B. Dougherty, who was then an executive with Baxter International. Charlie collected four of Baxter's hospital wristband VIP passes from Dougherty, and passed them to the coaches. "Put yours on yourself, Charlie," said J. B. "I know you know how to wear one of these."

Coach Graf suspected that the Super Bowl VIP tents would be Las Vegas and Beverly Hills all over again.

"So here we go into the VIP area with Tom Landry, one of Ken's favorite coaches from the Dallas Cowboys, walking past, and Hank Stram, the legendary coach of the Kansas City Chiefs. We walk into the Miller Lite tent because Coach Hollub knows another former student, Randy Martin, who's at the game and who works for Miller Brewing. We talked football for half an hour with former Oakland Raider Ben Davidson, a tough-guy lineman who was doing all the first Lite commercials. Talk about football heaven."

With a few Lite beers under the belt, the team snapped a flurry of photos in the VIP area. Even Charlie D cupped a Lite from Miller in his hand for the photo, just in front of a Super Bowl XXII banner. They then found their seats in the lower level of the stadium along with 73,302 football fans, around the 30-yard line, 23 rows up from the field and within shouting distance of USC all-American quarterback and Rhodes Scholar Pat Haden; the Kauffmans, owners of the Kansas City Royals baseball team; and Bud Collins, the NBC Wimbledon tennis commentator. Before they knew it, everything tasted great and seemed less filling. Bob Hope and the leggy Radio City Music Hall Rockettes dressed in white top hats provided on-the-field entertainment before the game. F-16s flew above the stadium during the playing of the national anthem and the Redskins and Broncos ran onto the field for the kickoff, the Blackshirts just behind the Broncos' sideline.

For any football fan, it was a dream game. While Super Bowls are historically never close games, Denver jumped off to a quick 10-point lead against the heavily favored Washington Redskins, making the game interesting. Elway darted a bomb to Ricky Nattiel that caught the Washington Redskins' defense by surprise, and followed it up by directing his team within field goal position on Denver's second drive. It was 10-zip, Denver. Washington's defense seemed to be sleeping on the field.

The Redskins came to life in the second quarter, scoring five touchdowns in only 18 plays, including two 50-yard-plus scoring passes from Doug Williams to Ricky Sanders, part of a wide receiver corps known as "The Smurfs." The touchdown-happy Smurfs leaped together like four musketeers after every score, doing a one-for-all high-five in the end zone. The Blackshirts talked that talk and walked that walk with them the whole game.

Many Super Bowl records were broken by the end of the Redskins' 42-10 victory. Williams, the game's first starting black quarterback and MVP, threw for 340 yards, breaking Joe Montana's record of 331 yards in Super Bowl XIX. A Redskins rookie named Timmy Smith, who was never heard from again as a pro, rushed for 204 yards, breaking former Raider Marcus Allen's record of 191 yards in Super Bowl XVIII. Smith scored on a dazzling 58-yard dash to the end zone to shut the door on any Denver comeback, and scored the final touchdown of the game from four yards out. Washington's five touchdowns and 602 total yards became new Super Bowl records. At that point, all the Blackshirts' Super Bowl bets hardly mattered, although Charlie D and the coaches had been right on the interception over-under and the final outcome of the game.

"There were so many things to bet on," said Coach Hollub, seven years after Washington had won their third Super Bowl in less than a decade. "I can't say how we really did. I know we got the interceptions right and bet on Washington. We also placed a bet that would have paid $20,000 if Doug Williams had been the first black quarterback to score. We figured if he had the chance, he'd run the quarterback sneak. So we also bet on that one."

The game ended with Super Bowl souvenirs and some legendary trading by Charlie D and another Super Bowl souvenir speculator. Coach Graf spent $500 on six Super Bowl hats, three Super Bowl sweaters, 50 Super Bowl key rings, and so much other stuff with Redskins and Bronco team logos that he can't even remember what he bought. Charlie egged him on the whole time, to do it bigger and better and with more style. Harley understood the meaning of money.

"I had 50 teachers who I supervised back in Waukesha, and my wife and kids," said Graf. "So what the hell? I put five $100 bills down on the counter and just started buying. Charlie was laughing so hard that he shouted to the VIP area: 'Look at this folks, this guy is going to set a record for buying Super Bowl souvenirs.' He loved it."

Charlie also had some fun with the souvenirs. A Super Bowl host, wearing a custom sky blue Super Bowl cap and commemorative pen, was leaving with his wife when the Blackshirts nearly sacked him. Charlie offered the bewildered man $100 for his hat. The hat was to be a gift for Coach Hollub. When the man said no, Charlie bid $120, $140, $160, $180. As the price rose higher, the man's wife nudged him in the ribs for his obvious stupidity. The hat and pen sold for $200 and ended on Coach Hollub's head, where Charlie wanted it.

Charlie then started bidding for the wife's cap. "Charlie, I don't need a hat," joked Coach Graf. "I've already bought up half a souvenir tent."

The Blackshirts left, talking about the strategy of the game, second-guessing Elway and Coach Dan Reeves all the way to the car. Says Coach Graf, "we always had a great time second-guessing everybody."

The night ended with dinner at a restaurant overlooking the ocean at Marina del Rey in Los Angeles, four high school football junkies enjoying each other's company. Their conversation rolled rhythmically like the waves of the ocean, not so unlike the comforting rhythms that came from Coach Hollub's voice, after he, Coach Graf, and I had talked for hours about his quarterback.

"We always let the quarterback call his own plays," said Coach Hollub. "I'd send something in once in a while if we saw an opening, but most of the time Chuck called his own plays. My coach let me call plays when I was quarterback, so I did it the same way with all my teams. This wasn't a time when football players were robots, as they are now. Probably Chuck's greatest game was the game against West Allis Central that decided the championship. They had one loss and we had one tie. Whichever team won that game would probably be the Suburban Conference Champion.

"West Allis, that year, had a defensive line that was bigger than most college lines. They had a couple of kids who weighed around 240 to 280. But if you ever wanted to build a team around a kid who was a student of the game, it was Chuck. He was confident. He was more confident in himself on the sideline than I was. He was like a coach out there, always one or two plays ahead of everyone else. He was a heady quarterback who always knew what he wanted to do with the ball."

atlas shrugged | 8

F riday, October 25, 1968. On a cool autumn evening on a plush green
and freshly chalked home field, the entire season for the Waukesha
Blackshirts had come down to this: first down on their own 17, 4:32
left to play in the fourth quarter, and the score tied 14-14 against the
West Allis Central Bulldogs. The next series of downs in the game would
decide the final outcome of the 16th Suburban Conference
Championship Game in Wisconsin. It would also determine if a promise
that Chuck DiFrancesca had made to his high school football coach, Ken
Hollub, whom he admired as a coach and teacher and loved like a father,
would be kept. Upon hearing from his father Vince that Coach Hollub
was considering an offer to become a college head coach, Chuck begged
him to stay to coach the team for his senior year. Chuck promised that
the team would make it a special year if he stayed. Hollub told Chuck it
was a difficult decision, which he needed time to think about. A few days
later Hollub decided to stay. Chuck couldn't forget Coach Hollub's sacrifice as he got ready that afternoon to play West Allis Central. By staying,
Coach Hollub had only enhanced his reputation as the George Bailey of
a Frank Capraesque Waukesha.

It was a wonderful life for Hollub and Chuck in Waukesha, but not at
the moment. The silver-helmeted Blackshirts had not scored an offensive

touchdown for Coach Hollub since their opening drive. The large-bodied Bulldogs in maroon and yellow seemed to be wearing down their lighter opponents as the game clock ticked. The last two and a half quarters had not gone well, but 8000-plus-strong Waukesha fans were nevertheless bouncing like stove-popped popcorn in the stands. The high school and particularly the football field were the heart and soul of baby-boomer housing developments that had risen from the outerlying farmlands. Houses in the area had been popping up like multicolored dandelions for the last decade to support a new generation of Midwesterners, and this field beneath the lights in the center of it all was a focal point for children and parents alike. Farmlands could be seen to the south, and invisible smoke in the night bellowed from the smokestack of an aluminum and brass foundry a quarter-mile south.

Surrounding Chuck DiFrancesca in the Blackshirt huddle was a scrappy but, pound-for-pound, leaner group of kids who had tossed the ball around with him since 1963. That year, his father Vince had become athletic director and head coach of Carroll College in Waukesha, and Chuck's foray as a quarterback in the huddle began. Vince had built a comfortable but modest four-bedroom house across the street from the main entrance of the high school on East Roberta Avenue. His three kids—Chuck, Janet, and John—were entering the postpubescent years of their lives.

Chuck could be on the field in a minute if he took the shortcut down the delivery road winding around the high school. Those in the huddle, including Chuck, were as close as their nicknames implied. And they all had them—names like "Bullets," "The Scooter," "Frog," "Little Shoes," "Ronald McDonald," "Sod Buster," "The Bear," and "The Streaker." Out on the sideline with an injury was Chuck's favorite target at split end, Mike Haas, a kid who wore number 85. Haas sprayed Firm-Grip on his hands so that he had sticky fingers and sure hands on the field. "Hongo," as Chuck called him, was out with a broken ankle after the first quarter of the game. Chuck had hit him with a 41-yard bomb to set up his own keeper around the left end and into the end zone a few plays later to score Waukesha's first touchdown. In for the injured Haas was Gary Koch, number 42, a receiver–running back everyone on the team called "Bullets."

Chuck was known as Di or DiFran or just Chuck, except when he sparked the team to victory. Then he was sometimes greeted by the ambivalent nickname "Son of Vince!"—which had the ring of football royalty, if there was such a thing in Waukesha. That name would be woofed and shouted enough times until it rocked a yellow schoolbus after the Blackshirts had beaten Shorewood 21-14 in the last 21 seconds of the game earlier in the season. Chuck didn't know what to think about it, but what else would you call the coach's son? And he was as proud of his Dad as his father was of him.

Over time he hoped something more personal and colorful stuck when he played college ball. He just shrugged and smiled on the bus and took a friendly slap from a couple of his teammates in the nearest seat, including 6'6" buddy Kirk Delzer, a backup tight end. Chuck was always happy to score a winning touchdown on a quarterback sneak or the option keeper. That's exactly what he had done in the game against Shorewood, scoring on a nine-yard run with the clock running down. He had sparked the team throughout that game by running the option cleanly and passing for 140 yards. After his winning touchdown, Chuck heaved the ball straight up in the air like a bottle rocket, relieved to sneak away with a victory against a heavy underdog. Neither Coach Hollub nor his Dad had much to say after that game other than at least the team had won.

This game, however, was a little different from playing a fired-up but lesser opponent like Shorewood early in the season. Chuck already had his bell rung this game by two tackles named Marv Waters and Dave Stanley. Stanley tipped the scales at 240 pounds, playing both sides of the ball, and Waters weighed in at a bovine 260. These heavyweights weren't lugs on their feet either. Waters was known for pancake blocks in short yardage situations whenever the Bulldogs needed a score or first down. Both bruisers had reached Chuck a couple of times in the back-field and had body-slammed or sandwiched him every chance they got when he rushed out of the pocket, heading upfield or scrambling for the sidelines. Chuck was banged up at this point, but his teammates never knew it by looking at him in the huddle. Although Chuck was playing the game with one injured hand, smashed in practice by another player's helmet earlier in the week, he stared each of his teammates in the eye and barked at them that there was no time like the present to score. The players had called a private meeting before the game without the Blackshirt coaches, just to remind themselves what winning the game would mean to Coach Hollub and to them. Chuck, his mother noticed, had a game face on that day at the breakfast table, a few hours earlier than normal.

The Bulldogs' beefiness had also done some damage to Chuck's teammates. But Chuck's game face never changed, even when his baritone signal-calling in the huddle sometimes got a little louder when it was time to make some big plays. The Blackshirts were into the game. The Blackshirts' band was playing their own hand-clapping version of a New Orleans jazz classic, "Oh When the Saints Go Marching In," substituting "Shirts" for "Saints." The Blackshirts' band and cheerleaders were rocking. But Chuck's voice had the huddle at attention. The players heard nothing except Chuck calling the plays and the snap count.

At the 17-yard line, with plenty of time, Chuck was prepared to take whatever yardage the competition gave him, even if it came in small increments. He called a play in the huddle. On two. Clap. Number 42 Gary Koch ran the counter from the slot for a tough two yards. He called another play. On one. Clap. No. 10 Chuck DiFrancesca snuck forward off the center's left hip for another seven yards, losing the ball for an instant in the scrum before alertly pulling it back in before the pile fell on him. The clock was running, less than four minutes left in the game. Chuck called another play on one knee. On set. Clap. Kyle Hilmer, number 22, turned the corner on a student-body left for another five yards to the 31. First down. As the Bulldogs' front four hunkered down, prepared to strip the ball on any Blackshirt running play, Chuck called a play he had been trying to set up with the run. With Tim Goralski on the sideline as a field-goal kicker who had missed only once during the season, the Blackshirt head coach seemed content to run at the Bulldogs. Judging from the play calling, Coach Hollub and Chuck both knew what they needed to do to move the team into field-goal position.

On first down at the Blackshirt 31, the Blackshirts clapped their hands, broke from the huddle, and set for the snap. Koch substituted for the injured Haas, wide right. Everyone expected more clouds of dust to be kicked up on another run. But Chuck's instincts told him that Goralski would be forced to convert on a fairly long field, assuming the

Blackshirts could keep moving the ball in the time left. His team was running out of gas and Goralski's luck might change under pressure. Hollub was worried too, toying nervously with his pencil and clipboard. Chuck had called a play that might catch the Bulldogs by surprise. He rubbed his hands together breaking the huddle. On two. Clap.

Chuck dropped deep in the pocket, rolling slightly to his right, his front line giving ground to the heavier Bulldogs. He waited for his receiver to break clear. His arm and body uncorked a throw after he pumped the ball once, two defenders whiplashing him in a head-on collision a split second after his weight had transferred to his front foot. The punishment after the release had not affected the zip on his throw. Coach DiFrancesca in the stands and Coach Hollub at midfield could only stand and watch a pass fly that Chuck never even saw to remember. The ball fell into the breadbasket of "Bullets" who had streaked up the field with half a yard advantage on the cover man. The pass play covered 38 yards, with Koch lassoed by the defender's outstretched arms at the Bulldog 36. The perfection of the pass, which seemed to lodge itself in the squarish hole at the center of the 4 on Koch's jersey, had not given the defender a chance at recovering. The fans in the bleachers lurched and swirled and shrieked and clapped. Chuck trotted upfield, seemingly in the eye of a Waukesha hurricane. He shook off the hit by listening to the cheers of the crowd as he jogged downfield. The Shirts were marching on.

The clock had stopped with little more than three minutes left to go in the game. Accepting a minor face-mask penalty at the end of this pass play, the Blackshirts had the ball on the Bulldog 31. On the next series of downs, Chuck escaped with his life on a quarterback keeper to his left, barely getting back to the line of scrimmage. Fortunately, he picked up five yards for his suffering on a Bulldog offsides penalty. Another keeper by Chuck gained two more yards, leaving third and three. Kyle Hilmer went up the gut for three more, killing more time on the clock and leaving the ball standing between the Bulldog 20 and 21. First down, pointed the referee. A couple more runs in the center of the field potentially set up Goralski perfectly for a field goal attempt, but the Bulldogs still had all their time-outs. There might be time enough for them to score as well.

Chuck called a play that looked, again, like another quarterback roll-out keeper to his right. An injured sophomore receiver with a sprained ankle wide right, number 24, Bob Keith, ran a down-and-slant pattern to the right goal line flag once the ball was snapped. Keith caused the safety to bite on his inside fake, leaving him three steps in the clear. Chuck hit him with a soft floater in stride. Keith limped the last five yards into the end zone, skipping in pain and dropping the ball without emotion beneath one of the scoreboard's wooden posts. Touchdown, with 1:33 left in the game. Keith's ankle was almost as bad as Haas's and his teammates helped him to the sideline. The Blackshirts heard the thunderous racket from the stands loud and clear. An extra point forced the Bulldogs to match the Blackshirt drive or lose. Goralski split the uprights. As Chuck trotted off the field after the game, a self-assurance came over him that he never forgot, long after he had stopped playing football. His promise to Hollub was fulfilled, and he had Coach Hollub's confidence in his play-calling to thank for that. Even Coach DiFrancesca did not really know what to say about his son's moxie in that last drive of the game. It spoke for itself.

Chuck's life continued to be that of a football player after that game. His play that entire season earned him the team's MVP honors, an all-state selection, and a high school all-American award in the opinion of one football magazine read by hard-core coaches, recruiters, and fans. Wisconsin head coach John Coatta offered Chuck a full-ride scholarship to play in the Big Ten Conference for the Badgers, along with nine other top recruits from the state. Chuck traveled to the University of Wisconsin the following September and began school. Over the previous winter, Chuck had considered the Air Force and the possibility of playing at Carroll College for his Dad, but neither offered the upside of Big Ten competition. Wisconsin was the place to be if Chuck wanted any chance of making it to the pros.

Chuck was playing in Madison on Wisconsin's freshmen team when a job for an assistant offensive coach became available. Chuck's Dad applied for the job, but never get a call back from the head coach, Coatta. Chuck resented the fact that Coatta hadn't given his Dad the courtesy of an interview and told the Badger coach just that to his face. Coach Coatta didn't know what to think; kids came and went through the Wisconsin program like leaves on a tree. It wasn't Michigan or Ohio

State, after all. A freshman just under six feet and weighing 185 pounds, Chuck was sticking his neck out pretty far. His words probably didn't sound like much of a threat to anyone on the Wisconsin coaching staff, including Coatta. The Wisconsin coach had other things to worry about, like his own job, and Michigan and Ohio State. But Chuck meant what he said. He cleaned out his locker. Didn't his father at least deserve an interview?

The next year Chuck transferred to Carroll College to play for Vince, a loyalty move that put him in football player never-never land. He played without a scholarship. He was a Vietnam-era kid with two devout Christian parents, living only a few blocks from the family home, in the TKE frat house. He wanted to let his hair grow and experiment with life like everyone else, but time and space seemed to be crowding him. It was all so awkward for Chuck in Waukesha. At Carroll, living almost in the shadow of the house where he had grown up, he would forever be known as Vince's son and seemed to have taken a few steps backward all for the sake of pride. He felt like a football player, but he wasn't so sure he was one—even if he was the team's starting quarterback. At night in the TKE house, however, he was having plenty of fun. At the TKE house, Chuck discovered that he was also the best poker player in his small universe of jocks and college buddies, making money for weekend dates with his high school sweetheart, Joy Batha, when he couldn't mooch a few extra dollars from the parents.

Vince and Chuck's football relationship was a complex one, particularly now. Chuck, in some sense, had been a player in Vince's locker room all his life, walking the field with Vince at practices with the Iowa State Cyclones in Ames. Vince's teams back then always got their butts whipped by the likes of Bud Wilkinson's Oklahoma Sooners and Bob Devaney's Nebraska Cornhuskers, but he was also regarded in the Big Eight Conference as a coach who recruited student-athletes, not football players who didn't go to class or sometimes robbed gas stations. Only a certain type of kid could play for Vince, whose integrity as an educator naturally precluded him from turning an institution of learning into a football factory. Vince had been a player once himself, serving as one of the co-captains of the 1946 Northwestern University football team. The team went 3-6 that year, but it did have some ball players who could scrum and bang with most any team in the nation.

Under a new coach, they had almost turned the corner. Vince played in the *Chicago Tribune* College All-Star game for outstanding college seniors, and the Northwestern players who suffered through that season played in Northwestern's only Rose Bowl appearance in 1947, at least, that is, until Gary Barnett's miracle turnaround season in 1995. After meeting Margaret at Northwestern and later marrying her, Vince became a thinking man's coach. He had written his master's dissertation at Northwestern on a concept he called *rule-blocking*. The idea behind this pigskin concept was that offensive linemen not be given a preconceived assignment in the huddle on who they should block. The play and the positions of the defensive players at the line of scrimmage dictated who blocked whom. Vince's innovation eliminated the possibility that defensive stunting could upset a play at the line of scrimmage. An offensive lineman himself, Vince conceptualized the notion after Northwestern had squeaked by Vanderbilt 3-0 the first game of the season. Vanderbilt's stunting at the line had turned what should have been a wipeout into a close one. Whenever one of Vince's players complained that rule-blocking was too difficult to learn, Vince asked one of his young sons, Chuck or John, to recite the fundamentals of rule-blocking to the player. Hearing these little-kid voices explain the concept was intended to show how easy it was and often silenced the player. Vince passed his novel idea to Coach Hollub's Waukesha Blackshirts. Hollub later admitted that such a scheme put his high school offense way ahead of the bell curve when it faced the suburban Milwaukee competition. "When we told other high school coaches about this concept at summer coaching seminars, they were surprised," says Coach Hollub. "It was easy for the kids to learn. But many other coaches didn't know what the hell we were even talking about at the time."

Coaching at schools with mediocre talent and limited football budgets, Vince won over 100 games throughout his coaching career and was selected as part of the Carroll College Hall of Fame after retirement. Vince tinkered with football fundamentals and gameplan strategies all his life, and his two sons picked up a lot of his chalk talks by osmosis at the dinner table or on the practice field, sprinting the sidelines when they were bored. A local sportswriter in 1968 would be so amused by Coach DiFrancesca's Carroll Pioneers that he wrote up all the new looks he had seen in the team's gameplan during its final victory of the season over Millikin.

"One thing which was different," wrote sportswriter Lee Fensin, for the *Waukesha County Freeman*, "was seeing a six-man defensive line with just one linebacker. Another change from the normal was seeing split end Bill Wick playing a flanker position. One play which you don't see everyday which had the fans oohing and aahing is what Coach Vince DiFrancesca calls the 'razzle-dazzle.' The 'razzle-dazzle' is used on kick-off returns. What happens is once a Carroll man catches the kick, about five more Pioneers come running over, huddling around the man with the ball. All of the players come out of the huddle making like they have the ball, and DiFrancesca hopes that someday, the man who is actually carrying the ball will slip away down the field unnoticed."

Vince DiFrancesca may not have been Steve Spurrier of the Florida Gators when it came to the vertical passing game, but it was also clear that he knew the game of football and wasn't afraid to dream up new schemes of X's and O's to score touchdowns with some flair or keep opponents out of the end zone. Such vast coaching knowledge and Vince's laurels as a player were not an easy shadow for his son to step out of, particularly in a small town like Waukesha. Almost every newspaper clip about Chuck's stellar play that final season included his father's bio as well. It most often came in the article's last sentence, as his son made headlines almost weekly for his skills at quarterback, reading something like: "Chuck DiFrancesca is the son of Vince DiFrancesca, Carroll College football coach and athletic director who was captain of the 1946 Northwestern University football team." These lines had to ring in Chuck's ears.

The father-son football thing wasn't all bad. Chuck and his Dad sometimes had fun rolling with it. They were both grounded, in some sense, by what they shared. The *Milwaukee Journal*, on October 2, 1968, would write about their relationship. In that article, Vince told sportswriter Bill Dwyre that having "a father who's a college coach is a tough situation for Charlie. He used to ask me when we were just joking around if I'd get mad if he didn't play for me. That decision is going to come hard. It's going to be frustrating for him." Chuck, on the other hand, could only tell Dwyre of one kid who played for his father, "Pistol" Pete Maravich at Louisiana State, a basketball player Chuck loved to watch on TV. Chuck added his own two cents' worth about the situation, perhaps in a moment of I'm-just-a-kid honesty: "I guess there are problems. If I played for dad, he couldn't build me up in front of the rest of the team, but then he couldn't tear me down, either." In that interview, Chuck expressed his desire to go away to college. His mother supported the idea, or so it seemed from another wry quote from Vince planted in the story by the same sportswriter to get a chuckle. But if he did pick the Carroll Pioneers? "That could be a tougher situation for both of us," Vince explained. "I've talked to coaches who have had sons on their squad, and they get in a corner where they're damned if they do and damned if they don't. Every time the boy throws an incompletion or misses a tackle, the catcalls start."

What happened to Chuck's football career probably played out in between the hash marks of life. Who knew what the gridiron crystal ball held in store for Chuck? He seemed comfortable as the "Joe Willie Namath" of Waukesha, both on and off the field. His hair blew a little longer in the '60s Vietnam-era winds of change and protest at Carroll College and other college campuses around the country. Who listened to their parents then? Students started to vocalize their ideas about the Vietnam War and the U.S. government. Naturally, Chuck popped a few cans of beers with his frat brothers once in a while, and sometimes stayed out a little too late with his girlfriend, Joy Batha, an attractive blonde who caught the attention of frat boys and football players every time she was around Chuck. As a child, she had lived just one house away from the DiFrancescas and was one of the high school's top swimmers.

Vince, too, was hearing cries of parental protest from the stands every time his son threw a pass that was off the mark or ran the option once too often without pitching the ball. The team lost only one game that season, but the Carroll College campus was becoming a very small place for both father and son. Something had to give.

Vince looks back at that year with some regret. Being a coach was a bitch of a headache. Everyone in the stands was a Monday-morning quarterback, particularly the parents who became as actively vocal about sports as their children were about war. "I was the one who made Chuck a defensive linebacker during the year he played for me," he says. "I had two or three quarterbacks. Charlie was a tremendous option quarterback and powerful runner because he weighed 200 pounds at the time. But if he missed a pass or did something wrong, you heard the murmur in the stands. So I said, 'Charlie, I'm going to make this move.' I put the kid in who was the best thrower on the team, but to this day, I still think Charlie was the better quarterback overall. We had an excellent season that year, going 9-1."

By the end of the season, the coach and son were angry at each other, one for choices made on the field, one for choices made off the field. "He was cocky. We had a father-son meltdown," says Vince. "I had a job for him handing out towels at the gym, and he told me he wasn't going to hand out towels to anybody. I was giving all these motivational lectures around the state about what it took to be a good man, and my own son was testing me. So I said, really? I ended up throwing a road atlas on his lap and asked him which college he would like to go to. OK, I said, it's your turn to make decisions for yourself. Let's go get in the car."

Chuck looked up at Vince, confused, the day of the meltdown. "Where are we going?"

Vince's voice took on a tone Chuck had never heard before from his father—just as cocky and defiant as him. "Son, we are going for a little ri-i-i-de."

The mediator in the DiFrancesca car on the trip down I-80, past Davenport, Iowa, past Lincoln, Nebraska, past North Platte, Nebraska, and into Colorado, was Chuck's younger brother, John. Not much mediating needed to be done, however. Vince let Chuck pick the school in which he wanted to enroll and gave him a ride there. Because he didn't play for Vince, he could do whatever he wanted—become the next Joe Willie Namath, if Joe Willie was who he really wanted to be. Recalls John about that trip with a remember-that family chuckle: "It was . . . It was . . . Let's just say there wasn't a lot of discussion between Charlie and Dad in the car." The final stop on that road trip was the school Chuck selected in Fort Collins, Colorado. Son of Vince, meet Colorado

State University, land of the 1-10 Golden Rams. *This is as good a place as any, Dad. Let's stop here. OK, son, fine. Good luck and don't forget to call us once in a while. Mom, I'm sure, wants to hear from you.* Actually, the whole episode wasn't that abrupt. Vince spent time introducing his son to the new coach at Colorado State, Jerry Wampfler, whom he knew. Coach Wampfler had taken over the job a year earlier after leaving as offensive coordinator for college blue chip, Notre Dame.

Two years of football eligibility down for the count, Chuck walked on as a defensive back the first day of practice. He pasted a couple of receivers to the turf and showed some great instincts on the field, even if he was a half a step slower than the coach liked. Perhaps because he had something to prove and no money to pay for school, it wasn't going to be easy to knock this kid off the team. And he seemed to have another burning desire: to show his Dad that he could make it, on his own terms. By the time the Golden Rams had their final scrimmage that season, Chuck had a football scholarship to replace the one he had sacrificed at Wisconsin. Playing for Coach Wampfler, however, would be an even worse nightmare for Chuck than playing for his Dad. Unlike Coach Hollub and Vince, the Colorado State coaches created a hyperaggressive atmosphere during practices. It wasn't uncommon for players to get injured before games, sometimes unnecessarily. If you weren't willing to play the game balls-to-the-wall, you were considered half a man and half a player. It was a violent smash-mouth game much different from Coach Hollub's or his Dad's teachings. Or perhaps it just seemed more that way since Chuck was on the defensive side of the ball, not by choice, chasing rather than running and passing. As far as Chuck was concerned, this type of violent coaching would never work. Only mindless idiots played this kind of football, if football was what you call it. Chuck quit five games into the season, leaving football for good. He was not alone; a number of other players bagged the Golden Rams in a mass exodus. The team, 0-5 at that point, was a joke. Students partied hard before games and showed up in small numbers with mute signs like Rah-Rah-Rah to do their cheering. There were plenty of empty seats, even near the 50-yard line, late in the season. Only Lawrence McCutcheon, a star running back who the coach loved to bench for not putting out 100 percent behind a weak front line, defied the internal inconsistencies of a football program that was all gas, no engine. He later starred as an All-Pro running back for the Los Angeles Rams.

Wampfler's football program hit rock bottom that season at the homecoming game. Eight games into the season, the less-than-Golden Rams battled Ivy League Brown University for the distinction as the "worst college football team" because of its zero and something record. The Rams saved themselves from total obscurity with three late victories in the season against other perennial doormats when no one seemed to care.

All through school, even without his scholarship, Chuck never lost confidence that he would again play quarterback on some team. He just didn't know what kind of team that would be, despite his grades. He did his share of skipping classes, dissatisfied with something. Dissatisfaction seemed to be in the air. Around him other kids, partying as regularly as they went to class, seemed to be spinning their wheels as well. The apathy, feigned or not, of this generation of CSU students was reflected best in the 1973 yearbook. The editors of the *Silver Spruce* wrote: "Naked were you born into the world, but then you came to CSU. Four out of five CSU students when asked at the end of the day what they had learned that day answered, 'Huh?' " The food-for-thought pages at the front of the 1972 issue were equally as disillusioning, saying "in four years you will set forth upon the world armed with a CSU diploma, and promptly get a challenging job in your field. You know what fat chance means?"

A fat chance named Chuck attended CSU from fall quarter 1971 to spring quarter 1973. Early on, he began dating a girl from Sterling, Illinois, Sally Elliot, who lived in Corbett Hall, the same coed dorm as he did, one story below. Just a freshman, Sally had her eyes on Chuck from the first day she saw him walk into the coed cafeteria after football practice in a half-T that showed his navel and stomach muscles. Chuck had continued to correspond with Joy, his girlfriend back in Waukesha since high school. He secretly worried that Joy might have the hots for some other guy at Carroll. While he was uncertain about Joy but sometimes jealous, she seemed to be the least of his worries. By November 1971, Chuck hit rock bottom in school and in football, uncertain about everything, Sally and Joy included. Only Sally, whose father and mother paid for everything for their daughter, including a car, seemed to offer him any emotional and financial security. Sally and Charlie became lost in a love that bordered on obsession. On dates that included Friday trips to the Longmont Dog Track with other college friends, it was not uncommon for them to end up somewhere alone in the dark, holding each other, with Chuck talking about his dreams. Chuck's dreams always seemed big to Sally, even if they were as distant as the stars on a clear evening. No one could have convinced Sally that Chuck wouldn't someday pull them off. She never doubted his self-confidence.

Chuck's problems exited the football field and entered a new zone: Joy came out to visit him in November, precipitating a breakup soon after. Chuck's grades in three classes that semester were 1.67, 2.02, and 2.33. Perhaps because it was 1971 and student rebellion was in the air, perhaps because of failures at football, perhaps because of one beautiful coed named Sally, Chuck was a highway over which two women who didn't know each other would collide. A year later, Joy said as much in a letter sent to Charlie dated October 19, 1972. She wrote:

Dear Charlie, I'm sitting here trying to formulate a million thoughts, but not succeeding well with even one. When you called last night, I sensed the frustration that you obviously didn't mention. You said that I knew you like no one else. So I'm taking the liberty to explain my thoughts.

I think your decision to quit football probably was the start. I know how much it meant to you. Now you have to face financial problems again, but even more you have to start playing a different role.

Charlie, you are a very brilliant and intelligent person. I hope that you will see that you can have success in other areas—scholastically especially, other than being a jock. Being a super athlete was good in high school, and good enough to get you some money for college. But you have realized for you that it's not a career. Now you should start planning a career; you've put that off long enough. You shouldn't ever feel Charlie that you ever have to prove your virility or masculinity or athletic abilities to anyone; you know yourself.

It's been a year now, Di, since we've been apart. Now I have managed to see my goal; I have three semesters left at Carroll, and then I'm on my own. And now I feel strong enough to tell you something about love. I love you very much. We did a lot of growing together. But in our own way, our own immaturities spoiled it. But the point I want to make is not about you and me; it's about you and Sally.

A friend related an analogy to me once that went something like this: loving a girl is like planting a beautiful flower, the kind of loving that a not jealous person will let grow. He will water and feed the flower with communication and trust—two of the most basic elements of a relationship, even above sex. And he will watch the flower grow and bloom and become beautiful and be proud of it because others appreciate it, and it's his very own. The selfish person plants the flower in the dark and when it sprouts crushes it, because he is afraid of its beauty and is afraid others will appreciate it. In the end, this man has the flower for his own, but it's broken and not whole.

Think of you and me, Charlie. Think of you and Sally. Don't put Sally in the dark or hurt her in any way; I've been hurt and that is something I would not wish on anyone. I know she loves you as I did for a year, for you are an easy person to love, and I know you must love her too. Never have I heard you speak so highly of one girl in my life and even more reinforcing is when you slipped and called me Sal. Sal I'll never be, Charlie; I'll always be Joy, Joy Batha and no else.

Somewhere out of the radar of Joy's universe and personal catharsis in Waukesha, Sally and Chuck were married after his graduation. He received a B.S. degree in psychology from Colorado State University on June 1, 1973. His wedding with Sally included a wedding cake topped with chrysanthemums and a clear-glass table decoration in the shape of a race dog named Whippet, the dog that had come home bigtime for Sally and Chuck on a Friday night, allowing him to buy a wedding ring. It was a romantic story that Sally's mom, eyes twinkling, loved to tell her friends. The only one who seemed to love Chuck more than Sally was Sally's mom. Sally's father, a wealthy businessman, played the magnanimous host at the wedding, but had questioned his daughter's decision with her mother in private. But his objection wouldn't fly with the two women and he knew it, so he offered to help Chuck on occasion. Chuck had his pride and a good head, even if his college grades hadn't always shown it. He found such offers of assistance as offensive as when Vince asked him to hand out and wash towels in the gym. He wanted to make his own decisions and could take care of himself financially. He and Sally would be just fine on their own.

Chuck began his career, in his words, as a salesman pushing "enema bags to nuns" for American Hospital Supply Corporation—a job he seemed to do well. But something was missing in both the job and the till-death-do-us-part relationship for Chuck and Sally. And it would get worse for two kids, only one having graduated from college at the time. Four months after the wedding, the 22-year-old Chuck and 20-year-old Sally lost an ally in Sally's mom, who died unexpectedly of a brain tumor. Her sudden death put pressure on the relationship that neither Chuck nor Sally was prepared to deal with. Sally needed love and support and a shoulder to lean on, but Chuck wasn't always there to be an emotional crutch. Hurting himself, he assumed even more responsibility than he seemed prepared to handle. To fill the shoes expected of him by Sally's Dad, he needed a bigger paycheck to give Sally the lifestyle to which she was accustomed. But Chuck sure as hell didn't want Sally's father—who sometimes struck him as arrogant and often rubbed him the wrong way— to give it to him.

It didn't take long before the couple grew tired of one another's fragile egos and lacks and needs, some of which cost money, some of which cost a maturity that wasn't there. A honeymoon in the Bahamas now seemed as if it had happened a long time ago, and medical supplies started to collect dust in every room of Chuck and Sally's modest apartment in Springfield. Short on furniture and patience, Chuck tried to turn things around by committing to get his MBA from Northwestern University and finding a job at Harris Bank in Chicago. Sally later got her degree from Loyola University. But Sally no longer felt a part, still grieving the loss of her mom. The whole situation led down the expected but painful path of divorce, Chuck obsessed with work and the loss of Sally's mother and a desire to turn things around; Sally obsessed with the same loss and annoyed by a husband whose drive to succeed made him impatient and resentful and sometimes angry at others and himself.

Sally never left the circle of the DiFrancesca family completely. Her bond with Chuck's mother Margaret remains to this day. I met her with the help of a call from Margaret. We set a time to visit in a coffee shop off the Eden's Expressway. Sally recounted some of the story I've told here, but hardly seemed the woman she described when she was married to Chuck at the age of 20. She was now Sally Winter, not Sally DiFrancesca, an attractive mother of four children. She wore jeans and drove a Chrysler mini-van to pick up her kids from school every day—her next stop after we had a cup of coffee at the Hill-Top Coffee House. It was easy for me to understand why Chuck had fallen in love with Sally, and why her husband Bob loved her. She was as stunning walking into that diner as she had probably seemed to Chuck over 25 years earlier. Her natural grace and beauty shone through in conversation as well. In her wedding photos with Chuck, I hardly recognized her. Seeing her in a wedding dress and Chuck in his tuxedo tails, it was not hard for me to blink and see them at the ceremony, with too little of life and experience crystallizing along with all that innocence into something that would last. But boy did they seem to be a couple in the photo, and what a wedding it was. There was Charlie D's best man, his nerdy-looking brother John, toasting the couple from behind the microphone and sipping carefully beneath the "classic" DiFrancesca nose. There was one of Charlie's best friends, Johnny Bollen, another football player who used to double-date with Chuck and Sally. When Chuck was short of rent money in college, Johnny gave his to Chuck, and later watched Chuck double or triple it in poker games more than once. Johnny never worried about losing it so long as Chuck had a deck of cards.

Between sips of coffee, Sally explained that her relationship with Chuck produced some of the best days of her life and some of the worst. After reading the opening paragraphs about Charlie D in a draft chapter about his boundless energy, she nodded.

"That's Charlie. He never stopped. Sometimes the DiFrancesca family and I would be up there sitting around a little dinette table in Deerfield, where Vince and Margaret lived, and we would just be hanging out. We would hear his car coming up the driveway, and we'd all start the countdown. 5-4-3-2-1. . . . The door would open, and it would be like a torpedo just blew into the middle of the room. He'd tap Vince on the shoulder. Getting a little fat around the middle, aren't you, Vince? He went around the table to Marge, to Janet, to John, to me. The humor that would fly around that room in about four minutes was amazing. I used to just sit back and watch it. They all have it, really. If Charlie hadn't had that, if he hadn't had that basic deep-down goodness about him, I don't know if I'd be here talking. But he also could go around the room like a machete. He could slice people in two. I truly will never know another person like him."

And what about before he became a success, Sally? "We lived on a shoestring when I knew him. I didn't know the Charlie D with all the success that you describe. I saw the other Charlie—the Charlie who was obsessed with being successful. On Friday nights at Colorado State, we used to dream. I would lie in his arms and he would plan his life out for me, tell me the whole thing. He would tell me, someday, I'm going to be big. Someday I'm going to make it like nobody has ever seen. It was a drive for him. In some ways, he was the smartest man I've ever met, a genius. You watch David Letterman, right? That's Charlie in a way. That's his personality. He could walk into a room and have more fast and funny answers than anyone. He also could go right at you. He's an enigma in that way. But that's the part of him I adored, that I loved."

And what was his master plan, beneath the stars of the Longmont Dog Track? "Part of his master plan was to be big, and to give. To give to the least expecting. To give to the needy. To make his mark. To show everyone. I don't think he had to prove anything to anyone, so I don't know where that drive came from. Maybe if he had married someone who had had far less materially than he had when he was growing up, it wouldn't have been an issue, but it was. My relationship with him was the most volatile thing I've been in. You loved and hated him. What you tell me about him after we separated doesn't surprise me one bit. Charlie was running fast and never slowed down. I don't know what he was running from. All that drive to get to the top was him running. He ran through life. I don't know what he was afraid of catching up with him. All I know is that the quiet moments were so infrequent. But when I look back he taught me more about life and my priorities than I could ever imagine."

Next thing, Sally is in a Big Bear Restaurant in Deerfield, explaining to Vince and Margaret why she is separating from their son. They give her their blessing. With a broken relationship with Sally behind him and the possibility of a new relationship in front of him with Ann and her two children, it was all quiet behind the glass in the members' gallery at the

Chicago Board of Trade in 1980, where he sometimes studied the markets, looking down at the trading pits. There Chuck could sit in relative silence and think about his future.

Only his efforts to make his own future a bright one might help turn things around. He was consumed by the muffled sound of men below the window in colorful trading jackets, trying to scream and shout to make a fast buck in the new bond futures trading pit in the northwest corner of the Board of Trade's South Room. He looked down and watched. It was an interesting game, fast, slow, exciting, some moments boring, like football. The best thing about it if you had the money to get in the game, he thought, is that everyone on the floor gets to play quarterback and to coach himself. He looked down at the bond pit even more intently, planning like a coach watching the game film of an opponent. By the time Charlie D emerged from behind the glass for good, he could read the activity in and outside of the pit and the faces of other participants in the pit the same way he read an opposing defense on the football field. It was all so effortless, once he came up with his own series of plays to call, depending on market situations. After a trader had made 5000 trades or so, you had seen almost every situation to which you would need to react; the rest was a quarterback's instinct. Some players had it. Some didn't. All that was left at that point was to stand in the pit and play.

Chuck DiFrancesca, son of Vince DiFrancesca and quarterback for Ken Hollub, was one hell of a quarterback. Charlie D was also one hell of a quarterback when the pigskin became bond futures contracts, representing a cash equivalent of $100,000 worth of U.S. Treasury bonds. He usually traded 300 to 500 contracts at a clip, once his capital built up, representing a notional value of $30 million to $50 million. It didn't matter anymore that he was too small, or too short, or too slow in this new game. All that mattered was his ability to read the field and react to what the market gave him. In time, Charlie found it remarkably easy to read the faces of other traders in the pit the same way he read a defense at the line of scrimmage. It was all so effortless, so long as he remained disciplined. When asked to describe Charlie D's trading success, many colleagues and competitors alike referred to Michael Jordan. It was based on instinct and practice. And he didn't back off even when the game clock clicked down. Most of the time he had the ability to make a trade when it counted most, but it was difficult even for him to try to describe his ability to work with imperfect information in the middle of chaos.

Neighbor and friend J. B. Dougherty came closest, perhaps, in explaining Charlie D's trading style by analogy. He would not describe it, however, in human terms. Charlie D was not your ordinary jock in a trader's jacket. He sometimes seemed to have his eyes on things in the market no one else could see. "In the trading pit," said J. B., "he was as natural as they come. It was like watching a bird dog sniffing and hunting and pointing in the weeds."

the other side of vegas | 9

A s a nationally known Christian radio broadcaster for WAVA in the Washington D.C. area, Janet DiFrancesca-Parshall does not mince words when expressing her views about faith, family, and related social issues either on or off the air. The microphone has taught her well how to encapsulate a situation for her audience in a few words. Thus, she can better explain the time period of a few days in July 1986 for the DiFrancesca family than I can. I see no reason not to just turn on my tape recorder and replay her words back to you. That would quickly eliminate any half-truths about Charlie D's donating blood to save his brother, as first recounted by the Merrill Lynch broker and swirling around in Chicago Board of Trade folklore.

Evangelical broadcasters often seem over the top to some listeners who may not share the same opinions, and I have been warned that even her brother Charlie sometimes liked to throw verbal kerosene on their philosophical debates about faith and God. But nothing Janet can say in our broadcast sounds kooky to me at all ("kooky" was Charlie D's endearing word to describe some of his sister's views he disagreed with, not mine). When discussing her family, she is merely a loving sister with broken chromosomes herself—barely on the other side of a medical mystery that is such a longshot-come-home it can only be code-named the Other Side of Vegas. Listen to the tape yourself—certainly, the story raises questions about God, faith, and family.

> *Here's my brother Johnny, this good-looking 30-year-old guy. We are all going, why isn't this guy married? He's dating his girlfriend Lynn and we are all thinking courtship and marriage. But the next thing we hear: Johnny, you have this thing with your blood, a problem. Next thing we know the doctor tells us he has a rare form of cancer known as hairy cell leukemia. What's that?*

Hairy cell leukemia is extremely rare. Its incidence statistically occurs in 4 out of 100,000 people, and is characterized by an overproduction of a specific type of abnormal white blood cells called lymphocytes. These abnormal cells have hairlike projections around their surface—hence the name. There is a corresponding reduction in all types of blood cells: the white blood cells, the red blood cells, and the platelets. A reduction in platelets increases bleeding tendencies, and liver and spleen enlargement are common.

More specifically, hairy cell leukemia affects lymphocytes which are made in the bone marrow and other organs. Bone marrow is the spongy tissue inside the large bones of the body. The bone marrow generates red blood cells (which carry oxygen and other materials to all tissues of the body), white blood cells (which fight infection), and platelets (which make blood clot). Lymphocytes are also made in the spleen (an organ in the upper abdomen that makes lymphocytes and filters old blood cells from the blood), the lymph nodes (small bean-shaped organs throughout the body), and other organs.

When hairy cell leukemia develops, abnormal lymphocytes may collect in the spleen, causing the spleen to swell. There may also be too few normal white blood cells in the blood because the leukemia cells invade the bone marrow, and the marrow cannot produce enough normal white blood cells. This can lead to infections. You should see a doctor if you feel tired all the time, or if your spleen is larger than normal, or if you develop an infection that won't go away. Or if you are John DiFrancesca.

Janet continues.

After John's blood results came back, Charlie went to my parents' condo and found out what the diagnosis was. He threw himself across my parents' bed, and as my mother told me, began to howl from the depths of who we are as people and as family. "Oh God, don't let it be Johnny. Let it be me." Charlie just sobbed there, just sobbed.

Then maybe two weeks later, Charlie goes to the doctor and they discover this mass. The doctor says that it has to be benign; nobody can live with a malignant tumor of that size for this long. And the doctor says he will do a biopsy. "I'm sure it will not be anything that we can't take care of."

And the day Charlie snuck in for surgery, I was back home in Waukesha, Wisconsin. Johnny called me and said, "Is the Lord in your life?" I said yes. He said you better sit down. When somebody tells me that, I know I'd better stand firm. Johnny says, "Charlie has cancer, and it's malignant."

Specifically, Charlie D was diagnosed with diffuse large cell lymphoma, one of about a dozen types of non-Hodgkin's lymphoma, one of the nation's fastest increasing fatal cancers. In 1996, the American Cancer Society estimated that 45,000 Americans were diagnosed with non-Hodgkin's lymphoma that year, and 21,200 probably would die. This compares to 153,000 Americans killed each year by lung cancer, the nation's deadliest type of cancer. In 1996, the overall five-year survival rate for all types of non-Hodgkin's lymphomas was 51 percent, according to *Scientific American*. But with low-, intermediate-, and high-grade types of lymphomas, the average survival rate belies the notion that the survival rates for certain types of lymphoma are highly variable. The probability cup isn't always more than half full.

Back to Janet.

As he's telling me this, I'm looking out the window and my son Samuel is falling off the swingset and drops to the ground. He breaks his arm. At that exact moment, my daughter Sarah is playing with her sister and pierces her ear drum with a pick-up stick. Boom boom boom. My husband Craig is at a court appearance scheduled somewhere in central Wisconsin. Johnny, I said on the phone, I think I have some cleanup here to do with the kids. I will come to the emergency room just as soon as I can. I call Craig to pull him out of the courtroom. We've got one arm in a cast, one ear patched, and then we drive, crying all the way down I-94, to go see Charlie.

We all had a chance to cry together as a family and buck ourselves up, and then we go into the room. Typical Charlie. There he is cracking jokes. "Well, I guess they misdiagnosed this one just a tad." I'm looking at one brother facing death in his bed, two weeks on the heels of my other brother's diagnosis. I'm watching my parents, thinking about what they must be thinking. Unbelievable, isn't it? The strength of character they manifested at that moment, and John's focus off his own diagnosis in his support for Charlie. It was unbelievable.

Roughly nine months later, my mother's blood count starts plummeting. We always joked it was the empathy that only a mother can have for her sons that caused her illness; she always wanted to be right there with them. My Dad and I are just sitting there as they are in the hospital and the doctors are looking for everything under the sun. We are a strange family, Bill. We tell this one doctor that our family's going to be the most unique set of laboratory rats he's seen, and I'm sure he's thinking, this is ridiculous; it can't be. And then he comes into the room with this long face and says that Mom has hairy cell leukemia. That's three out of five of us diagnosed with cancer in nine months, so there's an immediate rustle in the University of Chicago Medical School. Is this environmental? Is this genetic? What's the deal?

As a family, that was absolutely a secondary concern to us. My mom is supporting Johnny, Johnny's supporting Charlie, and Charlie's supporting Mom. As much as we all felt we were free-falling through the darkest period of our lives, the belief in God and the security and companionship of family just carried us for the next five years in what can only be described as the most bizarre roller-coaster ride that you can imagine.

After about an hour of listening to Janet tell the family cancer story, I turn my tape recorder off. Every time I hear her tell it, I go numb. I have heard various mutations of this story many times, but always watered-down or twisted into myth as it was with the Merrill Lynch broker. Janet's narrative pulls me out of the eye of this medical hurricane and plunks me down at ground zero of the Cancer Family. Holy random walk, holy fat tail, what in the hell happened?

I'm not sure I—or even any medical expert—can explain it. When it comes to cancer research, the progress is slow. The cost involves billions, and thousands upon thousands of people are affected. It is not a question that can be answered in minutes; it will more than likely take a few more decades, if it can be answered at all. On the other side of Vegas, however, these doctors can tell you a tale or two about the DiFrancesca family, particularly its gregarious leader Charlie D. After you crossed paths with him once in a hospital, it was difficult to swim your way out from under his wake without at least one or two mouthfuls of water and even more stories to tell about how he drove his boat. If he was going to be a patient, it would be on his own terms and his own schedule.

In Dr. Harvey Golomb's office at the University of Chicago Pritzker School of Medicine, I query Dr. Golomb, director and professor of the hematology/oncology section at the U of C's Medical Center and Dr. Funmi I. Olopade, a tall, dignified geneticist from Nigeria who is an assistant professor of medicine, about the family's medical mystery. While they cannot provide definitive conclusions, there is no question the powerful impression Charlie D made on both of them during the five years he battled cancer.

"When we first saw John," says Dr. Golomb, "he came to us for a second opinion [after blood tests at Highland Park Hospital]. We decided it was best to remove his spleen. Charlie was sort of the take-charge guy of the family, while John was more quiet and restrained. When I asked the brother about Charlie after he had left the room during an examination, he said he was a minor player in the bond pit. After we got to talking, he described Charlie as a big-league star. At the time, that really didn't mean that much to me. We did the surgery on John at our institution, and he did fine. But his mother called not soon after that and said they had another problem and could I help. I said sure. What's up?

"She told me that Charlie had a cough and had gone to the emergency room at Evanston and they found that he had a mass in a chest X ray and that they did a biopsy and found that he had lymphoma. A few days later, Charlie came to the clinic. He was still the same aggressive, dynamic person I remembered from our first encounter. He says I'm here; I want you to take care of it.

"I said something about John telling me that he was very active in the bond pit, and he said yes. During the examination, we got into what he did, because he had an incision in his side where they had taken the biopsy, and it was very tender. He was worried that he was going to have to get a metal vest in order to work in the pit, and I recall him saying that it was important for him to work every day. He said he was a large bond trader.

"I said if you're a large trader, then you ought to have a lot of money. He said, yes, I do. From people who have a lot of money, I said we certainly like help. And he asked what do you mean by help? I went to get a booklet we have called *Fund a Fellow*, in which we have pictures of each of our research fellows. I handed it to him and he flipped through all the pictures. OK, he says, I'll take that one. It was this doctor who I initially had see him, Barry Lembersky. It was probably $30,000 at the time to fund a researcher. He takes out his checkbook and writes a check on the spot. That was his style—to at first challenge you, and then to have this sort of banter going back and forth. After that, we had many encounters with him helping us with many things. I don't know if you know this, but he bought us a rather expensive electron microscope during the time we treated him to help us with our basic research."

That day in the clinic with Charlie D was the first sign that these doctors were about to experience something out of the ordinary, interlocked with one of the most unique set of medical circumstances a family has ever encountered. Up until this time, there had been only six cases of familial hairy cell leukemia (HCL) reported in the medical literature. According to a paper entitled "Familial Lymphoproliferative Disorders with Chromosomal Fragile Site Analysis," published in *Leukemia and Lymphoma* in April 1991 by Dr. Jill Moormeier and other contributors such as Dr. Golomb, the DiFrancescas were the seventh family to encounter such rare medical circumstances. Two of the other cases involved a parent and child, and the four others involved siblings. In those cases, the interval between diagnosis among family members ranged anywhere from six months to 14 years. The DiFrancescas, indeed, were every bit the laboratory rats they said they would be. "Interestingly, all three lymphoproliferative disorders manifested themselves within a nine-month period," noted the U of C doctors and pathologists who authored this paper. "The remarkable clustering of B-cell malignancies in a single family within a short period of time led us to question whether a common fragile environmental exposure in a family with a genetic susceptibility to developing neoplasms could explain this finding."

The research for this paper, released in 1991, would not start to take shape until the DiFrancescas were well on with their lives, lightning having struck three times. They quickly picked up the pieces and turned a great deal of their anguish over to their doctors and God. At different times, they all replayed the growing cancer screenplay over and over again in their minds.

John DiFrancesca first had come to the hospital with pain in the left upper section of his abdomen that he had been experiencing the last week in June 1986. During his second physical at the University of Chicago, his doctors noted a condition known as splenomegaly. His spleen now extended 9 centimeters below the ribs on the left side. A bone marrow biopsy at the U of C Medical Center showed his marrow to be 40 to 50 percent cellular with 60 percent of the nucleated elements being hairy cells. This contrasted with the statistics characteristic of normal blood. He was short on platelets, a key ingredient in making blood clot when we cut a finger on a knife, for instance. In response to John's diagnosis, University of Chicago doctors had successfully performed a splenectomy and John's blood had shown a hematologically positive response, his platelet count increasing from $98,000/mm^3$ to $227,000/mm^3$.

The splenectomy had improved the other vital statistics drawn from tests on John's blood and monitored by his doctors. By February 1988, all the critical statistics essential to healthy blood had improved in John—his hemoglobin (14.2 gm/dl) and platelets ($224,000/mm^3$) were in the normal range. However, his white blood cell count was $16,400/mm^3$ with 50% hairy cells and only 5% neutrophils (normal white cells), and this was of concern. For the next 18 months, he underwent interferon alfa-2b therapy, a drug treatment designed to bring his blood counts within an acceptable range and block the recurrence of hairy cells. Once again, his blood showed a good hematological response. His white blood cell count dropped to $5500/mm^3$ and he experienced a rise in his total neutrophil count to $1870/mm^3$. All the signs from the doctors' perspective were there for positive recovery. Although the blood count statistics were Greek to the DiFrancescas, the doctors were upbeat—this was a good sign.

John and Charlie's mother Margaret, in contrast, had been on her own roller coaster since March 1987. At that time she began to experience labored, difficult breathing every time she exerted herself. The peaks and valleys of the hairy-cell ride were literally taking her breath away. Upon examination, nothing seemed out of whack physically, but once again a complete blood count (CBC) produced some surprises. Her CBC was notable for a hemoglobin of 7.0 gm/dl with 6.2% reticulocytes; a white blood cell count of 4300/mm^3 with 87% neutrophils, 11% lymphocytes, 1% eosinophils, and 1% basophils; and a platelet count of 215,000/mm^3. A standard procedure known as the Coomb's test was positive, demonstrating IgG and complement on the red cells. Once again, this was Greek to the nondoctors in the caring crowd, but the test results prompted her doctors to schedule a bone marrow biopsy, which revealed infiltration of Marge's bone marrow elements with typical hairy cells. Like John, Marge went into surgery for a splenectomy, the hemolysis (dissolution or breakdown of red blood corpuscles with liberation of their contained hemoglobin) resolved, and things were looking up for Marge by July 1989. Also like John, she underwent interferon alfa-2b therapy to treat her progressive neutropenia (a blood disorder marked by a sharp reduction in the number of leukocytes). Her condition improved and stabilized. Another gray cloud seemed to blow past the family.

John and Margaret were hardly out of the woods with hairy cell leukemia, since you never say never with cancer. But compared to Charlie's more prolonged battle, they seemed to be responding positively to treatment and the overall seriousness of their illnesses decreased. At this time, it was not uncommon for Charlie D, the family heckler, to razz them for not being as tough as he was and wimping out in the family competition with their "kiddy cancer" diagnoses. It was dark humor only a family could appreciate; they knew Charlie D wasn't a quitter. Perhaps his spontaneous wish surrounded by all that sobbing had come true.

Relative to his own condition, his coined phrase to describe John and Margaret's illness may not have been too far off the mark. At the age of 35, he had followed John into the hospital about a week later (preferring to do so secretly so as not to cause his family unnecessary concern). He had had night sweats, lost some weight, and had asked his Mom, who was a trained nurse, to feel under his arm once or twice; but none of them suspected anything was wrong until John was diagnosed. Charlie shrugged all this off as nothing more than a common cold, until John's health gave him pause for concern. Even his wife Ann suggested he go in for a checkup, but he would wait until he could hardly lift his arm. He went to the hospital for a checkup without anyone knowing, and then decided to relax over the weekend with his family.

Sometime after the Fourth of July, 1986 (a holiday he spent in Las Vegas with his family and friends), Charlie drove himself to Evanston Hospital for a secretly scheduled thoracotomy. This surgery, later determined to be unnecessary, was dramatic. Why he chose this course of action no one really knew. The procedure permanently screwed up his golf swing. The doctor's cuts beneath his right arm went through rib and muscle and never mended completely. Later, after having been cut open and then stitched right back up again because of a grapefruit-sized tumor, he ended up at the University of Chicago in December 1986 after a subsequent period of treatment in Evanston. The physical examination was notable only for bilateral 2-cm axillary (armpit) lymph nodes. A chest radiograph revealed a large mediastinal mass. Biopsy of this lesion demonstrated an intermediate type of non-Hodgkin's lymphoma known as diffuse large cell lymphoma of the B cell subtype. A further staging workup by his doctors was negative, and Charlie D underwent treatment with methotrexate, doxorubicin, cyclophosphamide, vincristine, prednisone, and bleomycin (MACOP-B).

Dr. Barry Lembersky, now with the University of Pittsburgh Cancer Institute, was the first doctor to treat Charlie D at the University of Chicago. At the time, Charlie D was in good health, with one notable exception. If he hadn't paid a visit to a hospital in Evanston when he had, he might have died in less than a few weeks, or so speculation swirled around the CBOT. It was that serious.

"Our discussions at that point focused on chemotherapy," says Dr. Lembersky. "We discussed how aggressive to be with it. Charlie D approached treatment very much like it was a business deal; he felt that his integrity and competitiveness had served him well in business, and he struck me as wanting to approach his treatment the same way he did trading in the bond pit. He wanted to be aggressive."

Dr. Lembersky put Charlie D on the most aggressive chemotherapy protocol that existed at the time, MACOP-B. The six drugs that make up this treatment were given to him over a period of 12 weeks, Charlie D going into the hospital for treatment every Friday evening. Before going in, he would eat an enormous portion of macaroni and cheese, which helped him cope with extreme nausea soon after the chemicals were dripped into his blood stream through a catheter. It wouldn't stop him from trading. He ordered a flak jacket similar to the one worn by Houston Oilers quarterback Dan Pastorini to protect his ribs from other traders in the pit, and stood on the bond pit's top step just as he always had. By the time Lembersky left the University of Chicago in June 1987, Charlie D showed all the signs of being in complete remission. "I think he felt he was cured," says Dr. Lembersky.

It wasn't as if there weren't moments during this period that Charlie D might have felt better off dead. His brother John remembers trailing him like a spy a couple of times, only to see him puke in a parking lot behind the Museum of Science and Industry. It wasn't Charlie D's style to complain, or to make public his bad days. The world, other traders in the pit, saw the same man, albeit without hair. He could see the shock in their faces when he'd pull a patch of hair from his head just like it was a clump of grass, and drop it into their palm. He may have felt like crying, but somehow decided it was better to laugh instead.

Charlie D responded well to the chemotherapy and then received 4000-rad radiotherapy to the chest to kill off any residual malignant tumor not killed by the chemotherapy. He responded well until November 1987, when he developed a right upper quadrant pain and fever felt to be consistent with cholecystitis (inflammation of the gall bladder). Complications of this sort are a way of life for many lymphoma patients undergoing chemotherapy and radiotherapy. A laparotomy revealed a normal gallbladder without gallstones; a single nodule of recurrent large cell lymphoma obstructed Charlie D's common bile duct. Less than one year after chemotherapy and radiation, the cancer was back. The tumor nodule was resected (cut or pared off) and Charlie D once again received 4400-rad radiotherapy to the porta hepatis, the area of the abdomen just below the liver where the common bile duct drains into the intestines.

A second recurrence of the tumor was documented in August 1988, when an enlarging nodule was discovered in the right upper lobe of the lung on chest radiography. He was again treated with local radiotherapy. The situation became more complex as time passed, as it frequently does for lymphoma patients, and Charlie D was no exception. But he never lost his sense of humor. Sometimes when he went behind closed doors for more tests, he would let out a bloodcurdling primal scream to dramatize the moment. The other cancer patients in the waiting room outside must have been perplexed when he later emerged from behind closed doors with a smile. Can't you take a joke, he seemed to be saying, when the seriousness of the doctors and the cancer became too much of a downer. Yes, the doctors and some of Charlie's bond-trading friends had to laugh, but they also had to ask him to stop his pranks. It unnerved some of the interns and residents. Life moved slowly in the hospital and sometimes Charlie D didn't have the patience to wait. Not even a doctor in an austere white coat could tell a bond trader who wore a more colorful jacket what to do. The pranks never stopped completely.

What was Charlie D's frame of mind? According to Dr. Olopade, who cared for him during the toughest part of his illness, he clearly wasn't within the statistical 47 percent of those diagnosed with cancer who have a level of distress equivalent to that seen in a true psychiatric disorder. He seemed to exhibit little of the anxiety or depression, or combination of the two, that manifest themselves in a high percentage of cancer patients. He simply refused to let his life change, unlike many victims who often need professional assistance when their emotional state interferes with their medical care. Charlie D's mindset defied explanation. And, in reality, the doctors didn't mind hearing a few good jokes in the hematology/oncology clinic. Charlie D the stand-up added much needed levity to what they saw daily.

"Charlie was a model patient," says Dr. Olopade. "He was never down. He dealt with all the problems associated with his illness with both optimism and courage. Deep down, I think Charlie knew that his illness was serious. But he always approached it from the perspective of what treatment would allow him to maintain the quality of his life for as long as possible, not prevent him from dying. After some of his treatments, I can remember coming to the hospital on Monday to see how he was doing. Many times he had already left to go trade the opening, sometimes against our wishes. That was truly amazing, given the potency of some of his treatments. I can't say we always approved, but it was something we learned to adapt to."

The doctors knew statistically that Charlie D was far from out of the woods, even when he was in remission in 1987. "We had discussions with him at the time," says Dr. Lembersky. "The chemotherapy protocol that he was on had a curative rate at the time of somewhere around 30 to 40 percent. Although he was in remission, we advised him that at that time he may want to go directly into a bone marrow transplant combined with an even higher dose of chemotherapy."

As in the bond pit, this decision had to be made with less than perfect information. This experimental treatment was so new that even the doctors couldn't really be precise about the odds that it might work. In a nutshell, a bone marrow transplant uses very high doses of chemotherapy to kill resistant lymphoma cells in the body; these high doses, however, destroy most of the body's bone marrow.

To replace bone marrow, marrow is taken from a patient's bones before treatment and treated with drugs or other substances to kill the cancer cells. The marrow is then frozen, and the patient is given high-dose chemotherapy with or without radiation therapy to destroy all of the remaining cancer cells. The marrow that was removed is then thawed and given back to the patient through a needle in a vein to replace the marrow that was destroyed. This type of transplant is called an *autologous* transplant. If the marrow the patient is given is taken from another person, the transplant is called an *allogeneic* transplant. This can work as well, but the patient can potentially be threatened with infections and complications caused by his body's unwillingness to accept the donor's marrow.

The treatment decision for Charlie D was an extremely difficult one. It made the noise in the bond pit sound like the banter of a few intellectuals in a coffee shop, leisurely debating the meaning of life. According to clinical research being released in Europe in 1997, Dr. Lembersky estimates that the new, more experimental regimen has the potential to increase one's curative chances by 20 percent. But that claim could not be made in the late 1980s when the treatment was still quite new. It was just something better than 0 percent odds if the lymphoma came back. The flip side of this new chemotherapy regimen done in tandem with a bone marrow transplant was that the toxicity associated with the chemo had been known to kill patients before the body could recover. The doctors could make no promises about its curative possibilities. "It was a very high dose of chemotherapy," explained Dr. Lembersky, "a dose that was some eight times greater than the protocol that he had just been through."

According to Charlie D's doctors, he approached his decision seemingly with optimism and calculated care—his strategy in the bond pit also. But this wasn't a question about buying or selling. It was about how much time he might have to live and the quality of his life.

Dr. Lembersky talked to Charlie a couple of times from Pittsburgh in 1987 to see how he was doing, and he heard the optimism in Charlie's voice. The other doctors certainly tried to temper his initial positive responses to treatment with the realities of his illness, and the probabilities that it might return.

"I think he thought he was cured at that time," says Dr. Lembersky. "He thought perhaps he was part of the lucky percentage of patients who are cured, and why wouldn't he be? He struck me as someone who had this invincibility—a guy who never lost at anything. On the other hand, when it came right down to the final decision, I don't think he felt he could take that very high dose of chemotherapy. I think he had tested reality with his first chemotherapy treatment, and it had been the most difficult thing in his life. We had discussions with him. We told him that the odds were that he would have a recurrence sometime down the road. In all fairness to Charlie, none of us knew whether this new regimen would improve his odds. The side effects from his earlier treatment—nausea, vomiting, infections, hair loss—were difficult for any patient to cope with. I think he felt that a dose eight times larger might impair the quality of life he felt he still had. These are very difficult things for a doctor to try to discuss with any patient. But I would describe Charlie as extremely well informed at the time he made his decision, notwithstanding the investigational nature of bone marrow transplantation in 1987."

"The upfront mortality and toxicity associated with this treatment was just too high for him," says Dr. Olopade. "At the time he was making his decision, we had a number of patients with horrendous toxicity. It was a very tough procedure to go through."

Dr. Moormeier and Dr. Olopade watched over Charlie D as the critical period in his illness unfolded. Charlie D decided against the bone marrow transplant. Dr. Olopade met with Charlie D in May 1990 to discuss some X rays they had taken to monitor his situation. "From this first day I met him," says Dr. Olopade, "he just had this wonderful sense of humor. He came after regular clinic hours, after trading that day, so Dr. Moormeier had asked me to cover for her since she could not be there at that time. It was as if we had known each other for a very long time. He said, 'Just don't give me any bad news.' "

Dr. Olopade did not know how to candy-coat matters. She discussed the X rays with the same directness Charlie D expected from all his doctors, telling him exactly what she now saw as an umpire in the field. "It's not really my call," said Dr. Olopade. "I don't manufacture what appears on the X rays.

"Because I was a new doctor for him at the time, I think he felt we could sort of negotiate how the X ray would turn out. There's nothing I can do about the X ray, I told him. Even though I knew what was going on, he wanted me to say, maybe it's alright; maybe it's just scarring. But based on what we saw, I told him his cancer was recurring. He was very animated, full of life at that meeting. He was extremely brave and never once seemed to be afraid of dying, but he also knew what was going on. That's why from that day on I treated him like I've never treated any other patient in my life before."

Dr. Olopade did not see the extended denial that she saw in other patients, or the distress. "So many patients start with the supposition that everything is coming apart when they hear that type of news. But Charlie was different. He asked me to take care of his problem as best we could, and to do it within the framework of his schedule. 'I don't care whatever you do, as long as it fits my schedule. I want to work every day, to trade, so I can give you a day or two—my weekends. But that's about it.' At that point, we knew that if someone had multiple recurrences, odds were we couldn't cure them. So it was a question then of how we could help him lead the best life he could lead, given all the circumstances and his desire to live his life to its fullest."

Charlie D was not looking for miracles. "He made it clear that he wasn't going to be treated at all costs; to live at all cost to the quality of his life," says Dr. Olopade. " 'I want to live, but I want to live how I want to live,' he told me. 'And if that means I die sooner than you doctors want me to, well, that's OK by me.' That's how things really went with him."

Charlie D did not fall apart with self-pity. His life with his illness, if possible, was almost identical to his life without it. One weekend he'd go to Doral to play golf with his son Jake and his neighbors, delaying his chemotherapy until Monday. Dr. Olopade learned to appreciate what life meant to him, and took a step back, smiling when he showed up on a Monday, unannounced and ready to be treated. She learned to go with the Charlie D flow.

Dr. Moormeier's research continued. A few years later, the U of C medical research paper lumped the DiFrancescas together by reporting on their attempts to explore the genetic predisposition of each family member, zooming in on the fragile sites on their chromosomes that they may or may not have in common with the general population. It was a genetic study of the family that led the doctors to write: "Examination of the distribution of common fragile sites expressed in the members of this family revealed a similar pattern to that noted in the control population. This suggests that the high level of common fragile site expression did not predispose all three affected family members to a specific chromosomal rearrangement, but rather, may be simply an indicator of possible sensitivity to a wide range of mutagens. Finally, the temporal clustering of malignancy in this family raises the question of whether common exposure to an environmental mutagen acting on a background of a familial sensitivity to mutagenic damage played a role in the development of the lymphoproliferative malignant diseases noted in these patients." In other words, the fact that all their related cancers happened in such a short time was hard to explain purely due to poor family genetics.

It was a question no one could answer. The DiFrancesca family as a whole, and each family member individually, were simply trying to overcome their illnesses and get on with their lives as research for this paper continued. The first sign of Charlie D's indomitable and competitive will to go forward came after he ended up in the hospital and underwent his first round of chemotherapy. John and his girlfriend Lynn decided on a Friday that July to get married on a Sunday, so Charlie could stand in the wedding as best man. They really didn't care whether the wedding was in a hospital room or church. Sicker than a dog, dehydrated and inflicted with the constant aftertaste of chemo, Charlie D made sure the ceremony was at a church, standing next to John at the ceremony wearing a white corsage his wife had pinned to his lapel. He was too sick to do much more than show up. Photos of the two brothers were shot with each pointing at the spot of each other's "problems" under their suits.

It wouldn't be long before Charlie D was coming to the pit without any hair, covering his head with a baseball cap. The cap ultimately came off to a cheer in the bond pit, and the trading bell rang. Charlie D was at it again, trading with the same zeal and charisma that had defined his trading, whether he was healthy or sick, with hair or without. If you were in the bond pit trading against him, this was no time to trade with him out of sympathy. If you did so, he happily took the edge you gave him, emptied your pockets, and left you standing there sick to your stomach as the market passed you by. He didn't want any tears; he just wanted another opportunity to compete, day after day, as he always had. If he had ever taken anything for granted, he certainly did not now.

During this time Charlie D traveled—sometimes to the Doral Resort in Florida, sometimes to the Desert Inn in Las Vegas, sometimes to his summer cabin in Michigan with his wife and kids, and sometimes on a canoeing or camping trip with friends like Tom Gallagher and Kirk Delzer to Wisconsin. But it would be the Desert Inn, with the monographed DI on the handles of the hotel doors, that became his favorite refuge from the pressures of his illness and treatment—a place to socialize with a cadre of family and friends who would join him for a weekend. Somewhere in the midst of his battle with cancer, Charlie D befriended market analyst Tom DeMark during one of his many jaunts to Las Vegas.

On one such trip in 1988, DeMark was at the Desert Inn's cashier's cage on the casino floor making arrangements to schedule a flight back home. DeMark was accustomed to rolling the dice or playing a hand of blackjack for up to $1500, but the player behind a stack of chips on a blackjack table caught his attention. These were chip colors he did not often see piled on the green felt table. The guy pressing one between his index finger and thumb was obviously no ordinary risk-taker. He slid another one into the yellow betting circle.

"I had no idea who this guy was," says DeMark. "I saw this big guy wearing shorts with this bald head and bloated face. He looked to have something like $10,000, $20,000, maybe $30,000 at the table. I didn't know what some of those chips were, so I asked a stickman at the craps table. He told me $1000. This guy just kept raising the stakes at certain times in the game, so I had to stop and watch."

DeMark stood mesmerized as Charlie D's wife Ann kissed him and headed off somewhere else in the resort; but Charlie's eyes never turned from the game at hand. It was not always easy for an outside observer to comprehend the way Charlie D traded in the bond pit, or the way he played the gaming tables on the casino floor. His unit size, in either place, was simply a function of his competitiveness and confidence and understanding of the odds. DeMark was intrigued by what he saw in Charlie—a combination of daring and calculation. That Charlie varied his bet size at times suggested to DeMark that he was wagering according to some kind of system. This was a mind who never blindly took on the odds in any situation. Watching him piqued DeMark's lifelong obsession with market statistics and numbers and trends. He asked the man what he did for a living.

"I trade," said Charlie D, the bloated-face man on the stool.

"Where do you trade? The Chicago Board of Trade?" asked DeMark.

"That's right. How did you know?" asked Charlie D as he threw two pink chips worth $1000 in the circle in front of his stool. "Who are you? And what do you do for a living?"

"My name's DeMark. Tom DeMark," he replied, extending a hand to shake. I . . ."

"You're Mr. D-Mark? I thought that was a pseudonym for Deutsche mark. You're a real person, not a currency?"

"Yes, that's DeMark. D-E-M-A-R-K."

"The name's Charlie DiFrancesca. A pleasure to meet you."

The conversation did not last long. DeMark had a plane to catch. The dealer gave Charlie D a chance to cut the cards.

Tom DeMark watched Charlie play a few more hands, his pile of chips growing and shrinking, depending on the play of the cards. He remembered the dealer calling the man "Mr. D" and later being corrected by the man on the stool. "You don't have to call me that. Just call me Charlie." By the time DeMark left, the bald-headed man was a few thousand dollars richer.

"I recall he said he subscribed to my newsletter service," says DeMark. "I thought he was just playing games with me. But he swore he was a subscriber to my service. I had no idea who he was. So I asked around about him and someone I knew from Goldman Sachs told me he was the biggest bond trader on the floor. He also told me he was one of the nicest and had a brother who also traded. But Charlie wasn't talking much that day. I think he was feeling sick."

Approximately two years later, Charlie D and Tom DeMark met again coincidentally. In 1989, however, DeMark saw a man who was thinner, sporting a full head of hair, and looking very healthy. DeMark did a double take when he stumbled upon Charlie D outside the scorer's tent, his spikes scratching the concrete as they wandered into the pro shop. Both men had come to the Desert Inn to play in a Senior Tour pro-am event, compliments of the Desert Inn. DeMark's drive on one of the par-5s caught Charlie D's attention. Charlie D drove his golf cart some 50 yards ahead of his ball and made a comment to one of the pros. They weren't even in the same foursome. When he saw the name on the long-drive stake, he didn't match it with a face.

"This guy's got us all by 50 yards," said Charlie D, his left foot dangling off the side of his golf cart. "But he's also got our pro by at least 20. That's large—some might say Andrew Large." He stabbed the stick back into the ground, driving his cart forward to chase his partner's second shot.

The man whose name was on the long-drive stake and Charlie D crossed paths after the tournament was over. Neither the long-drive winner, DeMark, nor Charlie D remembered the other all that well from their passing encounter before at the blackjack table. But a passion for markets and golf and a fascination with gambling they seemed to have in common. Charlie D invited DeMark and his wife Nancy to join him and his wife Ann for dinner that night at the Portofino, an Italian restaurant on the Desert Inn's second floor, overlooking the hotel's gaming floor. Charlie D especially liked this restaurant because it commanded a view of the floor in a way that was not dissimilar from the way the member's gallery overlooked the trading pits at the Chicago Board of Trade. At dinner, the men discussed the art and science of gambling and, more important, their involvement in the futures markets as trader and market technician. When it came to the bond market, they found they had similar views, even though one analyzed the market from the perspective of an off-the-floor technician while the other screamed and shouted in the pit to make his living.

When it came to gambling, however, they were like oil and water. DeMark liked to go for home runs, playing the hardways bets with long odds more often than not. Every roll of the dice either sent the ball over the fence, or his wager was swept off the table by the stickman. Charlie D, in contrast, tried to put the statistical odds in his favor as much as he could with the first roll, freelancing from there in a nearly infinite number of patterns depending on how the game seemed to be playing out. He always enjoyed himself, but he wasn't whimsically foolish. He led more often than not with the DON'T PASS line, a .01 probability advantage over the gamblers who bet the PASS line. The odds were still in the house's favor, but sometimes Mother Chance moved in his favor, adding up to something sizable. The .01 difference between these two customary opening bets, both offering the house a 1.4 percent advantage, gave him the best chance of winning. If the dice played in his favor, then he might go for the jugular.

"Tommy, it looks like you play the game with the right side of the brain," said Charlie D, "and I play with my left. Let's go see if you can hit one playing craps as far as you hit that golf ball today."

Both men loved the casino floor. Both favored playing the table with Richie the Stickman. Richie and the other Desert Inn boys who ran the craps table began calling this twosome Big D and Little D, for their play at the table. Both men often dominated the table in the eyes of other Desert Inn guests because their bets were typically larger—especially

Charlie D's. Throw in a few bond-trading friends from the Board of Trade and it could become a very fast and entertaining game.

Whether Charlie D won or lost at these games hardly seemed to matter. Within 30 minutes he could drop or gain $30,000 to $60,000 playing blackjack, baccarat, or craps, or sometimes even poker. But no game seemed to hold his attention as much as craps, or provided the same level of entertainment to those who watched or played with him. According to those who experienced them firsthand, these crap games were unparalleled for theatrics and stoutness.

Among the Desert Inn employees who worked the tables, drove limos, cleaned his golf clubs or shined his shoes, Charlie became known as a King Kong George—Las Vegas lingo for a man whose tipping was equally as generous, no matter what happened with the dice or cards. Charlie D's bond-trading friends describe him as a world-class poker player who often took their money on the flight down and gave it back as the "designated tipper," never leaving a penny of it in his own pocket.

While at the Harris Bank, he had gained a reputation for cleaning up in smaller-stake poker games to augment his income. In 1978, he went to Las Vegas for the first time with Harris Bank friend, Tom Young. They sowed their wild oats playing every game under the sun, believing they had a can't-lose system at blackjack that seriously minimized their chances of ever going home broke. After one night at the tables, both young men learned a painful lesson. Charlie lost his last $30 and used a credit card to take out another $100. That $100, fortunately, turned their luck around enough that they could afford a plane ticket home and the luxury of joking about the trip later. The trip hadn't totally been a laughing matter for Charlie D. He would tell friends that losing his last $30 had caused him to lose his cookies that evening at the casino, before he had gotten the nerve back up to plunk down his plastic. It was a story he carried with him to the trading pit, as a reminder of the discipline it took to stand near the fire of money and not be consumed by the flames.

Charlie D was now on the other side of Las Vegas. He wasn't out there playing "systems" with friends like Tom Young, believing he might have the skill to earn some easy money as a professional gambler. He was there to have fun and relax with friends, perhaps sharpening his understanding of probabilities and his own nature as a trader in the process. In the long run, he always felt it would make him more competitive in his real market: the bond pit. No one more closely resembled the ideal poker player—described in Robert J. Hutchinson's *Absolute Beginner's Guide to Gambling* as one who has skill "in observing and understanding human nature, the ability to detect nascent greed or quivering fear welling up in the heart of an opponent"—than Charlie D.

Mark Droegemueller, another successful bond trader who sometimes went with Charlie D to Las Vegas, recalled at least one trip to the Golden Nugget when everyone else went off to see a show. "He got into this game with those types who haven't seen sunshine in about three years," Droegemueller explains. "It's one of those unlimited stakes games and all these guys have about $30,000 sitting in front of them, with $500 and $100 chips stacked into piles. Charlie just looks at me and says, 'My kind of game.' He sits down and loses about $8000 in his first couple of hands, and you see him trying to figure this game out. After a few more hands, he has a breakthrough. He ups a guy $4000, sucks him in deeper, and wins. He looks at us and says with a smile: 'I don't think I'm going to make the show.' By the end of the night, after we've returned from the show, he's up a huge pot against these Amarillo Slim types."

The treks to Las Vegas were about more than distracting himself from the cancer, though. While it was his stoutness at the gaming tables that swirled back to the melee of the bond pit and became a legend unto itself, close friends who made some of these trips claimed that as much quality time was spent off the gaming floor as on. Las Vegas was not just a gambling fest.

"Charlie was on a search at the time," says Johnny Musso, a close friend and fellow trader in the bond pit. "He was on a spiritual quest. People who don't know Charlie any better would be surprised to hear me say this, but that was one of my reasons for going to Las Vegas with him at the time. Inevitably, we had some of our best conversations about spirituality on those trips to Las Vegas. He claimed to be an agnostic. I don't know if that was to raise my feathers and get a reaction out of me."

So why did he bring up issues related to his illness and need for some higher purpose in life at the time?

"Charlie felt comfortable with me," says Musso. "He told me that I didn't wear religion on my sleeve. I told him maybe that was a fault;

maybe I'm not as up-front with my beliefs as I should be. He knew I had deep convictions. And he would challenge you about your faith in God. How could a gracious God kill 5000 people in an earthquake, or how could a Christian God be known by people starving in some part of the world that believed in a different God? He challenged you to explain how a gracious God could be involved in the universe where bad things happen every day. Believe it or not, we had some of our best debates about this in Las Vegas, because he was willing to challenge you. I think we had such a good relationship because he knew he could be honest with me, and that I wasn't necessarily going to judge him. No one had more integrity than Charlie; it was great to just be there with him. I told him you can't have a loving relationship with anybody—including God—that is mandatory to obey. To have a true relationship, you have to have a choice that you can make, or there is no free will in the equation. We used to debate man's condition in relation to God on those trips.

"I will say Charlie had a spiritual thirst and was on a quest that few people knew about or really saw. It was extremely important to him. It was one of his essential desires—a question to try to pursue and answer. I do know that it was in his character and drove the things he did. People who don't believe it have to question what drove him to be so generous and compassionate if that wasn't the case."

Musso's personal stories about Charlie D in Las Vegas were something I hadn't expected to hear, but he wasn't alone in seeing this side to Charlie D outside the bond pit, on the Other Side of Vegas. It is there that I came across Richie the Stickman; Smitty, a Conrad Twitty look-alike who ran the Desert Inn's casino floor; and Bill Barry, vice president of casino marketing at the Desert Inn, who pulled out the eye-catching business card of Jimmy Hoffa's son when we were sharing small talk about Las Vegas during its early years in the 1960s, all of whom attested to Charlie's overwhelming integrity and decency.

My trip to Las Vegas was nothing like Charlie D's trips, but it wasn't hard to see why he liked the Desert Inn casino. Like the bond pit, it offered a floor full of characters. I would awake in room 721 ($35 per night) at the Frontier Hotel and Gambling Hall, just across the Strip from the Desert Inn, for three mornings in October 1996. On my final day in

Las Vegas, the first two spent visiting every location I had been told about by Charlie D's family and friends, I finally had a chance to meet these characters. Good thing, too, as money seemed to be falling through an invisible hole in my pocket.

I awoke to a sunrise shortly before 6 A.M. in which the Frontier Hotel's neon sign glittered red and white against a dark blue sky. From my window, I could see the black elevators outlined by white showlights at the Desert Inn, crawling slowly upward to the top floor of the old part of the hotel, where Charlie D sometimes awoke in the rooms that had once been a temporary home to Howard Hughes. When executives at the hotel tried to kick Hughes out to replace him with some higher rollers around New Year's one year, Barry told me he did not take kindly to the snub. He retaliated by buying the hotel and more of Vegas. Charlie D no doubt found this story amusing. It was not hard from my watchtower at the Frontier to imagine Charlie D across Las Vegas Boulevard, watching the same eternal sunrise turn the sky from behind the mountains a spectrum of colors that finally ended in almost infinite shades of reds and oranges. Night desert shadows faded to disclose a mountain range and a green golf course, the sprinklers squirting the fairways at the Desert Inn resort to keep them moist and lush.

On New Year's Eve in 1991, a few months before his death, Charlie was again at the Desert Inn. He felt at peace. The desert and all its colors seemed timeless and eternal. Charlie was a realist—he knew he was dying, even if he didn't know exactly when. I could understand why this place was a sort of medicine for the mind.

At the Desert Inn, Bill Barry and Curtis Smith showed me the lay of the land and offered their thoughts on why the resort was one of Charlie D's favorite places. They eulogized him in the same way bond traders had—they too could not forget Charlie D.

Rich Lopresto had a special, intimate message about Charlie D he wanted me to hear. Richie the Stickman met me at the Desert Inn, on his day off, wearing a sky blue dress shirt, with white cuffs and collar, and silver suit slacks. The gold jewelry around his neck and the watch he wore were impossible to ignore, as were his black and white wing tips. This was the man who had witnessed Charlie D's trips to Las Vegas perhaps more than any Desert Inn employee or friend. Of course, I thought we'd probably discuss Charlie D's stoutness at the tables; I hardly expected to talk to a man who believed that Charlie D had changed his life forever.

Rich Lopresto had grown up around gambling as the son of a doctor who had taken care of a number of members of a well-known Italian social club in Brooklyn. He worked summers at the club as a kid, thanks to his father's connections, and later made a career in gaming. It was at the craps table that he came to know the true nature of Charlie D.

Rich drove me up and down the strip for miles, first close enough to see the planes taking off from the airport, and then back again within walking distance of the casinos. During that hour-long car ride, he spoke to me of Charlie's mythological risk-taking, but also about his generosity and spirit—traits Rich felt were more meaningful.

The most memorable night at the craps table was a night when the dice were cold. After 20 minutes or so, Charlie was $30,000 down. "That night," says Richie the Stickman, "he made a huge comeback. He turned that loss into a $40,000 gain. We had all made about $10 in tips because it had been such a slow night, and here he's tipping all of us $1000 each. I go over to thank him at the cage, and he ends up tipping us $2000 more. I was so embarrassed. I tried to give it back to him. But he wouldn't take it. You lived off this guy's tips."

Rich also recalled Charlie D losing $10,000 in a matter of minutes another time. Large losses in such a short time sometimes caused casino employees concern; people who lose aren't always the best of sports. But Charlie shocked Lopresto again. "Charlie may have had something like $800 sitting there at the table in front of him," says Rich. "But rather than place another bet or take it with him, he gives it to all of us at the table. Regardless of the outcome of the game Charlie was always generous. I think he figured that we probably needed it more than he did, and he probably considered it beneath him to gamble with such a small amount."

It is not the gambler who Rich remembers most, though, or his big tips. Virtually every time he came to Las Vegas there was a story to tell. On nights when the dice or cards worked in Charlie D's favor, more often than not he would leave something extra on the seat cushions of a limousine on the way to a restaurant or to the airport. What Rich remembers most is Charlie D's concern about him when his luck turned for the worst and he and his son were on the Other Side of Vegas.

Shortly after Labor Day in 1988, Rich's son Matt was swimming at a waterpark called Wet N' Wild just off the Strip. A few days later, he had a seizure and ended up in a Las Vegas hospital with encephalitis, a life-threatening condition. The pressure of that time in the hospital led Rich to experience health problems, pushing him into a deep depression that was equally as debilitating. It was at this low ebb in his own life that Charlie D called and opened his arms to Richie the Stickman and his son.

"There isn't a casino employee who doesn't remember Charlie," says Lopresto. "But this was something different than just money. Charlie knew how bad I was hurting at the time, and he was prepared to do anything he could to make the situation better for Matt and me. This guy had his own battles to fight, and here he's calling me about my problems to make sure that Matt and I were going to be OK. I know I could never pay him back for what he did for me and how he treated me, but I want others to know about the size of this guy's heart. There was absolutely nothing this guy wouldn't do for you if he could. It sounds stupid, but I feel God has put me in this car to tell you that. When Matt and I were down, it was Charlie D making the calls to see how he could help us."

Richie the Stickman and I found ourselves parked in some empty lot along the Strip, staring silently out his Camaro windows as we thought about Charlie D on our own. A ringing cellular phone beneath an armrest broke our pause for reflection.

"Hello. Hey Matt, how are you?" said a father to his son. "Listen, I'm just here now speaking with my friend from Chicago about Charlie D. I'm just going to go show him how Charlie D used to play craps, and then I'll be home to take you out to dinner. Does that sound OK? I'll be home at about 5:30. Love you. Bye."

Fortunately, Matt won the battle with encephalitis. His father and I talked about America's Game, a new company he was starting to run nationwide fantasy sports events. If the company ever flew, he said it was a given that 10 percent was to be donated to charities such as the Make a Wish Foundation. "It's not a company otherwise," he said, "unless it's giving something back." Rich started the white Camaro, drove me back to the Frontier, and taught me a few things about how Charlie D rolled the dice. He said the good news was the Frontier casino was offering 10 times odds, whatever the hell that meant for an amateur gambler like myself, so I just nodded my head. Each of us would pitch in $100 to buy $200 worth of chips to play a game of craps in Charlie D's memory. After downing two burgers and Cokes we hit the craps table.

"Charlie D always bet the DON'T PASS line," says Rich, putting our first $5 bet right where Charlie D put it. "There's about a .01 difference in the odds between betting the PASS and DON'T PASS line. Assuming you can get past the first roll, your odds are a fraction better on the DON'T PASS line. It's the closest thing you can get to the house. . . ." The game is moving faster than the bond pit, and I can't keep up with everything Richie the Stickman is telling me about Charlie D's methods.

Later that evening, I consult the *Amateur's Guide to Gambling* to double-check this fact about the PASS and DON'T PASS line. I discover that what Richie the Stickman was saying was true: If Charlie D bet $5000 a hundred times, this .01 probability edge gave him one more "free" shot with the dice. If you viewed the 1.4 percent advantage of the house as not being so unlike a brokerage commission, that one extra roll might come in handy at some point. At Caesar's Palace the day before, I spent half an hour listening to a craps "instructor" lecture on the benefit of betting the PASS line, without ever mentioning the DON'T PASS line. For what Rich and I were playing for, it hardly made a difference. But, for a risk-taker like Charlie D, it was a free pass for the end zone. You never knew what might happen with one extra roll. As Rich reminded me, the dice have no memory.

I continued to try to follow Rich's mimicking of Charlie D's craps play, but the game moved too fast. My eyes glazed over. I closed my notepad. It was time to enjoy our little craps troika with our silent partner. Next thing I know, Rich bets 10-to-1 on a hard six for the guys running the table. "Charlie D did that for me and the guys all the time," he said. "He'd do it for anyone at the table in the interest of a little fun." A potbellied man in a blue golf shirt rolls the hard six, paying off $50 for the guys running the table.

"Thank you, my friend," says Ronny the Stickman at the Frontier.

"Don't thank me," says Rich. "That's Charlie D."

Over the next four rolls, hardways and craps bets come up big. First it's snake eyes, paying 30-to-1. Then someone rolls craps, a one-two combination, paying 15-to-1.

"Now, if Tom DeMark was here with us, he'd be playing all these types of bets in the center of the table. After these three rolls, he would have just made a fortune and walked away from the table. Of course, Charlie's ribbing him for playing with the right side of his brain. Charlie D very rarely went near those bets with the big odds, unless he was putting a bet down to tip the stickman and other guys on the table, like I just did. He did that all the time for people he didn't even know. Pretty soon the whole table was pulling for him."

The DON'T PASS line, after 20 minutes of play, hasn't worked out that well for Falloon–Lopresto L.P., so Richie the Stickman jumps to the PASS line to shake things up and give me the privilege of rolling the dice. I roll once, not even knowing what number pops up. He bets the odds on the PASS line. Throwing the dice the first couple of times feels awkward, but fun. I remember Coach Graf's story about sending the boxman's chips flying and not even hitting the wall, so I make sure to backhand the dice both times with a little oomph. I roll the dice four or five more times before one of my numbers clears the table. So much for the Virgin Principle, a Las Vegas superstition about first-time rollers bringing good luck. After 45 minutes, we have each lost $45. It is not our night. Not unlike Charlie D in the bond pit, we cut our losses.

At the cashier's cage, I thank Rich for showing me the Other Side of Vegas. "Charlie didn't have a high regard for money," I hear Johnny Musso say in the back of my mind, as Rich is tipping the woman at the cashier's cage. "He used it to have fun, and to let people around him have some fun. He made Las Vegas fun for everyone, rather than sitting there stone-faced at a table, grinding it out. He did it at every game he played in the casino. He would bet a hand to tip the blackjack dealer, so instead of working, this guy would be having some fun. All this side stuff would be going on. If he saw a couple on their honeymoon, betting $3 bets, he'd put a $1000 bonus on whatever they were playing—just to give them a chance at some fun. Once he did that, and put down a bet to tip the boxman, dealers, and stickman, the table came to life. It wasn't before long that everyone was enjoying themselves and pulling for the same thing."

"Thanks Rich, for taking the time . . . ," I say.

"Anything for Charlie," he says.

Rich's look says it all. He pauses for a second, remembering, then gathers himself enough to smile and shake my hand.

As for our silent partner at the Frontier craps table, his final meeting on the Other Side of Vegas with Dr. Olopade came on the heels of his last chemotherapy treatment in March 1991. That New Year's at the Desert Inn, Charlie toasted his wife Ann at the craps table, taking a couple of sips of bubbly. At the meeting at the University of Chicago Medical Center, he and John sat facing each other, sitting on the floor of Dr. Olopade's office with their legs crossed like Indian chiefs. Neither of them said a word as they listened to Dr. Olopade talk about what was ahead. After Dr. Olopade went through all the possibilities, Charlie D looked John in the eye. He saw for a split second all he needed to see. That conversation with Dr. Olopade would have been even tougher if John hadn't been there.

"He had come through that round of chemotherapy well," she says, "but then it started to spread. We had to change plans and do something else. By that time, he was feeling weaker and wasn't doing as well. And he wanted to know what other things could be done. What else is available? We went through everything. But I told him: 'There is no choice left.' At that meeting, he really hurt. He believed to the end that he had the will to beat it. At that meeting, he realized that he was seriously ill, but he wasn't going to let anything get him down."

Charlie D saw Dr. Olopade's pain; it was equal to his own. It was time to move to the Other Side of Vegas. Charlie D challenged his doctor one more time with one of his most famous bets, a bet that funded in part a research paper that Dr. Olopade was preparing to present in Houston a few months later. If she kept him alive until June 1, 1991, he promised to donate another $60,000 to cancer research. If they didn't, it was double or nothing, like it was on the fairways. It was one final competitive challenge Charlie D set for himself: to accept Dr. Olopade's words, but not accept defeat. John and Charlie D looked across Dr. Olopade's desk at each other, the silence defining their bond.

Hey, Dr. Olopade, what rhymes with trouble? Double-Redouble. Charlie D thought about saying this to Dr. Olopade, but his Mona Lisa lips didn't move. He could see that she was hurting as much as he—that his final dress rehearsal, as he called it, had just started.

308 east roberta | 10

On the road to Waukesha: Population 56,985.

Why is it we feel compelled to find answers to life's tragedies? If we have the answer is it really a solution? Will it prevent future deaths, keep tragedy at bay?

Probably not. People will continue to get sick, sometimes unexplainably and without apparent reason. I am not so naive as to believe otherwise.

Yet, ever since first hearing the legend of Charlie D at the Wigwam Resort, I have been haunted by the DiFrancesca house at 308 East Roberta. Through the cigar smoke, I imagined it plucked down Wizard-of-Oz–style in Midwest farm country under streams of high-tension wires. Although first only an idiosyncratic connection the family's cancer tale brought to mind Carson's *Silent Spring* (perhaps brought on by the maternal resemblance between Margaret DiFrancesca and the dust-jacket photo of Rachel Carson with binoculars around her neck).

I first read this book a few years before the DiFrancescas were making their visits to the University of Chicago Hospital and have reread it often when thinking about Charlie and his family. The first page of its opening chapter, "A Fable for Tomorrow," seemed somewhere just beyond the grasp of memory, as was Carson's mythical town, until I

heard about Charlie D and probed his family's story. Driving into
Waukesha, I traveled to a place similar to the one Carson painted with
words, "where all life seemed to live in harmony with its surroundings."
In fact, the page-1, ink-dot drawing of her town in *Silent Spring* was not
so unlike the beautiful one I was visiting with the help of Joy Batha's
map. I wanted to know whether the DiFrancesca family's problems were
genetic and completely unavoidable, or whether unseen environmental
forces may have been at work. If you are a journalist, such as myself,
you feel obligated to investigate.

Often referred to by the DiFrancescas as Forest Lawn Cemetery, not
in deference to their bouts with cancer or Charlie's death, but as a joke
about its landscaping, the bi-level ranch house at 308 East Roberta was
surrounded by an unseemly number of pine trees. Hitting the front door
with a newspaper was a paperboy's worst nightmare; it was impossible to
toss anything through all those trees. The house appeared to be buried
beneath the bulkiness of all those pines.

The room that interested me most was Charlie's: an 11½' by 16' bedroom in the basement. The DiFrancescas never thought twice about the
rarity of their situation until the queries of University of Chicago medical
researchers prompted them to contemplate where and when they had
lived together for an extended period of time. Ever since, the room has
held special significance to the DiFrancesca family in their unscientific
attempts to explain their illnesses, as did the house itself and Waukesha
in general. In Margaret's mind, it was the precise location in which she
and the two boys had spent a considerable amount of time together. If
there was a place to search for environmental mutagens, it was this location to which motherly intuition pointed.

"The fact that the boys and I spent so much time downstairs,"
Margaret's voice echoed as I observed the room, "was the only way we
could explain why we got cancer and Janet and Vince didn't. They spent
far more time upstairs. We have no idea, but that is what we sometimes
think ourselves."

Except for the shag carpet, the room was empty when I inspected it.
Margaret's voice grew fainter. It struck me as ridiculous that I could discover anything in the house.

Just as Vince and Margaret claimed, 308 East Roberta Avenue was a nice family house, situated across the street from Waukesha South High School. When I relayed the Charlie D story about power lines to the grandmotherly woman who owned the house, she said that the floor of the basement family room was heated by underground coils. This might have posed a health problem, with John and Charlie lying there watching TV, just above an enormous electrical blanket buried in the concrete. But the coils were heated by warm water—obviously not hazardous. In short, the house was a house was a house, nothing more.

I looked outside through one of the windows in search of high-tension wires—perhaps rising before me in the backyard. It was certainly not the electromagnetic envelope of death I had imagined. I opened the curtains to a sliding door in the back of the house. As a result of the ground's tilt, it was only Charlie's bedroom that was below ground, two walls surrounded by soil.

The basement had to be checked for radon at one time or another, I presumed. The grandmother said it had never been a problem that she knew of. I left the house with no further suspicions aroused or confirmed, other than the idea that Charlie's room seemed cavernous and tightly sealed, with opaque glass blocks on one wall. Maybe radon was a problem back then, but radon seems to be linked to lung cancer, not lymphoma.

The power-line theory had appealed to me because it fit nicely with another Charlie D legend. Before he died, Charlie had supposedly made one final joyride on a Harley Davidson. I imagined power lines appearing in his rearview mirror one by one as he throttled up past 90 mph on an open stretch of road. In the rolling movie in my mind, planted by the Wigwam broker, I imagined those power lines a symbolic reminder of what had led him down the road to death.

The poetry of this power-line theory jibed with my romantic impression of Wisconsin as an environmentally conscious state. I had been told that Wisconsin had some of the highest environmental standards of all 50 states and I never doubted that it was true. The power-line theory also fit nicely with my reading list. A book written in 1993 by Paul Brodeur, a writer for *The New Yorker*, *The Great Power-Line Cover-Up: How the*

Utilities and the Government Are Trying to Hide the Cancer Hazards Posed by Electromagnetic Fields, was a concrete, reputable source I could point to and say, "See, he told us so."

Brodeur noted that 8 out of 11 childhood residential studies published in peer-reviewed medical literature over the last 15 years demonstrated that children living in homes near high-current or high-voltage power lines were developing cancer at significantly higher rates than children not exposed to such conditions. It was easy to imagine John and Charlie out playing football with Coach Vince in some open field, using these wires as an imaginary boundary to form a football field. But no such lines existed in Waukesha when I visited, and the coaches could not recall their presence in the 1960s either.

Many other theories had been posed about what caused the DiFrancescas' health problems. Charlie D's sister, Janet, suggested that radon levels in Waukesha in the 1980s had been written up as being in excess of the maximum exposure standards set by the Environmental Protection Agency (EPA). I later discovered she meant radium. The town of Waukesha and the EPA had reportedly locked horns over radium levels in the water during Janet's years as a Waukesha resident. Apparently the EPA had proposed a standard that put Waukesha's water above the acceptable safety standard as established in the Clean Water Drinking Act of 1974, potentially forcing the city to spend money to remove the radium before it went into people's homes. This was viewed by many in the town as an unnecessary and potentially expensive proposition, particularly since Waukesha was in the ballpark of complying with the standard anyway. The town's mayor priced water-treatment facilities at a stiff $69 million. And then there was the issue of what to do with the radium once it had been removed—another issue of concern and potential expense. Janet and even Charlie D's coaches recalled this problem causing somewhat of a stink in the local press. All remembered warnings and advisory reports being issued on Waukesha water bills to advise citizens of ways they could cope with this naturally occurring mineral.

Another theory about what may have caused the DiFrancesca family's health problems surfaced at Janet DiFrancesca-Parshall's 15-year high school reunion. In recounting her brothers' and mother's health problems to classmates, she was surprised to hear that others on East Roberta

Avenue had been diagnosed with various forms of cancer. By the time
Janet told this story to me, she couldn't remember the neighbors' names.
It seemed like an interesting list, but not a terribly long one. Janet's husband Craig told Janet about friends who recalled that the DiFrancesca
property on the steeply sloping hill once had been a farmer's chosen
dumping site. After treating his fields with whichever chemicals he may
have used, the excess was dumped on the hill to be washed away by rain,
or so Janet had heard through the grapevine.

At Janet's high school reunion, the stories flew. One neighbor reportedly had brought the issue of a cancer cluster to public health officials,
though no one knew which neighbor it was or when the complaint had
been made. The hearsay had swirled around to create a bona fide urban
myth. Charlie D's high school girlfriend Joy, like Janet, retold a version
of this myth.

"Supposedly this one neighbor in the area was going to get a change
in his insurance after he had been cured of lymphoma. The story was that
he went to collect his personal medical information to disclose to the
insurance company, but found out he could not get access to his own
medical records because some sort of secret investigation was going on. I
think his name was Tom . . . Rickens, something like that. He was
another one who reportedly lived in the Roberta Avenue area." Had any
correspondence ever been written to health officials by Rickens, or
someone else?

While the three members of the DiFrancesca family were sick, it was
not easy to investigate any of these theories. Janet, the only DiFrancesca
living in Waukesha at the time, was busy raising four kids. The other
family members had their own problems, to say the least, keeping one
another upbeat as they all dealt with different cancer treatments. The
DiFrancescas did not want to be hospital laboratory rats any more than
they had to be—particularly once the side effects of their treatments
kicked in. Thus, the contribution that environmental contaminants may
have played in their illness was a theory largely left unanswered in the
research paper written by the University of Chicago pathologists and
doctors.

"At present, we have a poor understanding of the environmental factors that may influence fragile site expression, nor do we know the dura-

tion of alterations in fragile site expression that may result from such factors," said the doctors in their May 1991 paper about the DiFrancescas. "With respect to the family that we have examined, there is no documented history of environmental exposure to mutagenic agents. . . . The role of environmental factors versus genetic factors could, in part, be addressed by an evaluation of fragile site expression in spouses of the siblings of our family, and in siblings of the father. Unfortunately, these individuals were not available for such an evaluation."

This unexplored conclusion was one more reason I returned to Waukesha. Never were my conspiratorial theories and personal biases of Waukesha more urgent to me than during a chance encounter at the Waukesha Historical Museum. Charlie's coaches had mentioned to me the same health notices about naturally occurring radium in the water, so perhaps the museum might have an exhibit about water.

Coach Hollub had sent me some old brochures and pamphlets stuffed in his files, along with his water bills. One of these brochures was a laundry list of one-line fun facts published by the American Water Works Association in Denver, Colorado. This trifold pamphlet was entitled "25 Facts about Water." Facts 2, 13, and 25 primed my pump. I thought of all the possible things that might have leached into the DiFrancescas' water supply.

Fact 2 was shocking: "In 1989, Americans dumped 365 million gallons of motor oil, or the equivalent of 27 Exxon Valdez spills." So was unlucky 13: "Industries released 197 million pounds of toxic chemicals into waterways in 1990 alone." The final fact that caught my attention, number 25, made me wonder about one teeny-weeny gallon of anything being mixed up with our water supply. "One gallon of gasoline can contaminate approximately 750,000 gallons of drinking water," it claimed matter-of-factly. Did the DiFrancescas drink anything like this, unknowingly, for extended periods of time?

The possibilities for water contamination were many and varied. I imagined Chuck, Blackshirt helmet under the arm, gulping water after a football practice at a bubbler near the field. If anyone had a passion for water, it was high school jocks like Chuck, John, and their buddies.

It was time to learn a bit more about Waukesha's water supply. One of Coach Hollub's pamphlets, entitled "How Safe is Waukesha Water?," was dated August 29, 1989. It turned out to be a curious read. On the front cover, it said with institutional confidence: "The Waukesha Water Utility furnishes safe and high-quality water for home, commercial, and industrial use." Inside, this trifold brochure explained that "Waukesha water is drawn daily from a deep sandstone aquifer which lies under much of south and central Wisconsin, eastern and northern Illinois and extends into northern Indiana, Iowa, northern Missouri and southeastern Minnesota." It informed me that "most water drawn by Waukesha enters the aquifer in western Waukesha and Jefferson counties, after being filtered through miles of sandstone before reaching Waukesha's ten deep municipal wells." This filtering process generally made the water that reached the tap in any home a hard water rich in natural minerals, including iron, which gave it a distinctive reddish or brownish discoloration.

The brochure hinted at the radium issue that had surfaced at Janet's high school reunion and indicated that it was being addressed: "A low level of natural radium was recently identified as being potentially hazardous. While there is no immediate threat to life or health, the Utility is in violation of the EPA's proposed standard. The Utility has agreed with the Wisconsin Department of Natural Resources to follow a prescribed schedule in meeting their standard."

Surely the problem had been resolved, I thought. After all, this was 1996, not 1989, the year the brochure was apparently released.

Reading further, I found a section called "Future Concerns" that was even more distressing. On a little hand-drawn map, tiny pictures and arrows—labeled pesticides, herbicides, fertilizers; acid rain; chemical spill; road salt; and landfill—were resting above a thick crisscross set of lines labeled top soil, limestone, and dolomite. This little diagram was a pictorial island surrounded by written text that hardly put my mind at rest.

The quality of Waukesha water is protected by a generally impermeable layer of shale. This layer is located between water contained in dolomite rocks and sand and gravel deposits (on the top) and water contained in sandstone (on the bottom). The layer of shale inhibits flow of shallow ground water and contaminants from moving into the deep sandstone which is Waukesha's water source. There is no guaranty that the future supply of water will remain unspoiled. The Utility will respond to the evidence of ground water pollution with appropriate treatment devices or well abandonment and substitution.

It was quite impressive to see such an enormous potential problem encapsulated in a mere five sentences complete with a helpful picture. And, admittedly, a journalist equipped with so little information is a bit like a loaded gun. Upon entering the Waukesha Historical Museum, I discovered a lecture was about to take place on one of the subjects I hoped to investigate further. I had happened upon a slide presentation made by Mrs. Marilyn Hagerstrand, a local historian and antique collector. Her speech that day, entitled "Dunbar's Great Discovery: Waukesha Springs Era," was an absolute pleasure. I decided that perhaps Mrs. Hagerstrand might be able to answer my questions about Waukesha's water supply.

"I'm curious about the possibility that Waukesha's water supply is polluted. I know you are about to make a presentation on the natural springs of Waukesha and their historical significance to the community, but I'm wondering if you know anything about the drinkability and safety of Waukesha's water drawn from the city's municipal wells today."

Marilyn and her husband Milt were polite. But after that question, they looked askance. In the few minutes they had before the lecture was to begin, they explained that the city's water no longer came from natural springs. It poured from deep underground wells that, as far as they knew, were safe and pure.

Waukesha claimed a rich past when it came to natural spring water. Crystal clear water used to just bubble to the ground's surface, ready for drinking, almost everywhere nearby. The Waukesha city streets converge at a location known as the Five Points, where a replica springhouse stands as a nostalgic reminder of the purity of the town's natural spring waters.

Waukesha's reputation for its spring waters began in 1868, although Indians had known about them for years. At that time, a gentleman named Colonel Richard Dunbar, who was ill with diabetes, came to

Waukesha and discovered their "healing effects." Despite his infirmity, he had come to town to attend the funeral of his wife's mother. On that trip he built up such a thirst that he stopped beside a spring on a carriage ride across his sister-in-law's farm. Over that day, he drank approximately 12 glasses from the spring. "I felt then," he later said, "and expressed the opinion there was something wonderful in the water, as I felt it working a great change for me." He returned from New York the next year, suffering from the same poor health. Again he found his health restored, drinking from the same natural spring. So moved was Dunbar by this experience that he claimed the water had healing powers and began to bottle it on a national scale. Five springs on Dunbar's property bubbled drinking water to the surface; he filled in four and left his favorite open for business, dubbing his spring "Bethesda."

Dunbar soon had followers. Resorts sprang up and Waukesha became known as the Saratoga of the West. Business in water boomed. For the next four decades, people from all over the country, including Mrs. Abraham Lincoln and President Ulysses S. Grant, came to the plush resorts to vacation and drink the miracle water. So did Chicagoans by the trainload. As many as 25 trains a day left for Waukesha.

Dunbar began shipping barrels of the water throughout the United States, beautifying the grounds around the Bethesda Spring and intending to build his own resort hotel. In 1871, the cornerstone for that resort hotel was laid by U.S. Supreme Court Chief Justice Salmon P. Chase, who claimed that his health was improved with Bethesda water. The hotel was never built, although Dunbar remained in Waukesha and promoted the Bethesda Spring until his sudden death from a heart attack in 1878.

Waukesha's nostalgia for pure spring water has never really died. Nor has the belief that its purity was more than a half-truth. Mrs. Hagerstrand's lecture and the words of Joseph E. Ryan in the Special Springs Summer/Autumn 1992 issue of *Landmark* are testament to this belief. "As a long-term Pewaukeean," wrote Ryan, "I think there was something to that spring water. We base our conclusion not on science, but on a healthy respect for aboriginal intuition. . . . There should be a special hell for those who destroy illusions. We'll take Colonel Dunbar and the Indians . . . [and m]ost of all . . . a swig with the marshy taste of our own now vanished spring. Perhaps because our youth and hopes lie back there, we set high values on 'uncut' materials."

Joy and Joe, her biologist husband, dispelled the notion that Waukesha's water was the DiFrancescas' problem. Joe's reasoning made sense. He explained that the recharge area for Waukesha's water supply was actually in Jefferson County, west of town. That water supply was drawn from municipal wells 1300 to 1800 feet below ground level, going through many layers of sandstone and limestone. He suggested that people such as he and Joy, who drank from shallower private wells, were more at risk. Drinking water drawn from private wells as little as 150 to 200 feet below the surface was potentially more vulnerable to pollutants. While pollutants such as pesticides and herbicides may contaminate shallower private wells, the city water supply was constantly monitored and safe to drink. "We don't drink a lot of groundwater that actually comes from here," he explained. "Groundwater is so strange because it can go up and down and all around, depending on the natural geography of the soil. Just because we live up here on this hill, for example, we can't assume that the water in our well is safer than the water of someone living in a lower area. Pressure underneath the soil can push water up. It's not like an underground river; groundwater moves all over the place."

For another perspective on Waukesha water, Joe suggested Ellen Langill and Jean Penn Loerke's book, *From Farmland to Freeways*, a history of Waukesha County. He said this book could provide better answers to my questions about water and potential pollutants in Waukesha. Joy also seemed skeptical about most of my theories about what caused the DiFrancescas' illnesses. She knew that the old Roberta Avenue neighborhood had always been on municipal water. That eliminated the possibility that the DiFrancescas drank from a fertilizer-contaminated well before it was detected.

Joy did not dismiss my theories completely, however. She had attended the same high school reunion as Janet. If you were a former neighbor of the DiFrancescas, it was natural to listen to any ideas about what caused their cancer. I told her that University of Chicago doctors had at least explored the idea of the DiFrancescas' exposure to some harmful environmental mutagens.

Joy recalled the names of some neighbors in the immediate vicinity of her parent's house who also suffered or died from various forms of cancer. First there was her father, who had been diagnosed with colon cancer. There was Mrs. Carlson, who had been diagnosed with breast cancer. There were Wayne and Theresa Meehan. Wayne had been diagnosed with colon cancer and his wife Theresa with breast cancer in the 1980s. She remembered Tim Vrakas, the son of Waukesha's mayor, who had died from leukemia. She promised to send more names to me later. A subsequent letter from her included Mike Gross who had died of leukemia. Another kid, Tom Bertacchini, had been diagnosed with Hodgkin's lymphoma. Joy recalled that he had been the one who was the subject of the town's urban myth, not someone named Tom Rickens. She wasn't sure if he was still alive or not. A few days later, Joy mailed off another list of names, adding five more to the count. But the details were sketchy. Her addendum list read: "Mr. & Mrs. Linderude? (deceased); Mr. Robert Younger (deceased); Dr. Brent Behrens; Mrs. Ralph North? (deceased); and Mrs. Don Stouffer (deceased)."

As more names came from Joy, I didn't know what to think. I started calling some of the neighbors she named. The first to call me back was Bobbie Bertacchini, the mother of Tom, the urban myth. I told her the DiFrancescas' story, and she told me the story about her son, who had been diagnosed with Hodgkin's lymphoma at the age of 14. Thankfully, he was alive and living up north somewhere.

Bobbie recounted more families affected by the big "C" in the DiFrancescas' old neighborhood. My list grew longer and became more detailed. Bobbie provided the names and phone numbers of five other neighbors, some of whom were on Joy's list. I later discovered that many of those who had been diagnosed with cancer, like her son, had types similar to the three DiFrancescas.

Many from Bobbie's generation felt suspicious that the neighborhood had more than its fair share of cancer, but life was simply moving too fast for any of them to sit down and think about the past. I suggested we team up. With the help of 10 other neighbors we rounded up, including Joy, Margaret, and Bobbie, in less than four weeks we came up with 80 cancer diagnoses within a few-block area surrounding the old DiFrancesca house. As we had agreed, we sent the information off to the Wisconsin Department of Health.

During those weeks of research, I called Linda Knobeloch, a toxicologist at the Wisconsin Department of Health and Family Services in Madison, Wisconsin. Linda passed me to Beth Fiore, an epidemiologist with the Bureau of Public Health. I asked Beth questions about a possible cancer cluster. I inquired whether she had ever received any other queries or correspondence from neighbors in the East Roberta Avenue area. The thought crossed my mind that she might know about the letter that had supposedly been sent by a neighbor years ago, asking about a possible cancer cluster in the neighborhood. Beth searched the files and informed me that nothing had been reported, based on records going back to 1990. When I suggested that she check further back into the 1980s, she renewed her search. This time she came up with two letters from a man whom she could not publicly identify.

When Beth said she could only send me the Bureau of Public Health's reply letter to this Mr. X, I became incensed. She had just told me that the Bureau of Public Health was reliant on concerned public citizens to gather information related to potential cancer clusters, but a wall was going up. Why waste time making me duplicate work? Beth snapped back that I "knew nothing about cancer clusters." To hit home the point, she added rhetorically: "Don't you know that 30 percent of us will be affected by some type of cancer over the period of our lives?"

Beth was right; she knew far more than I ever would, and that is what made me feel helpless and angry. I fired off a letter requesting additional public health records and the letter from Mr. X under the Wisconsin state "open records" statute. My first request was denied for statutory reasons. I was informed that the Bureau of Public Health was following Wisconsin public disclosure law in denying my request. A week or so later, Beth's correspondence to Mr. X arrived, the date curiously missing. As I read Beth's cover letter, it seemed to contradict what I had come to believe, issuing me an indirect challenge: ". . . the type of cancers identified at this site in 1986–1989 were not attributable to a common cause. It was, therefore, determined that this site was not a cluster. If you feel you have additional evidence of cancer cases which may be linked to a common cause, such as a carcinogen (a cancer-causing substance) in the environment, we encourage you to report the findings to the State of Wisconsin."

I didn't have a common cause. But the "cancer" map Bobbie and I worked on seemed frightening. The penciled-in dots blanketed the streets near East Roberta almost as well as the pine trees in front of the DiFrancescas' old house. I sent another "open records" request, this time making it clear that I was requesting Mr. X's correspondence and not public health records.

That second letter turned out to be both therapeutic and frightening. While the letter's author could not be legally disclosed by the Bureau of Public Health, I suspected that it had been written by Wayne Meehan. Ms. Fiore, in our first conversation, told me it had been written by a man on the 1300 block of East Roberta. The address matched an address on Bobbie's cancer cluster list. I now also had a clearer picture of why it hadn't been sent the first time. Mr. X's first letter, dated January 7, 1985, had never been replied to by the Waukesha County Health Department—an obvious embarrassment.

As a result, his second letter had been sent to the Wisconsin Division of Health, along with the first. Ms. Fiore promptly replied to Mr. X's letter, dated April 28, 1989, to the Wisconsin Department of Health. In Mr. X's memory, particularly since his first letter was "lost," I present portions of the text of Mr. X's original correspondence.

Dear Sir:

My wife, [name deleted], and I were residents of Waukesha from November, 1959 to July, 1979, during which time we resided at [address deleted]. In 1975 our good neighbor, [name deleted], died of cancer of the pancreas. . . .

In 1982 we learned that both [name deleted] and [name deleted] had both undergone surgery for cancer. . . .

During a routine physical exam in late Dec., 1983, we learned that [name deleted] had a malignant tumor. . . . In May last year I began to pass blood in my urine and after a series of exams it was determined that I had a malignant tumor in my left kidney. . . .

We know of others in that area who also developed cancer. [Name deleted], who lived behind us on [street deleted], had leukemia which was in remission some time before they moved elsewhere, [name deleted] had a mastectomy, and [name deleted] died recently of cancer of the ovaries. We have heard recently of others in the area, some much younger than we, who have developed cancer. . . .

My reasons for writing this letter is to bring to your attention the curious fact of so much cancer in that small area of Waukesha and to wonder if you might have an answer. Speaking for [name(s) deleted] and ourselves, none of us ever smoked and the use of alcohol was minimal if at all. The one thing we had in common was a garden and during our lives we did our share of removing paint and refinishing various items. [Name deleted] smoked an occasional cigar.

Almost every week or so reports are issued about how doing this or eating that or not doing this or not eating that will result in getting cancer in one type or another and what is always so disturbing to us is that in all cases we have been acting and eating properly. So what caused the cancer? Were all the foundries a factor? Was there something in the soil or in the air which contaminated the food we raised in our gardens? How about the air we breathed? What about cancer elsewhere in Waukesha?

Perhaps you have already studied this situation and have arrived at a conclusion which you can tell us about. We trust you will keep us informed.

Very truly yours,

[name deleted]

Mr. X followed up this letter four years later. He wrote to the Wisconsin Division of Health.

Dear Sir or Madam,

After reading an article in the April, 1989, issue of *Wisconsin Natural Resources* on the subject of potential cancer clusters I want to send you a copy of a letter I wrote to the Waukesha County Health Department on January 7, 1985. When I spoke to them later in person none remembered having received the letter or could find a copy in the files. It was discouraging as I imagine everyone would like to know how or why he got cancer. . . .

Shortly after the letter was written [name deleted] died. We moved away in [date deleted], so cannot provide any information regarding any other individuals who reside or resided in that neighborhood.

I would appreciate it if you would not throw this letter away as the Waukesha County Health Department apparently did. It was a shock to learn that something which killed three clean living individuals and affected the lives of several others did not deserve more consideration. . . .
Respectfully yours,
[Name deleted]

In total, Mr. X had identified 8 neighbors with cancer. The cancers he reported occurred over a nine-year period from 1975 to 1984. He reported breast (3), colon (1), kidney (1), leukemia (1), ovarian (1), and pancreatic (1) cancers. To its credit, the Wisconsin Bureau of Public Health responded intelligently in 1989, unlike the Waukesha County Health Department. Beth's letter to him was both thoughtful and educational, responding to the facts as they were then known:

"A true cluster caused by a carcinogen (a cancer-causing substance) in the environment usually results in a higher risk for only one or two different types of cancer. If a suspected cluster includes many different types of cancer, it's almost certainly not a true cluster and cannot be attributed to one toxic substance present in the environment. The apparent cluster described in your letter includes six different types of cancer. This means that the situation you describe in that neighborhood of Waukesha would almost certainly not be a true cluster of cancer caused by one common type of pollution in the environment."

Beth and I are in agreement on some key points: It is difficult to know if this is a cancer cluster, or if it was caused by one specific carcinogen. Like her, I also know it probably isn't a good idea to report a cancer cluster that isn't one. Why falsely scare the public? I do *not* know if Waukesha has anything to worry about, but I believe there existed in Waukesha a number of possible carcinogens that could have contributed to a high incidence of many types of cancer in the East Roberta neighborhood.

It is the story of the DiFrancescas and other neighbors that health officials must consider. Whatever the Bureau of Public Health decides to do with the information we've provided, neighbors in this area deserve some intelligently researched answers. More than one long-time

Waukesha resident believes that research needs to be done. Remarked one neighbor: "I received your package & am amazed at all of the cancers in this area plus the 'fingers' that go off these streets we have mentioned. Thank you again for drawing this to the attention of the health authorities."

So what might the environmental mutagen or mutagens have been? *From Farmland to Freeways* had some useful answers. Around the time the DiFrancescas moved into Waukesha, a great shift in population and land use occurred between 1950 and 1970. Suburban living, supported by a healthy economy, automobiles, and highways, turned low-cost farmland into real estate development projects. The population of Waukesha County jumped from 85,901 in 1950 to 231,334 in 1970, up 169 percent.

During that time, farmland such as that on which the DiFrancescas and other neighbors built their houses diminished. The number of farms in the county dropped 60 percent by 1969. Seitz's pasture disappeared to the south of the DiFrancesca house and became a high school, and Downing's farm to the north became streets lined with houses.

The outcome of this changeover was uncertain but potentially dangerous. "Development has moved faster than knowledge of its real costs to individuals and to society," editorialized *From Farmland to Freeways*. "If left alone, problems would worsen. Clearly there was a need for some control over haphazard land use and an attempt to balance the rights of the landowner with the needs of society. People were learning the hard way that no one individual's manipulation of the environment stands alone but that the ramifications of individual acts could and would affect others not only immediately but also for years to come."

One Waukesha resident who saw this confluence of factors rolling over the DiFrancescas' old neighborhood in the 1960s and 1970s was Bobbie Bertacchini's friend, Bob Schuett. A farmer turned real estate developer in the area, he watched as many of the houses in the area were built on Downing's farm and Seitz's pasture. Schuett recalls that Downing's farm was approximately 120 acres and rotated crops. It was not uncommon for the land to be planted with 40 acres of strawberries, 40 acres of alfalfa, and 40 acres of corn.

"Atrazine was about the first chemical we used in this area as farmers," he recalls. "It killed everything but the corn. We started using it around 1960." While Schuett cannot quantify what volumes of atrazine were sprayed on crops at the time, he adds that "the pesticides and herbicides we used back then were much more potent than the ones we use today."

Since that time, atrazine has been categorized by the EPA as a class B carcinogen, causing mammary tumors in laboratory rats at exposure levels of 3 parts per billion. Although atrazine is still used today, farmers are specifically trained to follow safety procedures and use lower concentrations of this herbicide on corn fields. An estimated 5 percent of well water in one major corn-producing area in Wisconsin—Dane County has high levels of atrazine. As a result, a large part of this county is prohibited from using atrazine. Nitrates, another known group of carcinogens, show up in significant amounts in approximately 10 percent of Wisconsin wells. In the case of the DiFrancescas, it is impossible to know what airborne exposure to pesticides and herbicides they may have faced as the neighborhood evolved from farmland to an urban environment.

Other potential concerns in this growing Waukesha neighborhood existed. Barclay's Brass and Aluminum Foundry, for example, spewed out a number of things that Schuett has more questions about than answers. When houses were being built and needed additional dirt to place next to concrete foundations, it was not uncommon for builders to buy blackened silica sand from the foundry as dirt. This sand was white as snow before it was used to form casting molds, but turned black in the furnaces. Other foundries brought "dirty" sand into the neighborhood to sell as fill, sand that was considered safe underground. Airborne, however, it posed the threat of silicosis, notes one foundry owner. "It was probably the late '50s and early '60s that we started using foundry sand for fill," Schuett explained. "They'd bring it in along the bottom of the foundation of the houses. I'm not saying all of the houses used it, but some of them certainly."

Schuett cannot remember the sand being considered unsafe, but he wonders if it should be investigated by health authorities. "This was the late 1960s, maybe the 1970s, when someone put the kibosh on it. All of a sudden they stopped hauling it out, as I recall, and I can't say why."

Was the black sand a potential health hazard—after it came out of the foundry? Were some of the batches of sand that went around the houses a health threat because of some residues resulting from the foundry process?

It seems plausible, however, that Charlie and others had been exposed to high levels of radium and other man-made toxins that may have had a synergistically harmful effect on their health. A radium advisory pamphlet published by the Wisconsin Department of Natural Resources has some hypothetical answers on how this might have happened.

You may be exposed to high levels of radium if you live in an area where it is released into the air from the burning of coal or other fuels, or if your drinking water is taken from a source that is high in natural radium, such as a deep well, or from a source near a radioactive waste disposal site.

Radium, once it is breathed or swallowed, can stay in the body for months. It is transported via the bloodstream and thus carried elsewhere, especially to the bones. It is estimated that 80 percent leaves the body in the feces, the remaining 20 percent carried through the bloodstream to other parts of the body. That is why the EPA regulates the amount of radium in drinking water.

Another concern posed by Schuett may be that some dumps could contain or might have been built in areas already containing volatile organic compounds. At least one of these dumps has caused problems in Waukesha. An apartment complex built on top of it has since been abandoned, sinking some two feet in spots due to methane bubble problems. According to Schuett, there was no such thing as a landfill when farmland around Waukesha began to be developed, only dumps. One dump, John DiFrancesca recalls, was probably within a mile of the neighborhood, to the east, near the old foundry.

While I have no idea what's in some of these dumps or the foundry sand, or whether the DiFrancescas were exposed to dangerous levels of atrazine or other farm chemicals during the 1960s and 1970s, there is no question that radium is in the Waukesha water supply at levels above the EPA's clean drinking water standard. According to the Wisconsin Department of Natural Resources, approximately 50 of 1300 community water systems in the state exceed this standard. Most of the water supplies that exceed this standard draw water from the same deep sandstone aquifer as Waukesha. These communities are located in a narrow band which stretches from Green Bay to the Illinois state line.

What health risk does radium pose in these water supplies? The Wisconsin Department of Natural Resources answers:

The National Academy of Sciences has concluded that a long-term exposure to elevated levels of radium in drinking water does indeed pose a "higher risk of bone cancer for the people exposed." The U.S. Environmental Protection Agency estimates that long-term consumption of water containing five pCi/l radium will cause 44 added cancer deaths for every million people exposed. The risk doubles to 88 per million at 10 pCi/l, triples to 132 at 15 pCi/l, etc. . . . [This] is approximately the same as the risk of dying from lightning strikes, or tornadoes and hurricanes.

There is no clear solution to the radium levels in Waukesha's water. Notes the Department of Natural Resources:

The most inexpensive treatment method is likely to be synthetic zeolite ion exchange such as used in home water softeners. This water softening process is expected to remove about 90% of the radium. It produces a pleasing water supply that reduces scaling in pipes. However, it increases an average daily sodium intake by 200 to 400 mg compared to an estimated average daily intake of 2,000 to 7,000 mg. . . . Numerous treatment plants may be necessary for community systems with multiple wells. Other possible treatment methods include lime-soda ash softening and reverse osmosis. Comparatively high start-up and operating costs may make these options impractical for most affected Wisconsin systems. . . .

All treatment processes produce wastewater and solid waste (sludge) containing radium in varied concentrations. These treatment by-products must be disposed of properly. Radium waste disposal issues are relatively new to Wisconsin, and the problems they raise are complex and difficult. State officials, however, are working to establish environmentally safe waste disposal criteria.

Peter Wood, a municipal engineer for the Wisconsin Department of Natural Resources who monitors the Waukesha water supply, says that since the early 1980s when the Clean Water Drinking Act of 1974 started to be enforced, radium levels in Waukesha's 10 public wells have averaged 10 pCi/l. What is puzzling about this is that the EPA standard for radium isotopes 226 and 228 has been 5 pCi/l since the standard was established in the 1980s. Through legal wrangling, Waukesha will not have to comply until the EPA formally releases its new standard.

"We went to court to pursue enforcement," says Wood, "but we are currently in a holding pattern. Right now, the Waukesha Water Utility has to provide quarterly statements to citizens to make them aware of the radium levels in the water and the possible health consequences. There's been some talk that the EPA might raise the permissible levels of radium exposure considered safe in drinking water, which is something they don't typically do, or that they might hold the standard right where it is. The utility's view has always been that it would be a costly problem to solve, and one that may be unnecessary. As we speak, the drinking water in the city does violate the radium standard levels established by the EPA as safe. But as a result of the court decisions, that standard is not something that we can enforce on the Waukesha Water Utility."

Woods tells me that because Waukesha has had the same wells since the 1920s, it would be an excellent site to determine the long-term effects of radium in the water on population. A scientist couldn't possibly find a better natural laboratory to conduct research and attempt to reach some definitive answers. Would it be that expensive for the Wisconsin Bureau of Public Health to explore some or all of my theories? Could such research save lives, or put more directly, is anyone's life near 308 East Roberta still in danger if research isn't done? In a world of imperfect and limited information, I'm not sure I have an objective answer.

An answer did come on June 24, 1997, from the state of Wisconsin's Bureau of Public Health. Thomas L. Sieger, chief of environmental epidemiology and prevention for the bureau, replied to the information that I submitted on behalf of 10 neighbors, including Margaret DiFrancesca and Bobbie Bertacchini. "With regard to your Waukesha concern," he wrote, "the variety of cancers occurring over many years (as indicated by your list) does not suggest neighborhood exposure to some environmental cancer-causing agent. . . . Again, based on the information available to us, we will not be proceeding with additional investigation into this situation."

I cannot help but wonder what Charlie D might think about Sieger's reply. After all, Waukesha was a special place to him—and to the entire DiFrancesca family. The key to his success was his ability to assess a situation, often with limited information, and then make the best decision possible. For all I know, he too would dismiss the information I've gathered about the possible synergistic effects of environmental mutagens in his old neighborhood with two words: bad genes. But then, again, he might have been inclined to pick up the phone and cut through the red tape by funding research himself.

full throttle | 11

A s Charlie D watched *Flatliners* on one of the movie channels at the Desert Inn in 1990 with Tom DeMark, he had a special sort of empathy going with the characters in the movie. He sat there quietly, seemingly absorbed by the characters' views of death. It was one of the rare times he had ever sat still in Las Vegas for more than a few minutes. The doctors in this movie toyed carelessly with death, not unlike the manner in which traders sometimes played with bonds. In the end, the doctors discovered that even their experience of death did not necessarily bring them any closer to God and "His white light." It had, however, put them in better touch with their haunting guilt for unvanquished sins. Kiefer Sutherland, who played the first Harvard medical student to flatline, soon felt the retribution of Billy Mahoney, a childhood acquaintance who accidentally fell from a tree to his death at the hands of a group of rock-throwing boys. About the time his doctor friends joined him, the snot-nosed, baseball-capped Mahoney took on a nearly super-human demeanor, revisiting and pummeling the doctor at every chance. Wearing the physical scars and bruises of Billy Mahoney's wrath, the doctor chose to flatline one more time in the hopes of reconciling himself with his guilt for mistreating Billy Mahoney. By movie's end, they had switched places in a tree, the site of their violent conflict.

Charlie D had to have found special meaning in this movie, knowing his own death was imminent. DeMark walked to the suite's bathroom, gone for not more than a minute. The movie credits were still scrolling on the TV screen when he returned. A strange feeling, perhaps even morbid, had come over him during the film. Charlie was sitting in a recliner, motionless and seemingly far off in a world not visible to DeMark. It was quite a movie to watch when you were dying, but even a scarier one to watch if you weren't dying but were with someone who was.

Charlie was frighteningly quiet. DeMark tiptoed closer to him, fearful that the worst had just occurred in the time it took to shut a bathroom door, pee, and flush the toilet. He moved closer to Charlie, his heart pounding against his chest. Charlie didn't seem to be moving at all. Less than five feet away, Charlie's eyes flew open saucerlike, as if he had just been hit by some incredible pain. When he saw the look on DeMark's face, he could not help but rescue his friend from his own mind games with mortality.

"Just practicing, Tommy," he said, only half apologetically.

"Come on, Charlie. That wasn't funny."

"Sorry if I scared you, Tom, really. I didn't know you had left the room."

DeMark knew this wasn't true and felt like punching his friend, the flatlining fool. All Charlie D could do was recline some more, smiling and laughing at his own dark humor. In some ways, laughter was all he had left. Soon they were both laughing at a joke well timed and conceived, no matter how morose. DeMark knew, or felt he knew, just what it was like to be in Charlie D's shoes. In some sense, he felt Charlie D hadn't just been flatlining like the doctors in the movie for up to three or four minutes, but had done so for over four years in a less-sterile place—the bond pit. The movie had provoked some personal reflections, but Charlie D never once let anyone feel sorry for him, including DeMark. Charlie D hit the remote and the eerie final hymn from the movie was gone. The room was silent.

"Guess the movie got to you a bit, too, huh Tom?"

DeMark glared at him, refusing to respond, angry that Charlie had taken him over the edge into such darkness with his joke. When Charlie was up, moving about like usual, playing golf or poker or trading, it was easy for DeMark or anyone, really, to mistake him for Gandhi, except he was wearing a golf shirt and Bermuda shorts. The shape of their heads, thought DeMark, seemed remarkably similar. The only thing missing were those small wire-framed glasses, a gift DeMark just might buy him as payback, if he could find a pair in Las Vegas. As the men had done many times, they sat and talked about everything they had in common, especially their deeper appreciation for some of the subtle nuances of markets and life. At one time they had talked about going into business together, but both of them knew that was not practical at the moment, given Charlie D's health.

It was getting late. Charlie D was particularly looking forward to a round of golf the next day. Of course, DeMark was wild off the tee, but he also hit the long ball better than many scratch golfers, winning a long-drive contest here or there in his golfing prime. Before he had hurt his back, he could claim a single-digit handicap, but that was years ago. It made for a good 18 holes and a lot of fun wagers, particularly when Charlie could knock it on the green first and see what DeMark did with the short sticks in his bag under a little pressure. The air presses by Charlie D kept the laughter flowing, and so did both men's errant iron shots. The laughter never stopped with these two, especially during their final rounds of golf together.

Despite the joking and fun that evening, Charlie D was clearly unable to shake the cobwebs of flatlining. His death-joke with DeMark was only partly in jest. He began to talk to DeMark about his own "Billy Mahoney," a kid of some unknown age and name he had roughed up in his youth. Charlie D wasn't too specific, but he seemed particularly troubled, enough to tell DeMark that he intended to apologize to this kid as soon as he possibly could. It was well past midnight in the Midwest and far too late to place a well-meaning phone call; Charlie D claimed that he would call the kid in the morning and apologize. He even told DeMark he planned to send his Billy Mahoney a monetary gift as some sort of recompense for all the trouble this fight may have caused. Charlie D didn't give names or specifics, but clearly he saw someone from his youth with remarkable clarity and empathy. That kid, whoever he was, had crept completely beneath the thick skin and steely nerves of a toughened risk-taker.

Charlie D mumbled only the parts of the story he wanted DeMark to hear. DeMark stared at his friend in disbelief. He didn't know what to tell him.

"Charlie, that was such a long time ago. He's not even going to remember you when you call. That's the last time I ever watch a movie with you. Next time we're watching golf videos. Now, that would do you some good."

There was more laughter and joking that night, but Charlie was focused on some reexamination. As a director, he no doubt wished the scriptwriter could change one or two scenes that bothered him, but he surely knew they were forever part of his personal history. Of course, his history couldn't have been all that different from any of ours. But imminent death caused him to recall rather than bury past sins. Even though his skill as a trader had always been defined by his ability to learn from a bad day and then move on, it had not always been true for him outside the pit. He sat deep in thought as DeMark said good night.

DeMark reminded Charlie D that their tee time was scheduled for 7:45 A.M. Charlie D nodded, turning off the TV to get some sleep. In the morning, the bright desert sun woke him from his reclining-chair slumber. It was much easier sleeping at a 45-degree angle, head above the chest cavity, given the fluid buildup in his lungs that the cancer and treatments sometimes caused. He coughed periodically to clear his throat and lungs.

Fifteen minutes before they were set to head for the first tee, Charlie D emerged from the pro shop wearing white spikes and Bermuda shorts. He was all smiles, ready to play some high-handicap golf, with a couple of extra sleeves of golf balls already stuffed in the golf cart's cubbyhole. Jumping in the golf cart with DeMark, he picked up exactly where they left off the night before. He explained that he had just gotten through to the kid and set things straight with him, as best he could. He even told DeMark that he had sent the kid some money. It was a little lotto that Charlie D dropped in the mail for good measure.

"Charlie, are you getting kooky on me or something? You've got to be kidding. Well, whatever you thought you had to do, I'm glad you did it. You scared the hell out of me last night."

DeMark drove down the cart path to get off hole No. 1. That round, Charlie D the flatliner played as if his heart had truly stopped, ice in his veins. He birdied 3 out of 18 holes to take a few skins from DeMark, despite his share of double bogeys and even a one-legged snowman on one of the par-5s. Charlie D never laughed at one-legged snowmen, but he did this time. When DeMark asked him his score on the hole, he quipped, "Give me a quad, a quadriplegic." When he heard DeMark's laughter at his expense, he promised to get it back.

"Air Press, Tommy."

DeMark couldn't recall Charlie D having played this well before, despite one 9 after a couple of bad passes at the ball. Charlie D played the putting greens that day with all the precision of a pool shark.

"Guess Billy Mahoney must have been a golf pro," joked DeMark. "He must have forgiven you this morning, or given you a putting lesson when I wasn't around. If I were you, I'd stop right now, before someone hits you with his driver."

Charlie D sliced a six-iron to the center of the green on the next par-3. He laughed at DeMark's frown and made some crack about the Senior Tour in 2001.

"2001 seems like tomorrow. Double-redouble that Air Press, Tommy."

The two men never discussed the phone call to the kid again, but it turns out that phone call of atonement was not the first or only one Charlie made. Sometimes he did more than call and apologize. A few weeks before Ken Hollub's retirement party on May 4, 1988, Joy received an unexpected visit from Charlie D. It was the first time the two had spoken since their relationship ended in 1971. That breakup hadn't been easy for either of them, and there was something in the way Charlie D had handled it that bothered him. Roughly 19 years later, Joy heard the roar of a motorcycle pulling into her driveway on a Saturday. When the doorbell rang, she had no idea who it would be. And when she saw him at the door, the man in the leather jacket who had just parked his Harley, there was no holding the tears back.

Seeing Joy cry like that shook Charlie to his core, though he remained composed. Despite his flaccid right shoulder, weakened from surgery and years of cancer treatments, he lifted Joy like she was made of feathers, somehow popped the door open, and set her down gently on the couch. He hadn't had time to think. All he had done was react to a situation, like he did on the bond floor. It would take a few moments before either of them regained their composure, until the smoke and flames of years had finally dissipated. Joy excused herself from the couch only after the phone rang a half hour or so into their conversation. It was her boyfriend Joe, ready to take her to the weekend softball game. She explained to Joe that she had a surprise guest, telling him to pick her up in about an hour. Joe knew from Joy's tone not to ask questions. He would see her in an hour. They were in love as deeply as Joy had once been with Charlie.

Joy and Charlie got reacquainted with some small talk. Joy told Charlie about Joe, the man she had put off on the phone. In turn, Charlie talked about his wife Ann and his two stepchildren, Jake and Maggie. Thrown into the conversation was some talk about his career as a bond trader and her career as an elementary school teacher. But Charlie hadn't come for chitchat. Joy offered some beer to break the emotional tension in the air. He thanked Joy for the drink, but Charlie's beer remained untouched for an hour, sweating on a coaster on the table until the moisture had evaporated.

When Joy asked Charlie why he had come to see her after all this time, his answer bespoke a fear he had always held in his heart. His pause told Joy that he was searching for words, something she had never seen him do. He couldn't say at that moment; he asked his own question instead. He had no idea what to do with this outtrade, if that is what you wanted to call it.

"Why are you still crying?" Charlie D asked.

"I don't know. I guess it's because I just didn't think that I would ever see you again. But you still haven't told me why you are here."

Charlie was speechless. He knew the answer to the question, but it just wouldn't dislodge itself from his throat.

"I wanted to make sure that you were okay," he said, unable to cry in front of Joy, though he may have cried for sheer peace of mind while riding his Harley back to Chicago.

That wasn't the whole answer, either. Finally, Charlie brought up Joy's trip to Colorado in November 1971. He told Joy there had been some ups and downs in his life. He discussed his success, his wife and kids, and admitted to a handful of private regrets. But of all the mistakes he cared to share with Joy, he said there was none more shameful and hurtful than how he had treated Joy on the trip she made to see him in Colorado. It was something he had never completely forgiven himself for, and he was there to tell her that now.

He didn't even care whether Joy accepted his words as sincere; he knew that they were. Charlie did not fumble his words now. Pointedly staring at Joy, he puked more than money all over his shoes. He puked it all out, the 19 years of silence, like he never had with either bonds or chemo or radiation. His look told Joy that whatever she said, it was clear that he had just taken a loss from which he knew he could not recover without her help. It was clear to her, then, that his pain had been equal to hers—perhaps even greater. Despite all this, he emphasized that he was only there to see that she was okay. They both cried with all the anguish of something invisible lost and perhaps something new gained. Only Joy's forgiveness could make it right for Charlie. Something in her tears told him his trip may have been worth it.

Charlie D then moved the conversation forward, seemingly embarrassed that he had lost control of the situation. When Joy asked about his health, he spoke almost effortlessly, the opportunity to move on a welcome relief. His guard went up again just a bit.

He described the treatments he had been through, some of the side effects, and explained to Joy that he did not intend to go through them again. His descriptions of the treatments and what they did to him, however, were not nearly as memorable to Joy as was Charlie's final admission. Despite his apparent good health and full head of hair, all was not as it seemed. He was just grateful that he could see her at a time when he felt good, all things considered. He touched on his illness and his future only indirectly.

"Joy," he said, in the company of someone he truly considered one of his closest friends, despite the 19 years, "if I drank that beer, I couldn't even taste it. I'm just waiting for the other shoe to drop."

Charlie D's cards were on the table, fully exposed.

When I asked Joy about that surprise visit, she was not sure she could fully explain the meaning of Charlie's motorcycle trip. She told me, however, of a donation he had made on her behalf, a donation he did not tell anyone else about. It was a sign he wasn't there to lie, as he felt he had once done to her before.

"I'm not a little fly hair of a woman," she explained, describing the moment she greeted Charlie on the porch. "When I think about how sick he was and how he picked me up: That physical effort to lift me when I was crying had to kill him. When we sat down and I said that I didn't know him anymore, he said that I knew him as well as anybody ever had. We had grown up together."

Charlie did not let the conversation end on a low note. When Joy indicated that she planned to go on to graduate school, he promptly offered to pay for it. He seemed embarrassed by the offer when Joy thanked him but refused. It was something he had done many times for many friends in sickness and in health, including the son of his cleaning lady back in Wilmette. The ice of 19 years continued to melt. It was not long before two friends were traveling back to the best parts of their shared past. As high school sweethearts, they joked that if things had been different, they'd have had a litter of boys together—enough to form a basketball team. That wasn't enough for Charlie, Joy later joked. Remembering what he said brought a smile to her face, a reaction that told me she did perhaps know the complexities of Charlie D as well as anyone.

"He said that would be fine," she recalls, "so long as there were also one swimmer in the bunch like me. Yes, I felt good after we talked. I didn't want him to leave at that moment, but I knew he knew he had to go. After we talked, I didn't think I'd ever see him again. I wish that I had gone to see him in the hospital, but I just thought at the time it would be inappropriate."

Joy provided the missing pieces to Charlie's personality in a way no one else had—virtues and faults. Her view showed a side of Charlie that although not visible from the bond pit no less contributed to his success. Charlie lived and traded larger than life; in dying, his trades were equally sizable, but contemplative and private. It did not strike me how important this motorcycle ride to see Joy had been until I realized that it was the only part of his "legend" that I had not heard. It was important because of all the unspoken things it told about the man. From that day on, I never saw Charlie D as someone larger than life in the bond pit, defined by legend. Instead, I saw him more complete, three-dimensional, if you will—faults and attributes. Perhaps this explains Johnny Musso's comment that, unless I knew him and had actually *been* with him, his spirit would be next to impossible to capture on the printed page. And his spirit was what ultimately made him so successful.

"I was thinking about our first phone conversation about Charlie, when you asked me if he would be happy a book was being written about him," said Joy. "It's so hard to say. I think the final time I saw him he had an idea that what he did wasn't nearly as important as what Ken Hollub had done for him and a thousand other kids in Waukesha. I remember in that conversation how he kept saying that if he had another chance to do it over again, he probably should have tried to be a coach like his Dad or Ken. I think if you asked Charlie, he'd probably say that a book should be written about Coach Hollub. Then again, Charlie always wanted to be a player on the field; he told me that is why he enjoyed bond trading. It was the closest thing to playing in professional sports that he could find. I don't think he would ever have been a good coach."

Fortunately, Charlie D's life would not end before he had a chance to express that sentiment himself. On his trip to the Super Bowl with Coach Hollub and Coach Graf, he began to make plans with Coach Graf about what he wanted to do for Coach Hollub on May 4, 1988, the night of his retirement party. In Charlie's mind, the coach was truly larger than life, not because of fame or fortune or the size of his bond positions, but because of his integrity. On a trip with Coach Graf to Burlington, a small town north of Waukesha, Charlie D bought a mobile home for his coach and then swore Coach Graf to secrecy. As he had explained to Coach Graf, he did not want to take credit for the gift; it was to be given to Coach Hollub by all of the kids he had helped prepare for the ups and downs of life over the years.

On May 4, 1988, with the Jayco 27-foot camper parked outside Zorba's Restaurant in Brookfield, just northeast of Waukesha, Charlie D made a short speech representing all of Coach Hollub's players from the

1960s. The new camper had been parked everywhere around town to keep it out of Coach Hollub's radar for a week. Parked in front of the doors to Zorba's, it sat shiny as a new penny dropped on the ground, disappearing partially into the darkness as the sun set. Coach Graf's camera would be running to capture the moment on video while there was still some light, and all he could do as he filmed it was laugh like a kid, narrating the moment hours before when he gave Coach Hollub the keys. "A beeaauuty," he'd say to Ken for his viewing pleasure out there in the parking lot, the food and beer and conversation at the retirement party already flowing inside. Life doesn't get any better than this, he thought.

That evening, Charlie D recounted what Coach Hollub meant to him: The coach was someone who made a difference. Charlie D was introduced that night by the referee-shirt-wearing MC as "the kid who ran the school in the 1960s."

"I was thinking about Coach Hollub," said Charlie D at the banquet, "and the thing that impressed me most about playing for him is that it took me until I was about 36 years old to realize that he's only about this tall." As Charlie D put his arm at chest level, a howl rose from the hundreds of friends and family and coaches and teachers and students gathered at Zorba's to honor Coach Hollub. Charlie D never paused to stop the one-liners about this very little big man, sounding much like a coach himself.

"I can remember one time, I can remember saying this guy was a *big* guy. He used to call me over to the sidelines because he always used to yell at me. When we'd call a time-out, he'd bring me over to talk with me, and I'd bend over like this, and he'd say, 'Son, aren't you in shape?' And I'd have to bend over even more like this and say, 'No, Coach, I can't hear you.' But it just never dawned on me at the time just how much I had to bend."

Charlie D again waited for the laughter to stop after his second punch line, some of his words drowned out in the noise of the crowd.

"But Coach was a quarterback," he started again. "I have very fond memories of Waukesha High School. The college recruiters still refer to it as Quarterback U. That's because Coach would typically take someone from the senior class, usually the best athlete, a lot of times the kid who was most intelligent or most popular, and usually the best looking, and make him his quarterback."

Coach Hollub had seen this before. He began laughing at Charlie D, who'd deliver his own punch line about his *own* good looks. "Remember, I was a quarterback back in 1968. The standards to be his quarterback were much lower back then."

The crowd laughed again, as Charlie D started to get serious.

"I think Coach Hollub's program worked. I checked his record because I was supposed to represent the players from the 1960s, and he had an 83% winning percentage during that decade. I looked back at the long list of names of quarterbacks who played for him, and they are all good-looking, intelligent, popular."

More laughs.

"Coach had a policy of letting his quarterbacks call their own plays, which is a little bit different than the way football was played elsewhere. I can remember playing Tosa, and I was calling my own plays. And at a certain point as a quarterback, you figure it isn't all that much fun to hand the ball off. So I started throwing the ball. I threw about eight incomplete passes in a row. So Coach takes a time-out and calls me over and says, 'Son, you've been watching too much TV. Now get in there and hand that ball off.'

"Because we don't have much time, there are lots of stories about his toughness. But suffice it to say when your football coach has a tougher summer job than you do, you know he's a tough guy. I can remember we all had jobs in the juvenile delinquency program, or jobs in lawn service, and we asked Coach what he did that summer. He said, 'I drove a steel truck.' And when a guy that short says that to you, well, even you can see him driving that truck." Charlie lifted both arms above his head, driving an imaginary steel truck. "It's a *very* frightening concept."

The jokes were now over, almost. He spoke directly to his favorite coach.

"The thing that I remember most was the winter of 1967. There were about 40 juniors going to be seniors, and we all were finally going to get a chance to play for you. And then a college was going to steal you away from us, so we went to your office and begged and cried. And I can remember getting down on my knees. We said if you stay we'll win you a championship. You stayed, and we won. So now you can retire whole.

"Coach, I'm happy you're retiring. But I wish you weren't; because you always had so much to give, and you always meant so much to all of us. I know everybody here loves you. . . ."

Sometime that evening, Charlie D returned to the sidelines of the party with his family, as Coach Graf handed Coach Hollub the keys to something in the parking lot, monolithic in the evening shadows. At the moment he made the handoff, Coach Graf distinctly remembers the fear that his friend Ken might have a heart attack. All he could do was pat him on the back and wish him a happy retirement. But in the darkness, he shuffled behind Coach Hollub and was prepared to catch him, just in case his knees buckled as he stared at a retirement dream. Fishing and hunting in Wisconsin and beyond was running through his head. Outside the door in the darkness stood a symbol of the community's love for the coach, but more specifically Charlie D's notion of how to treat one of life's heroes.

"When I got the mobile home, I didn't know where it came from. No one told me at the retirement party," said Coach Hollub. "I thought Chuck might have something to do with it, but I really didn't know. I was in shock. When my high school coach, Harold Shumit, came along, all he said was, 'Ken, you'd better go talk to your quarterback.' I went in there and said, 'Chuck, what's going on? Level with me.' 'Coach,' he said, 'I don't know a thing about it. He'd never admitted to me that he'd basically done the whole thing himself.' "

From that moment forward, if it were true that Charlie D valued the meaning of his coach's life, the opposite might have been equally true. Coach Hollub realized then that he had also crossed paths with a man who represented a part of life that often appears invisible to us all—an ideal of a different kind in his own right. That night, he saw a kid who never gave up, even in the fourth quarter when things weren't going well. At the Second-Guessers Banquet to celebrate the Blackshirts' championship season on November 14, 1968, an appreciation entitled "What Is a Football Player?" was written on a program for the event and was still tucked away in one of Coach Hollub's scrapbooks when I had a chance to speak with him years after Charlie D's death. That appreciation describes not a coach, but a player, and it is something Coach Hollub and Coach Graf feel to this day describes a kid they knew as just Chuck.

"Between the innocence of boyhood and the dignity of a man, we find a sturdy creature called a football player," reads the appreciation, sealed in plastic slips along with other memorabilia from the 1968 championship season and Charlie D's funeral. "Football players come in assorted weights, heights, jersey colors and numbers, but all football players have the same creed: to play every second of every minute of every period of every game to the best of their ability."

Other things in that scrapbook could make Coach Hollub speechless. It was a player's individual heart and competitiveness that was seen by everyone who encountered Charlie D, whether he was a kid playing football, a bond trader in the pit, or a cancer patient in the hospital. These were intangibles in a player for which nobody, including that player's coach, could give me an explanation.

"I'll tell you, we will never know how great and how generous and kind a person he was," said Hollub, in the *Waukesha County Freeman* on June 1, 1991, in a eulogy entitled "Unforgettable Character." ". . . The motor home and that trip will no doubt be the highlights of my life forever. I still can't believe somebody would do that for me."

bozo bonds | 12

On Saturday, February 19, 1991, Charlie D attended the 40th annual benefit dinner-dance for the University of Chicago Cancer Research Foundation auxiliary board. Attending the $250-per-couple dinner were 300 other guests who had packed themselves into the balconied ballroom at the Hotel Inter-Continental on Michigan Avenue. The annual dinner-dance typically raised $75,000 to $80,000 by auctioning off anything from a day with Oprah and Paul Simon tickets, to luxury vacations and baseballs autographed by Hall of Famers.

In attendance were Dr. Stephanie Williams and Dr. John Anastasi, two doctors whose research was earmarked to receive the lion share's on the funds raised. Williams, a mother of three, had discovered some new ways to boost bone marrow regrowth after transplants. Anastasi, in contrast, was being introduced at the predinner cocktail as a researcher who had developed a unique technique for analyzing chromosomal abnormalities. Anastasi's technique was aiding the precision with which malignant tumors could be diagnosed and treated.

Sitting at Williams's table was a completely bald bond trader, attending the fund raiser with his daughter and friend Tom DeMark. Showing a flair for bidding that brought a familiar spark back to Charlie's eye, Dr. Williams cleared the market at $900 for four tickets to go see Bozo the

Clown with her children. Bozo bonds, thought Charlie D, admiring the doctor's confidence in a crowd. Make them puke them on their shoes, he must have thought, enjoying every minute, as Williams upped her bid another $100 and silenced her competitors. Sold!

The good doctor was interrupted later that evening by a *Chicago Tribune* reporter, Johanna Steinmetz, who also attended the fund raiser.

"Now that's something I've never seen before," said someone at the table, toasting her effort with another dinner guest by hoisting a full glass of wine. "A doctor who supports her own cause."

"Not exactly," said Dr. Williams, who was approached by Steinmetz, with notepad and pen in hand. "I had a benefactor."

Williams looked out of the corner of her eye at a man who closely resembled Gandhi, only he was wearing a tux. The man she smiled at that evening was someone the doctors knew well from his frequent trips to the University of Chicago Hospital. Charlie D had once been identified as a candidate for a bone marrow transplant, but he had privately refused such treatment long ago, despite the medical advice of his doctors. He wasn't a terminal patient, only a trader, working with imperfect information. The $900 he antied up for Dr. Williams was not his most significant donation, but certainly one of his most heartfelt. Dr. Williams and her fellow researchers were developing procedures that at one time might have been able to save his life—procedures that have since been refined so that they now no longer involve the same toxic effects he had once chosen to avoid. That made these doctors special in his mind, even if they too worked with imperfect information. These doctors were a sound investment, even if a tad speculative.

That evening Maggie posed for a photo with her father. Charlie D's smile was undeniable—no Mona Lisa lips here—and so was the comfort of his daughter at his side. Sometime that night her hand rested in her father's like a wounded bird, but his sense of humor carried them forward. It was simply a time to hold hands, give some more, and wait. Both Charlie D and Maggie looked into the camera, illuminated more by their love than the camera's flash. Invisible to the camera was the terrifying velocity with which Charlie D's death approached.

It is in that moment that we should remember him—a father, a courageous cancer patient, and a legendary bond trader who had no peer. Integrity and honor were something he expected of himself, and losing in the pit was nothing to fear. He was a winner not because of his winnings, but because of how he competed when he played, all the way to the very end.

Like Coach Hollub and Joy, I often find myself at a loss for words in trying to explain why I am here telling you about Charlie D. It is still a mystery to me how someone I never met could guide a pen across an empty page, sometimes in ways that I cannot explain. All I know is that after speaking with Joy and Coach Hollub about Charlie D, the pen somehow seemed to stop late one night, just before I had fully mapped out another chapter about Charlie D's funeral. I could not get it to move again.

That moment seemed to me as good a time as any to pull out the cigar I had saved from my trip to the Wigwam and give up the pen. The cigar smoke that night disappeared almost as soon as it was exhaled, and nothing larger than life appeared in the smoke. All I could do was watch it rise upward, lost in the dim light of a sky full of stars. I felt that I had come to know someone, though I wasn't sure exactly who, or that I could prove it to anyone. I suppose Johnny Musso was right: Charlie D was only a legend that those who knew him could ever truly claim to see.

What made him successful? We will never truly know. But it started with all those intangibles that we refer to simply as guts and heart, as if two words could encapsulate the Herculean efforts and small gestures of a lifetime. Charlie D will always be admired from a distance, like some of the athletes to which he has been compared, but there will never be another like him. May remembering him always remind us to celebrate what is known but never totally visible—in a man both ordinary and exceptional.

epilogue

by thomas r. demark

Stationed on the top step of the Treasury bond futures trading pit stood Charlie D. Like a policeman directing traffic at a busy intersection, his arms were outstretched, his view unobstructed, his demeanor pensive, and his resolve determined. In contrast to the view from the top, situated at the outside bottom of the pit was an old, worn carpenter's bench. Occasionally runners, traders, and other floor personnel would sit on it and rest for a moment before catching their breath and resuming their busy activity. Charlie called the bench "the lounge." Although physically and mentally drained during the trading day, not unlike the professional athlete during a game, he refused to succumb to the temptation to sit and rest from his frenetic trading for even a short moment. To interrupt his trading would suggest a vulnerability or weakness he refused to allow his opponents to see. Charlie preferred to stand above the crowd at all times.

Charlie was able to trade until a month before he died. However, his deteriorating health forced him to withdraw to the bench after the closing bell on his last day of trading. He had to recuperate from the day's exertions before he could tackle the tedious walk to the elevator and then down the hall to his office. It turns out that Charlie was human after all.

True to form, he made money that day scalping trades, just as he had done so many times before. As Charlie sat uncomfortably on the bench, other traders stopped to greet this trading legend—some seemingly oblivious to his struggle. Charlie's life, reeling quickly by like the movies he enjoyed watching so much, was nearing the end, the credits rolling across the screen. It took nearly an hour for him to travel from the floor to his office. His speech was labored and almost inaudible. As he lay down on his couch to review the day's trades and market action, as he had done many times before, it was apparent that he was overcome by a tremendous exhaustion. While he would no doubt prefer we remember him as he was on the top step in rare form, this last day is no less a testament to his spirit, his competitive drive, and his perseverance.

There are certainly many successful traders, both on and off the floor, who are worthy of our examination. Many have been at least as successful as Charlie was in his all-too-short career. Why should Charlie's story be of special interest to us?

As a market technician, I have spent the better part of my years studying the markets, in search of accurate indicators and winning trading systems. It has been my job to provide traders both large and small with an edge. Yet, even I, the die-hard technician, know that a truly great trader is not successful because he or she has some special insight into the markets or has discovered the holy grail. Rather, what separates the greats from the merely mediocre are the intangibles—intelligence, drive, hard work. In essence, what makes traders like Charlie successful is not their system but their spirit—a largeness of mind and heart. And, most important, a strong belief in themselves—call it self-confidence. For if you are not confident, the markets will take you out in a second and cause you to question your very existence. No system can overcome a lacking from within. This unassailable truth was brought home to me with Charlie.

Charlie possessed a voracious appetite for trading knowledge. He would attentively absorb every aspect of any trading hypothesis I would conjure. Not only would he quiz me thoroughly, but he would also apply it on paper to real-time situations. I recall one episode in particular: He was amazed at how well a specific technique had performed. At his insistence, he convinced me that he wanted to trade it in real time, on the floor. We rehearsed repeatedly. Finally, every bit as confident and excited as I was since I knew that with his fearless style of trading he would be enormously successful, he took to the floor. That trading day I tracked the market, trade by trade, pleased with the performance results. Anxiously, I awaited his trading report. Much to my dismay, when he called, I could sense a level of disappointment. True to Charlie, he prefaced the conversation by extolling the virtues of the trading method and actually recited numerous instances in which it had worked well. Then he interjected, "you know, Tommy, I could never get myself to trade it. It's good, but it's not me. Maybe you can trade it for both of us. I'll put up the money."

Charlie made his own calls—on the floor as with his cancer treatment. If the call was good, his success was his own. And if he made a poor call, he had no one to blame but himself. In all the time I knew him, I never heard him criticize or blame another—trader, physician, family member, friend, or foe—for the outcome of any situation. Charlie controlled his own destiny, made his own trading decisions, and dictated his own fate. I wish we could bottle his spirit. Unfortunately, it's a bit like groping to catch smoke. At the same time it appears to be within one's reach, it is impossible to grasp.

acknowledgments

Three faces popped immediately to mind after I finished this biography. My wife Juliana allowed "Uncle" Charlie to live with us for four and a half years, and that sacrifice rose above all others once I was done with his story. I love her today as much as when we intertwined our hands beneath a ceremonial white cloth almost 10 years ago, and I cannot thank her enough for her support. My children Elena and Danny, who first heard of Charlie D when his spirit wandered through casual conversation at bedtime, were often as confused by him as MJ first was. *Who is this guy?* they also asked. Finally I can answer them in earnest—*A part of you, I hope*—now that pages of words and photos can be thumbed.

Beyond this troika, so many others shared their gifts of conversation, encouragement, and insight. I do not really know how to summarize all their contributions succinctly, so I will pluck a couple off the very top of my list and leave the rest to be acknowledged in some other equally dignified way in the future.

I could not have finished this book without the help of the DiFrancesca family. I will forever be indebted to this family for their entrusted faith, which came with no strings attached. At times, my research must have been an awkward intrusion into the past, but that never stopped them from offering their help whenever I asked.

In almost the same breath, how can I fail to mention the box of hand-made cigars from my brother Virgil? These custom stogies arrived at just about the time I was running on empty and smoked up the basement with a good vibe long before they were ever lit. Thanks, Virgil, for reminding me of the original joy in my journey and for the countless times you have played the role of Charlie D to Mary, Mark, Tom, or myself when we've needed a pep-talk.

My father and mother are with me at this moment, as always, and so too are Baba, Deda, and the Tetkas. I thank them, on behalf of all my family, for their sacrifices and support.

Thanks also to my friends Dave Nusbaum, Carl Rudorf, Jim Biery, Ruth Young, and Rayjohnclayjohn. When I just needed to say something nonsensical, they were there to drop the spaghetti rope from above.

Last but not least, I thank my agent Jane Jordan Browne of Multimedia Product Development for believing in Charlie D and my editor Pamela van Giessen for bringing his spirit to life.

While this book appears no larger than a little white ball against a backdrop of trees and sky, and while its ultimate flight path is so uncertain, I take this opportunity to shout "Air Press!" to the one man I hope is listening and to double-redouble my thanks to all those who have honored his memory.

permission acknowledgments

Grateful acknowledgment is made for permission to use the following:

Dustjacket photos by Gordon Halloran. Copyright © 1986 by Gordon Halloran. By permission of Gordon Halloran and Robert B. Moore.

Charles P. DiFrancesca obituary, *Chicago Tribune,* May 24, 1991. Copyright © Chicago Tribune Company. All rights reserved. Used with permission.

Excerpts from "Charlie D., 'the Sultan of Scalp,' Passes Away and the Bonds Close an Important Chapter," from *Bonen Reports,* volume 5, issue 100, May 24, 1991, by Thomas K. Bonen. By permission of Thomas K. Bonen.

Lecture by Charles Paul DiFrancesca on March 22, 1989, for LIT Commodity Training Seminar videotape. The author thanks John DiFrancesca for providing me with his personal copy of the videotape for use in the book, to Ann DiFrancesca for her permission to use Charlie's words, and LIT Clearing Services, particularly its president John Ruth, for his support of this biography.

Excerpts and background materials from Ken Hollub Retirement (May 4, 1988, videotape) and home videos of the 1968 Waukesha High School football games against Shorewood and West Allis Central. By permission of Kenneth J. Hollub.

Excerpts and background material from Harley Graf's personal Super Bowl scrapbook, including reproduced photos of his Super Bowl trip with Charles P. DiFrancesca, Mike Haas, and Coach Ken Hollub. By permission of Harley Graf.

Background material from family home video, "It's a Wonderful Life, Part II (Parshall Productions)." By permission of Craig and Janet Parshall.

Excerpts and medical background material about Margaret, John, and Charles DiFrancesca's illnesses from "Familial Lymphoproliferative Disorders with Chromosomal Fragile Site Analysis," *Leukemia and Lymphoma,* volume 5 (1991, Harwood Academic Publishers): 316, by Jill A. Moormier, Mary Elizabeth Neilly, James W. Vardiman, Michelle M. LeBeau, and Harvey M. Golomb. By permission of Dr. Aaron Polliack, editor of *Leukemia and Lymphoma.* A special thanks to Dr. Harvey M. Golomb for mentioning this medical journal article to me and to all of Charlie's doctors for reviewing "The Other Side of Vegas" chapter.